# THE GENTLEMAN AND THE JEW

Twenty-five Centuries of Conflict
in Manners and Morals

# THE GENTLEMAN
# AND THE JEW

*Twenty-five Centuries of Conflict*

*in Manners and Morals*

MAURICE SAMUEL

*A Jewish Legacy Book*

BEHRMAN HOUSE, INC. *New York*

A JEWISH LEGACY BOOK

Series Editor: Seymour Rossel

First BEHRMAN HOUSE edition, 1977

Published by arrangement with Alfred A. Knopf, Inc.

**Library of Congress Cataloging in Publication Data**

Samuel, Maurice, 1895–1972.
  The gentleman and the Jew.

  (A Jewish legacy book)
  Autobiographical.
    1.  Samuel, Maurice, 1895–1972—Addresses,
essays, lectures.  2.  Jews in the United States—
Biography—Addresses, essays, lectures.
3.  Judaism—20th century—Addresses, essays,
lectures.  4.  Bible.  O. T.—Criticism, interpretation, etc.—Addresses, essays, lectures.
5.  Zionism—Addresses, essays, lectures.  I.  Title.
[BM755.S243A3  1977]  296'.092'4[B]  77–6666

ISBN  0-87441-264-1

Manufactured in the United States of America

10 9 8 7 6 5 4 3 2 1 83 82 81 80 79 78 77

*To the memory of my brother*

JOSEPH SAMUEL

[1904–1949]

*whose spirit was deep-rooted*
*in his people*

# Contents

# CONTENTS

## BOOK THREE

## *JEW AND ISRAELI*

viii

# The Gentleman and the Jew

# CHAPTER I

## *Public and Personal*

❀

FORMALLY speaking, this book is a statement of my views on certain public matters: the crisis in the body and spirit of our civilization; the uniquely significant position of the Jewish people and of Judaism in this crisis; the relations between Jew and gentile, or between Jewry and Christendom; the possible meaning and possible consequences, in these connections, of the establishment of the State of Israel. Informally, it is a personal document and to some extent a personal history. What I believe in regard to the above-mentioned matters, and how I came to believe it, are not, for me, two separate subjects, and I cannot present the first without the second.

My ideas concerning the Jewish people and its place in western civilization are not simply external, intellectual, and "scientific." I hope they are intellectual and scientific in the sense that they conform to correct reasoning on the basis of historical probability; I hope they are external in the sense that they will be intelligible to some who have not had my experience. But these ideas are also the expression —or substance—of my life philosophy as a whole, and my life philosophy was not born of the objective contemplation of historical records. Records, historical and personal, have their share in it; but so have my experiences with the world about me. A life philosophy that does not issue from both these sources, and does not establish a congruence between them, is no philosophy at all; it is a fantasy; and nothing could be remoter from fantasy than my present concern.

One of the basic experiences that have woven themselves into my thinking and my teaching is the difficulty of overcoming, in readers, an initial prejudice against books on "a Jewish theme." It is an astonishing circumstance that while a Jewish Book is regarded by the western world as—at least —one of mankind's universal utterances, a book on a Jewish theme is instinctively classified as something limited and parochial. This attitude has nothing to do with literary merit; the proportion of inferior writers attracted by Jewish themes is the same as that attracted by other themes, and a good book at large is just as rare as a good book on a Jewish subject. The conclusion I have reached, after more than thirty years of observation, is that the resistance is part of that general complex of the western mind with which I deal in this book. People approach a Jewish book as if they were going slumming, and a first-rank publisher has told me, more than half seriously, that his books on Jewish subjects would sell twice as many copies if they could be sold at night. Almost invariably when a Jewish book makes a hit, it is one devoid of Jewish content, in which a general theme is attached to un-Jewish Jewish personalities.

I rehearse in the following pages some of the steps which led me to the conviction that an understanding of the Jewish episode in civilization is the key to the western world's intellectual and spiritual difficulties. But I cannot make an issue of the extraordinary feeling of isolation and futility which has pursued me during all the years that I have given to the exposition of this conviction. By a neat piece of logical inversion, preoccupation with "the Jewish problem" was equated with narrowness and perversity, while preoccupation with *evasion* of the Jewish problem was equated with breadth of outlook and liberality of sentiment. And even now, when certain facets of Jewish life have acquired a kind of respectability—really little more than front-page status—they have done so, it is assumed, by relinquishing their Jewishness in order to become "universal." Jewish life is becoming intelligible by losing whatever called for the exercise of the intelligence. I do not know which attitude is less satisfactory: "Now don't bother me with that question, it is really too, too provincial," or: "But my dear fellow, that question has been settled, why do you keep pestering me with it?"

Long advocacy of an obscure or unpopular point of view is an excellent discipline. It is also a test. If a man turns sour because he cannot get a hearing for his truth, there is something wrong in the relationship between him and his truth. If, in expounding his truth, he cannot speak simply and naturally about himself, but is driven to assume an attitude of objective omniscience, he properly becomes the less convincing; for then his truth is obviously not one that can sustain him in adversity. Consciously or unconsciously, every writer who presents a set of beliefs also presents a personality; and the interweave between the personality and the formal beliefs is the real, three-dimensional thesis. These are the principles that have guided me in the writing of this book.

I have called this "Chapter One," rather than "Preface," to give it a better chance of being read.

# BOOK ONE

# The Pagans and I

# CHAPTER II

## *Beginnings*

❀

I WAS BROUGHT to England out of Roumania at the age of six in the first year of this century. The migrating Jewish group of which my family was a unit, and which settled in the district of Strangeways, Manchester, belonged to the lowest economic level of the respectable poor. There was no tradition of wealth even in collateral branches of these families. There was also no recollection of scholars, rabbis, or saints. There have been poor Jewish communities with a high level of scholarship; ours was not of them. Roumanian Jewry in general was culturally one of the depressed areas of the Diaspora, and we were a depression within Roumanian Jewry.

We were concentrated in humble and monotonous streets —Norfolk, Suffolk, Bedford, and Trafalgar—with tiny outposts in Choir and Enid and Teneriffe Streets to the south and west, in Waterloo Road to the east, up Hightown to the north, beyond the queer range of scrubby hills which defaced the middle of northwest Manchester. These were largely Jewish districts, but not of Roumanian Jews. A few wildly courageous individuals had cut loose, like the relative who lived in the clog-resounding region of Rochdale Road, and the groceryman who had somehow landed in the impenetrable gentile wilderness of nearer Salford. Those other Jews were Lithuanian or Litvak, Polish, Galician, and Russian. There were also some utterly fabulous oriental Jews, who lived in a garden-like area called Didsbury, which I heard about in my childhood but did not visit until I was sixteen and began to attend Manchester University, in that vicinity. Somewhat incongruously, oriental Jews are now associated in my mind with my teachers, Ernest Rutherford and Niels Bohr.

Litvak and Polish Jews were our neighbors, for the colonies interpenetrated. But we did not have much to do with them. A certain shyness kept us apart, in spite of the strong Jewish bond. They were also a little queer. The Litvaks said "*der ferd*" instead of "*dos ferd*" for "the horse," and "*die meidel*" instead of "*dos meidel*" for "the girl"; it was told of them that they liked to eat salt herring together with sponge cake. The Polish Jews said "*fly-sh*" instead of "*flaysh*" for "meat," and "*gegannen*" instead of "*gegangen*" for "went." Some of the Polish Jews produced the *r* from the uvula instead of from the palate, which we thought charming in children but rather backward in grown-ups. English Jews were an even remoter species to us immigrants than oriental Jews.

Among us Jews, as I remember vividly, the attitude toward England was one of intense admiration, respect, gratitude, and affection, troubled, however, by certain perplexities. For Roumanian villagers like us—I mean my immediate family—and in a not much smaller degree even for those who had come from Braila and Yasse and Galatz and other sizable towns, emigration to England had been translation from the Middle Ages into modernity. Stone houses and paved streets even in the slums! No mud, no swamps in the spring and autumn, no blinding clouds of dust in the summer. Running water, flush toilets (outhouses, to be sure, but not just a hole in the ground under a flimsy roof), coal, gas illumination. No more petroleum lamps (though some of us clung to the habit), no more wood-stoves in the middle of the room. And tramcars everywhere! Fantastic things they were: a wire overhead, a pole from the tramcar to the wire, and that was enough to send the tramcar speeding along the rails. Electricity! These were some of the physical marvels of the new world.

But reaching far deeper into the emotions of wonder and gratitude were the spiritual achievements of this extraordinary English race, whose name had been a portent and a beacon even in the wilds of Roumania. More remarkable than the tramcar was the spirit of the man who drove it. I remember how my parents would describe it all to new arrivals.

"And who do you think drives that tramcar? Some self-important, puffed-up official, like the captain of the ferry-boat between Macin and Braila, before whom you have to bow and take off your hat? Nothing of the sort! A simple, friendly *goy*, who takes your penny or your ha'penny and says '*Kew!*' and gives you a ticket. Unbelievable!"

And from this subject the discourse would widen out:

" '*Kew!*' and '*Next!*' Those are the first things you must learn here in England. Politeness—and order. When you go into the pharmacist's here, you don't have to stand hat in hand for half an hour until the young snot behind the counter says: 'What do you want, Jew?' The pharmacist here may very well be a Jew himself. And even if he isn't, he's polite. You keep your hat on your head, the pharmacist says '*Next!*' you buy your bottle of iodine, he says '*Kew!*' and it's finished. Always '*Next!*' No pushing, no shouting, no bootlicking, no favoritism. Everything with a system. Quiet. Polite. That's freedom.

"It's so in the schools here. Jew or *goy*, if you're bright you get the prize. You're next, no matter who your father is.

"And if you happen to get into a quarrel with someone, don't hit. The first man to hit is in the wrong, no matter what words passed between you. And don't be afraid to call a policeman. And never try to slip something into a policeman's hand; woe to you if you do. It's not that kind of country. It's not *Valach* (Roumania). It's England!"

The briefing on conduct in a quarrel was theoretical. Jews did not come to blows, in public or in private. But— and here I touch on some of the perplexities—there was a section of the gentile population which was given to excessive drinking, particularly on Saturday nights, to occasional fighting and even to wife-beating, indulgences unknown among us. The poorer parts of Salford contiguous with our neighborhood were not particularly criminal, but they were rowdy, often to the point of ugliness. We did not assume that they were typically English; on the other hand we did not absolve England of responsibility. If these wonderful islanders could have tramcars, flush toilets, gas lighting and honestly administered schools for everyone, why could they not train the poor in better ways? As for the poverty, that was no excuse. We were poorer.

I will not suggest that it was as an explicit criticism of England that our parents sent us to *cheder*, or private Hebrew school, every evening after attendance at the regular school; but certainly there was an implied reservation. A shilling a week my father paid the *Rebbi*, or teacher, for my tuition, in days when a shilling was a solid slice of the family budget. From families as poor as ours, or poorer, two or three boys would exact one and ninepence or two and sixpence (reduction for quantity) weekly for their Jewish education. As I think back I am profoundly stirred by this heavy sacrifice, which our parents accepted as a matter of course. It was not, as I have said, born of a conscious reaction to England's imperfections. It was affirmative. It was a refusal to file a petition in bankruptcy even in the face of England's greatness. We were not spiritual paupers. With all our extravagant admiration of England we did not consider ourselves raw human material for even the most advanced of nations to place upon us the obliterating and recreative stamp of its culture. The humblest and least intellectual representatives of the Jewish tradition, we knew ourselves to be at least the matrix of higher things. We, on our level, were also the guardians of great values.

I must not understate the extent of our cultural resources. True, nobody that I remember in our fairly large clan could read and understand a page of the Bible or the Mishnah in the original. No one had a picture of the framework of Jewish history. Maimonides and Rashi and the Baal Shem Tov were only portentous names, symbols of vague supernal achievements in knowledge and faith. The exodus from Egypt and the Babylonian exile, the kings of Israel and the prophets and the Pharisaic sages, were not always placed in the right order. The Talmud was an enormous, an immeasurable realm of such wisdom as no gentile nation had ever possessed; but a person who could "learn a page of *Gemara*" (Talmudic text) was as remote from us intellectually as Rothschild was economically, and regarded with the same degree of awe. The Torah (meaning here only the Five Books of Moses) was nearer to us, because every one of us, we, our fathers, our grandfathers, had gone to *cheder* and had chanted the Hebrew text together with the Yiddish translation, at least from the age of six to the age of thirteen; we had also chanted in the same way the learned and penetrating commentary of Rashi, the great medieval exegetist. But the knowledge faded from us as we grew up, for two reasons: it was badly instilled, in the wretched one-room schools, by the utterly incompetent if conscientious pedagogues; and in later years the struggle for existence was

13

so exhausting that there was little energy left for the retention and development of these enjoyments. That is the obvious excuse, which does not explain why other Jewish
groups, as poor as we, did better. And yet—

No one was illiterate, and nearly everyone did a little
reading, almost exclusively in Yiddish. A one-eyed Jew on
Moreton Street had a Yiddish lending library and made
some sort of living out of the pennies and twopences that
he collected weekly from his subscribers. With two hundred
of them he may have grossed two pounds, or two pounds
ten, out of which less than half could have been profit. He
also sold prayer-books and prayer-shawls. Somehow he and
his family lived. It is something to be remembered that our
drab and harassed and not too intellectual little world could
maintain even this meager cultural institution. The books
were, as in all lending libraries, a wild assortment, with a
preponderance of rubbish: sometimes we got Sholom Alei-
chem and Peretz, more often we got the driveling novels of
Shomer. There was also a Yiddish daily from London, the
Express, and there were Yiddish periodicals from America.

A primitive Yiddish theater erupted occasionally in Manchester (I am speaking of the early years, before the visits of
Maurice Moskowitz), but many of us could not afford even
the sixpenny seats. We were fond of music, but pianos were
rarities and symbols of luxury. Our religious life would have
seemed grotesquely eclectic or haphazard to an orthodox
Jew. None of us admitted un-kosher meat of any kind—let
alone pork—into the house; but I do not recall a single
family in our clan keeping the requisite sets of two dishes
for meat and milk. We went to synagogue on the important
festivals, but not on Friday evenings and Sabbaths. No one
in our circle put on prayer-shawl and phylacteries every
morning, as pious Jews do. As far as I remember, every
mother of a household lit the Friday-night candles, but few

fathers said the Friday night Sabbath benediction over the wine. We fasted on the Day of Atonement and—in part— on the Ninth Day of Ab (for the destruction of the Temple), and we went to hear the reading of Lamentations, where we wept; but we ignored the minor fasts and festivals. Of course the *Kaddish* and the *Shivah* for the dead were rigidly observed; and sometimes the scapegoat rooster ceremony— the waving of a rooster over the head in a symbolism of vicarious atonement—was popular with a family. We re- cited Psalms (without knowing the meaning of the Hebrew words) on solemn and critical occasions, like births and serious sicknesses. Formally, then, it was a rather skeleton- ized Judaism, nothing more than a system of mnemonics. And yet—

The Day of Atonement, with its fasting and praying and— on the part of the women—copious weeping, was a tremen- dous annual event; and the Passover, with its scourings and its unleavened bread, its colorful opening ceremonial eve- nings round the family table, its new clothes and its old legends, has left with us—with the now long-since grown-up children of that world—memories of indestructible beauty. Few of us, in Manchester, actually built a booth on the Festival of Booths; often we failed even to observe the ritual of the palm branch and the citron; but somehow, from the observances of others, a breath of the oriental fields and harvests was wafted to us.

Muted ancestral voices reached us, speaking an exalted and half-intelligible language. Moses, our teacher and rabbi, was alternately a bearded colossus on the summit of Sinai and a sympathetic familiar, at home in our Rouma- nian Yiddish world. Elijah the prophet, renewed for us as a folk-figure by fragments of Chassidic lore—there were no full-fledged Chassidim among us—was not the violent and vehement "troubler of Israel," the fiery desert moralist and

15

scourge of kings; he was a kindly and ubiquitous magician, disguised now as a mendicant, now as a billygoat, turning up in the lives of the humble and pious in the last extremity, when the waters had come up to their soul. All these themes wandered about in our home-talk, leavened it, and redeemed it from vanity. And at all times the Messianic theme was implicit in our view of life—a restoration of the Jewish state, the redemption of the Jewish people and of all mankind.

For a long time I thought that a thoroughly Jewish Jew could not be wealthy; poverty and Judaism went together. I was not wholly wrong. But I clouded the truth by also thinking that Judaism went together with a low cultural level (in the formal sense) and with ignorance of the surrounding world. Years of alienation intervened before I corrected the error, and before I understood, for that matter, that the cultural level of my childhood surroundings had not been so low as I believed in my adolescence. And in a certain sense it was not low at all. It was in fact extraordinarily high for a social group with a minimum of schooling and a maximum of economic harassment. It was a long time before I could see the world into which I was born in its proper perspective, before I understood that its spiritual resources could not be stated solely in æsthetic and intellectual terms.

For who were these cobblers, tailors, carpenters, peddlers, small shopkeepers of the Manchester ghetto, or of that part of it which I knew? They were, I learned in time, the eternally faithful poor of the Jewish people. They were in the line of the weavers and water-carriers of Davidic Jerusalem and Hasmonean Judea. They had reached Manchester by a long trek across centuries and continents and civilizations. They had never lost contact with their origins. Few of us could trace our family line back for more than two or three generations. We had no records of our sojournings.

Yet the picture is fairly clear for anyone with an elementary knowledge of Jewish history: in the time of Nebuchadnezzar to Babylonia and Egypt; from Jerusalem in the time of the Romans—beginning with Pompey, and through successive expulsions up to the time of Hadrian—to Rome and the western world; by way of the Black Sea into southern Russia; by way of Spain into France and western Europe, with backwashes to the east; eastward into Poland and middle Russia in the time of the Crusades—and so a perpetual wandering through the time of the Renaissance and the "Emancipation," with a last strong westward tide across the Atlantic. The prayers, the legends, the folklore, persisted even among the lowliest—I do not speak of the instructed. A Jew of the time of Hillel would not have felt much of a stranger at one of our *seder* ceremonies; a Jew of the time of the Crusades would have felt very close to a simple Jew of the time of the Kishinev pogrom.

With the modification I have noted, I was not far out in associating Jewish survival with the self-respect of the poor. Particularly was this true of recent times. I did not know anything, in my boyhood, about modern Jewish assimilation and its relation to wealth. I did know, however, that the Anglicized Jews, those who had settled in the country long before us and were now well-to-do, were not as Jewish as we. They were, it appeared, good, benevolent people; they were the *Budagaren* (the Board of Guardians), to whom we might apply for interest-free loans in desperate times. But while they helped us economically, they let us down spiritually. They were more like the gentiles than like us. They made us feel our foreignness as much as the others did; perhaps a little more, because they were, in spite of everything, part of us. They also made us feel that they regarded our mores as inessentials—and worse: as outlandish impedimenta that were unnecessary to Judaism and a deter-

17

rent to good English citizenship. They helped us—but we embarrassed them.

Years later, looking back and savoring the richness of the inner life of my childhood world, I have been struck with wonder that any adult Jew should ever be able to adopt the slogan: "Workers of the world, unite! You have nothing to lose but your chains." These workers and peddlers, and their blood-brothers in Poland and the rest of eastern Europe, had a great deal to lose, besides their chains; and why, in an appeal to union and freedom, one should deny those treasures which freedom ought to safeguard is still beyond me.

# CHAPTER III

## *The Union Jack*

❀

THE HOMAGE that my elders paid to England's greatness was a pallid thing compared to the blazing loyalty that
was awakened in me. I would listen with a continuous in-
ward chuckling to their rehearsals of the wonders of the new
world—a favorite topic of conversation—and in my delight
there was the condescension of an insider, as though I had a
greater share in England and her achievements, as though
I was also in some way responsible for them.

It seemed to me proper that my parents should be dumb-
founded by the marvels of my England; and it also seemed
proper to me that the marvels should be lumped together,
the trivial with the significant, the natural with the man-
made, and credited indiscriminately to the master-people:
toast and tramcars and fogs and freedom. One laughed up-
roariously at toast, of course; it was simply burned bread.
One stood aghast before, or in, the fogs. But like the tramcars and the freedom and the order and the politeness, toast
and fogs were intimate features of the singular race which
in those days was considered the highest manifestation of
civilization.

My proprietory attitude was in one sense justified: I
learned English very quickly (the older generation learned
it slowly and with various degrees of imperfection) and was

soon reading furiously. Oddly enough, I did not feel the less English for not knowing any English people, any gentiles or Christians. Throughout my early boyhood and well into the teens all my friendships were within the Jewish colony. But we youngsters created an English colony within the Jewish colony; and like many colonials we outdid the inhabitants of the mother country in pride and love.

Our integration into England was effected by two instruments, the school and juvenile literature; and since the second was, as it seems to me, infinitely more important, I shall devote most of my attention to it. I call it the "Union Jack" literature, partly because a penny weekly of that name was, I think, the first material that I learned to read outside the school curriculum; and partly because the name itself is a summary and symbol. Other halfpenny and penny periodicals (twopence for the gloriously colored and appetizingly bulky Special Holiday Issues) were the *Boy's Friend*, the *Boy's Leader*, *Pluck*, the *Marvel*, the *Gem*, the *Magnet*, *Tom Merry*, *Greyfriars;* and if I am now confusing names of periodicals with names of their central characters—perhaps to the keen distress of other surviving addicts who happen to read this—it is of no importance.

Some of us could not afford a periodical every week. A twopenny double number was beyond anyone's single reach. We clubbed together for many of the purchases, and an immense system of exchanges, extending through school and *cheder*, enabled us to read something like ten periodicals a week.

This juvenile literature has not, as far as I know, been properly evaluated. It has been written about, but nearly always either indulgently or facetiously. It does not seem to have been regarded seriously as a powerful influence in the maintenance of England's moral tradition. Yet such it was. Alfred Harmsworth (later Lord Northcliffe) and the other publishers of these periodicals were not simply conscience-less businessmen. They had a mission. It is true that they made a successful business of their mission, but they did not deviate from a well-defined set of principles.

The magazines were produced for sale; therefore their contents had to be entertaining, and we found them irresistibly so. But they were produced within the rigid framework of a folklore and outlook that were profoundly and irreproachably English. While they held the youngster spellbound with stories of adventure and high jinks in public schools (English public schools; i.e., private schools), they indoctrinated him powerfully with English ideals of fair play, honesty, respect for the throne and the county nobility, pluck, cheerfulness, loyalty, and cricket. They were Kipling brought down to semi-slum levels, as Kipling was Shakespeare's Henry the Fifth brought down to Victorian levels, as Shakespeare's Henry the Fifth was Castiglione's *Courtier* transplanted to England, and as *The Courtier* was the ideal man of the classical Greeks reinterpreted by the Italian Renaissance. With this line of descent I deal more fully below; I must mention it here to show that the Harmsworth juvenile periodicals were based on no mean or upstart philosophy. They were in a great and universal tradition, something that is obscured for us—for those of us, I mean, who were brought up on them—by their primitive literary quality and their peculiarly English ideological argot.

I suppose "cricket" comes nearest to summing it all up. The impact of that word on us youngsters—the little Roumanian Jewish immigrants who became little Englishmen without mingling with English boys—was overwhelming. A thing that wasn't cricket was of course shocking and shameful; but these adjectives do not convey the force or flavor of the condemnation to an outsider. That "it" was not cricket did not simply mean that it was morally wrong. Something deeper was involved: the disapproval of Harry Wharton, Tom Merry, Darrel Figgis, and all the other decent fellows of Greyfriars and St. Jim's, the right people—no, the only possible people, all other people being outsiders.

That these people never stole and never lied goes without saying. They were frank and aboveboard, just as they were fearless and full of japes. Nevertheless, when they wanted to emphasize the truthfulness of an assertion, they used the formula "Honor bright!" If you said that, it was caddish of anyone to doubt your word. "Honor bright" did not actually mean "Otherwise I am possibly a liar." It was just a reminder of one's consciousness of the code, it was a salute, a Masonic signal. "I'm from St. Jim's." "I'm from Greyfriars." Among us Jewish youngsters "Honor bright" was used as often as in the stories of Greyfriars. It was a source of deepest chagrin to us that we could not explain the phrase and all its vast implications to our parents, or to our *Rebbi* in *cheder*; and it certainly made us feel that they were irretrievably outsiders.

The code also included "the stiff upper lip," which was as tacitly a part of a decent fellow's equipment as it was unthinkable to be a bully. It would have horrified us to be told that a bully could keep a stiff upper lip, just like Tom Merry or Harry Wharton. Bullying was among the unforgivable sins; but some sins were merely venial, hardly more than misdemeanors, like Billy Bunter's comical greediness. The genuine criminal was of two types, with a social distinction that is best brought out by a comparison between the words "poacher" and "cad." (Of course we knew poachers only from the books.) A poacher was a low-class person in both senses. He was something like a burglar, but with a special touch of reprehensibility because he concentrated his criminality on the county gentry. He was a churl, a rascally villein, in whose dishonesty there was something

22

of the disrespectful and contumacious. Besides being dis-
honest, as a thief, he was in his low way subversive; not
only did he steal from the squire; he showed an ugly disregard for the sporting code, which demands that hares be
shot or hunted down by gentlemen at the proper season, and
not trapped by ungrammatical vagrants at any time of the
year. We little Strangeways Jews had a lofty disdain for
poachers; however, it was nothing like the wordless contempt that the cad inspired in us.

For the cad was a horse of a different color. He had to
belong, by birth and upbringing, to the Tom Merry social
class. A member of the lower orders could not aspire to be
a cad; it would have been presumptuous, as well as futile.
A cad was something more than a thief, a liar, or a sneak.
One could be all of these, and even a bully to boot, and yet
not quite a cad. The full-fledged cad, the cad in good standing, had to be a traitor to the essential notion of a Tom
Merrydom and a Harry Whartondom. Thieves, liars,
sneaks, bullies could be redeemed. Not so the cad. He had
sinned against the Holy Ghost.

The crimes of a cad, like those of a poacher—but more
odiously, since he, unlike the poacher, had orginally been
"one of us"—implied a corrupt disregard for the *structure*
of things. It is the difference between the amoralist and the
sinner. A cad was one who accepted a bribe to sell out the
game in the great annual cricket match between Greyfriars
and St. Jim's. He did not care who was the winner even
when he had no special interest. He was capable of sabo-
taging a boat race by tampering with the oars. What these
things mean, how far they go beyond the ordinary transgression that is motivated by greed, or cruelty, perhaps only
a public-school Englishman, or a former reader of *Pluck* and
the *Union Jack*, can feel. I prefer not to linger on this distasteful subject.

The gulf widened steadily between us and our parents as we, the youngsters, sank deeper into the traditions of Grey-friars and St. Jim's. Our parents remained, till the end, incapable of understanding that a game was more than a game, and that "playing the game"—untranslatable concept!—was morality itself. They had a more somber attitude toward youth than did their Christian neighbors. At most they were willing to concede to youth a certain playfulness, a coltish need to scamper about and make unnecessary noises. But to invest this release with a tremendous moral function, on a level with the law of Moses, was wholly beyond their capacity. They lived out their lives in England, from early middle to old age, without so much as a glimpse of the English attitude toward sports; and until the end they were baffled by the extraordinary phenomenon of grown-up, often elderly people passionately addicted to football and cricket. In those early days there was one famous cricketer, G. W. Grace, who was bearded like a rabbi. His picture once appeared in the *Yiddish Express*, which on rare occasions had a few lines about Test Matches and similar national solemnizations. My father looked long and earnestly at the bearded man in the white flannels and kneepads, posing in the worshipful attitude of a semi-genu-flection before the three wickets; he looked, pondered, sighed, and gave it up. Neither he nor the other grown-ups knew what to make of this whole aspect of adult English life. At that, they were not aware of its depth and extent. It was, even in their imperfect picture of it, one of those perplexities which I have mentioned as troubling their extravagant admiration of England.

At a distance of decades the problem invites facetious treatment, or at least the light touch. Invariably it is in fact so treated. This is evasive, unsatisfying, and unilluminating. We youngsters were reconciled to the idea that our parents would always be aliens, that Englishness would never be theirs as it was ours. What wounded us was the completeness of their exclusion. For there were gradations of alienness. There were lesser breeds without the law which could achieve a certain semi-acceptability. Hindu and French boys turned up at St. Jim's and Greyfriars, and in time came to be voted "rather decent fellows." They even acquired a special merit because they had become rather decent fellows without really having to, not being English. But their admission to this status of associate human being was always won at cricket. Even a Jewish boy (Goldwasser: I remember the name because of the mingled discomfort and pride it awakened in me nearly fifty years ago) was once permitted to score a century at the wicket. There was also a Hindu boy who made a creditable record in an interschool match. Such persons, in spite of their organic handicaps, could be admitted as guests to the inner circle; they had undoubtedly perceived, if only in a dim and rudimentary way—something like the mathematical propensity in an exceptional horse—what cricket meant in the cosmic sense. What, however, was I to think of my *Rebbi*, and of my parents, who did not know by which end to hold a cricket bat, and to whom the higher symbolism of cricket was forever inaccessible?

It might be inferred from the foregoing that I became a little anti-Semite. This was not the case. I accepted the division of the universe into two worlds. How these two worlds accommodated themselves within me is beyond my powers of anaylsis or even of description. I never developed a contempt for the Jewish world, or a hostility toward it, and this still surprises me. It had powerful attractions, which I have in part described; but they are not the kind that one usually associates with boyhood. On the other hand it was a world which, apart from certain spiritual difficulties it

25

created for me, might have become repellent by reason of its severe disciplines.

From the age of six till the age of thirteen I was "robbed" of two or three hours every day (except Friday), confined to an evil-smelling room with thirty or forty other youngsters between those ages, and compelled to learn the Pentateuch in Hebrew by translation into Yiddish. Regular school took up from nine to four thirty, with a two-hour break; the *cheder* took up from six to eight or nine, depending on the age of the pupil. Saturday afternoons and Sunday mornings and afternoons were similarly pre-empted. So self-enclosed was our Jewish world, so little did it occur to us to compare our lot with that of gentile boys, that we accepted the discipline as self-understood. I must also remark that none of the people who went to *cheder* with me (I have kept in touch with quite a number of them) seem to be any the worse for it. We might, indeed, have been a great deal the better for it; but the *Rebbi* was no teacher. His scholarly attainments, I ascertained in later years, were respectable; his pedagogic instincts—training he had none—were rudimentary in the extreme. Conceding that I resisted my Jewish education, while I eagerly welcomed my English education; conceding also that I "repressed" the Jewish side of me until the age of nineteen or twenty, I still should not have found myself, after seven years of steady tuition, so wretchedly equipped in Jewish matters as I did, and compelled to go back almost to the beginning.

I say "almost" because I know it was not a total loss. As I read today the Hebrew Bible and the Mishnah, many passages reverberate with the arresting but elusive overtones of resuscitated memories. Five and a half of our *cheder* days were devoted to the mechanical repetition of the weekly portion of the Pentateuch, with secondary additions: Yiddish writing, the daily and festival prayers, special passages

26

like The Song of Songs and the Book of Esther. But Saturday afternoons were on a higher plane, and during those hours we sometimes enjoyed *cheder*. For then we would be regaled with the legends of the Jews, and we would learn *The Ethics of the Fathers* from the Mishnah. I should remark that twenty-five or thirty years ago I did not have as clear a recollection of my *cheder* life as I have today. In my sixth decade I am recapturing many details of the Jewish elements in my first and second. I can now remember clearly reading in *cheder* certain passages in the Pentateuch and Mishnah which a quarter of a century ago I would have said I was learning for the first time. A great many other passages are vaguely though powerfully evocative, like the *petite madeleine* in Proust. In the same way I now remember the profound impressions made on me by the Jewish festivals—impressions that I would have denied in my twenties. In my twenties I remembered only that attendance at synagogue with my father had been an ordeal.

That Jewish world of thought in me should have been, I suppose, constantly at war with the English world of thought. As I have said, it was not; and I do not understand how the two failed to join issue. The mutual incompatibility of those two worlds comes back to me with peculiar vividness as I reconstruct, with inescapable certainty, the moral instruction I received in *cheder*. This was both general, as issuing from the study of the Pentateuch, and specific, as condensed in *The Ethics of the Fathers*. When I place it side by side with the moral instruction that I derived from the *Union Jack* books, I am astonished not to find myself in the care of a psychiatrist.

It so happens that even in my Jewish moral instruction there was a division, that between the prophetic morality and the wisdom morality, as I explain in Book Two. That may be ignored for the moment. I will only recall that from

27

the age of seven or eight on I had the following precepts drummed into me in Hebrew and Yiddish:

"Thou shalt love the Lord thy God with all thy heart and with all thy soul and with all thy might."

"Thou shalt love thy neighbour as thyself."

"By three things the world is sustained: by truth, by judgment and by peace."

"Keep not aloof from the congregation, and trust not in thyself until the day of thy death, and judge not thy fellow until thou art come in his place."

"Let the honor of thy fellow be as dear to thee as thine own, and be not easily provoked; and repent one day before thy death."

To this last our *Rebbi* added: "How subtle were our sages! Since no man knows the day of his death, this really means that you must repent at once." I encountered this comment again years later in Browning's *Rabbi Ben Karshook*, a name otherwise unfamiliar to me. *The Ethics of the Fathers* gives Rabbi Eliezer as the source.

We learned further:

"Consider three things and thou wilt not fall into transgression: Know whence thou comest, and whither thou goest, and before whom thou must give account and reckoning. Thou comest from a stinking drop, thou goest to a place of dust, worms and maggots, thou wilt give account and reckoning before the King of kings of kings, the Holy One, blessed be He." All of which we understood, except "the stinking drop."

The insistence on moral self-conquest and death's inevitability may seem excessive for youngsters of seven to thirteen, but I remember discussing some of the precepts with fellow pupils.

We also learned: "If a man puts his fellow to shame publicly, he has no share in the world to come." I have a special reason for remembering this precept, as I shall shortly tell. Likewise we were instructed: "Be exceedingly lowly of spirit, for the portion of man is but the worm."

Then there were passages with a lilt: "Who is wise? He that learns from all men. Who is mighty? He that subdues his evil nature. Who is rich? He that rejoices in his lot. Who is honored? He that honors mankind." And then, gloomily: "The more the flesh, the more the worms; the more the money, the more the worry; the more the women, the more the witchcraft; the more the servant girls, the more the lewdness; the more the servants, the more the thieving." A cheerful antistrophe followed: "The more the study of the law, the more the life," and so on.

Perhaps these passages sank deeper into us than most of the other *cheder* instruction because they were taught on Saturdays, when we had no regular school; perhaps also because there was a festive air in the *cheder*, and on that day the *Rebbi* did not use the cat-o'-three-tails. But I was aware, even in those days, of the hopeless incongruity between this code and the moral code of Greyfriars and St. Jim's.

At Greyfriars and St. Jim's, too, it was taken for granted that a man ought to be modest and kind, that one ought not to put on side, one ought not to be a rotter. But that was not the point, really. Where, in the *cheder* code, was the cheerfulness, gaiety, and magnanimity of life at St. Jim's? Where was the gallantry, where were the affirmations: "Carry on, carry on, carry on, till the field ring again and again!" "Play the game!" "Hurray for St. Jim's!" "Hurray for the Fourth Form!" There was no hurraying in the Mishnah, no feeling of loyalty, attachment, camaraderie. There was, in short, no cricket.

Less intensely, because it did not grip the imagination like St. Jim's, our working-class school on Waterloo Road also contrasted in spirit with the *cheder*. At school we learned

English history as in *cheder* we learned—though much less systematically—Jewish (mostly Biblical) history. English history was adorned with poems like *The Charge of the Light Brigade* and *The Revenge, a Ballad of the Fleet*. There was nothing like this in the bits of Jewish history and legend that we got on Saturdays and, as contained in the Pentateuch, on weekdays. There were Jewish wars, Jewish victories, and Jewish heroes. There were also wild songs of triumph. We knew something about the valiant men of King David's *corps d'élite*, and something about Bar Kochba and his rebellion against Rome. Concerning the latter we were told thrilling things: that every man who enlisted with him had to cut off a finger to demonstrate his courage, and had to be so strong, and so skillful a rider, that he could at full gallop uproot a sapling without being unhorsed. And yet Jewish wars and Jewish heroes and Jewish songs of triumph failed to strike the right note.

Jewish wars were gloomy things; Jewish heroes, though impressive in their way, were without form and style; Jewish songs of triumph were too furiously triumphant. Where in Jewish history was a Hereward the Wake or a Black Prince? Where was a Sir Francis Drake singeing the beard of the King of Spain, or gaily finishing his game of bowls on the green at Plymouth before proceeding to polish off the Spanish Armada? Samson was obviously quite a fellow, but it did not seem that he ever set about the business of killing his enemies with the gallant and modest smile which would have illumined his features if he had been an English gentleman—an old St. Jim's man.

I read very early a verse of Newbolt's:

> *To set the cause above renown,*
> *To love the game beyond the prize,*
> *To honor, while you strike him down,*
> *The foe that comes with fearless eyes.*

That was exactly what I meant. When Jews used to go to war, thousands of years ago, they did not kill their foes in that fine spirit. And Jews, teaching and learning their own history, did not begin to understand the deficiency. How could one convey to them the spirit in which an Englishman did his killing? It was almost not killing. It was— well, it was rather like cricket.

"A good clean fight, no hitting below the belt, may the best man win, and no hard feelings": on the battlefield as in the ring. One could put these words accurately into Yiddish, but they would be gibberish. Jews looked on all fighting, private and public, personal and historic, as such a disgusting business that they could not associate it with an affirmative code; and I felt this so strongly even in my boyhood that I despaired of ever giving my parents a glimpse into the sunny combativeness of the St. Jim's *Weltanschauung*. How could I begin to reconcile it with the somber thoughtfulness of the Pentateuch and *The Ethics of the Fathers*? Where, within that subtle and perceptive discipline, could you find room for the dashing buccaneer type, who could make his prisoners walk the plank, but who, beneath everything, was something of a gentleman because he knew the meaning of "a fair fight"? And in what terms could I present to my *Rebbi* the honorable features in the characters of a Captain Kidd and Claude Duval?

For a long time I was deeply convinced that in the churches of the Christians there were wonderful prayers and rituals which expounded and expressed the code of St. Jim's; that for the gentiles there was the same congruence between their divine services and the ideal secular life as there was for us. In the church the sights would be set higher than in daily practice, even as they were in the *cheder;* but the direction would be the same. What glimpses of an apotheosized Tom Merry those Christian rites must afford the worshippers! And this belief of mine was fortified by the difference in externals. How different the churches were from our synagogues, which at best looked squalid from the outside, and sometimes consisted of nothing more than a rented room upstairs in a private house. If, among our Roumanian Jews, in such surroundings, and in connection with such a prosaic moral code, the overwhelming effects of the Day of Atonement could be produced, what must be the glories of the church services, with their stained-glass windows, their organs, and, above all, the radiant possibilities of the English public-school philosophy of life?

But it is with a church service, the first I attended—the second was not to follow for many, many years—that I associate the beginnings of my understanding that the Christian world is not the simple thing I once took it for. It came about thus:

I was in love with a little Christian girl in my last class at Waterloo Road School. I had never spoken to her. One did not play with girls, or do more than exchange a few words with them, at the age of twelve: that is, if they were Jewish. With Christian boys one played on rare occasions; with Christian girls one did not even speak. We did not go into the houses of our occasional Christian playfellows, we did not invite them into ours. So I worshipped this little girl from afar, and indulged in ecstatic visions of the two of us walking together, doing our homework side by side, and exchanging copies of the *Union Jack*, *Pluck*, the *Boy's Friend*, and other sacred publications.

Girls seldom appeared in the stories of Greyfriars and St. Jim's. When they did, they were the feminine counterparts of Tom Merry and Harry Wharton and Darrel Figgis: without the boisterousness and combativeness, they represented as profoundly the spirit of the game. How thrillingly right I found it when, one day, passing down the little street where the object of my adoration lived (a daring indulgence that I permitted myself occasionally), I saw her playing cricket on the sidewalk with a man who wore the reversed collar of a curate. I did not nod or raise my cap; nor did she acknowledge my fleeting and feverish presence. We never reached that stage of intimacy. But my heart thudded, and the sound of her laughter filled the whole world for me. They were playing cricket with an improvised bat and a soft ball; they had no wickets, only chalkmarks on a lamppost. But it was cricket, it was fittingly and exhilaratingly cricket. How unimaginable that my *Rebbi* should ever play cricket with one of us—much less with a girl! How unimaginable, for that matter, that any Jewish adult should play cricket with a youngster, or cricket at all! And here was a grown-up, a man of God to boot, probably—who could tell?—as much as thirty years old, playing cricket with a girl, and it was all so natural, so gloriously matter-of-fact. My heart swelled with loving envy—no, not envy: one does not envy the saints in heaven, the divinities on Olympus—it swelled with a loving and unuttered salutation from afar, the *un*envious, ungrudging salutation of an eternal outsider, hurrying past the gates, accidentally ajar, of an inaccessible paradise.

I tried to imagine conversations between the man and the girl, exchange of views, in the clipped but so meaningful dialect of Greyfriars and St. Jim's; I also felt the seamless unity of outlook which made conversation practically superfluous. How different from the hopeless division between me and my parents; how different from the whole tenor of the life of us Jewish boys!

I formed there and then a resolution the daring of which is perhaps as incomprehensible to a Christian as the manly jollity of *D'ye Ken John Peel?* was to my *Rebbi* and my parents. I was going to attend Sunday service in the neighborhood church, where undoubtedly the adored one worshipped and perhaps this curate officiated. I was going to penetrate into the forbidden place which pious Jews never passed without the prescribed muttered formula of indignant repudiation. I was going to witness, for once, the exalted ceremonies that were the highest expression of the English way of life.

The incident—for I actually carried out my resolution— remains in my mind after more than forty years as a great confusion whirling about a single point of astonishing clarity. I was so terrified, when I sneaked in among the last of the worshippers; I was so lost and helpless in the dim light; I was so busy trying to conceal from someone (whom?) that I was a little Jew committing a mortal sin, that I could not have given a coherent account of my general impressions ten minutes after I escaped into the sunlight. The point of astonishing clarity came toward the end; and it became more and more vivid with the passing of the years: I was utterly confounded by the sermon preached from the pulpit (it was not, alas, the minister who had been playing cricket with my beloved). The sermon, in which the name of Jesus appeared and reappeared with—to me—terrifying frequency, had nothing whatsoever to do, in spirit or in substance, with that gay, magnanimous, adventurous and gamesome world which I had come to hear glorified. It did not proclaim, in new and unimaginably attractive phrases, the cosmic rightness of the life of Greyfriars, *The Revenge*, *The Charge of the Light Brigade*, and the cricket team. In a most unbelievable way it rehearsed what I had been learning in *cheder*! It appeared that among the Christians, too, the meek and the humble were blessed. It appeared that when someone hit you, you did not answer laughingly with a straight left, and you did not invite your friends to stand around in a circle while you carried on with the Marquis of Queensberry rules. Not a bit of it! You turned the other cheek! And what was my stupefaction on hearing that anyone who called anyone else a fool was in danger of hell-fire —a straight lift from *The Ethics of the Fathers*! It appeared that the peacemakers, not the soldiers, not the manly, laughing killers, were the blessed. This was not Tom Merry's world at all. It was my *Rebbi's*.

I simply did not understand. It was beyond my power of insight at that time to perceive that some sort of fraud was being perpetrated, that someone was misrepresenting something. I only felt that this English church, and so-English St. Jim's, and what we learned at school, did not go together, as I had supposed they would; and I was ready to believe that I was at fault; I assumed that I was too stupid to get at the higher unity. I did not know that this was the faltering start of a search which was to occupy me most of my life and provide the substance of many of my books.

# CHAPTER IV

## *Tennyson, Kipling, Shakespeare*

❀

Tennyson and Kipling took me by storm in my thirteenth year, and stayed with me until my sixteenth or seven-
teenth. I thought Tennyson the greater of the two; he had
passages quite beyond Kipling's reach; yet it was Kipling
who hit me the harder. He had a double appeal, especially
in his poetry. He expressed with far more skill and verve
than Tennyson the ideal Englishman who was adumbrated
in Tom Merry and Harry Wharton; and he was more personal than Tennyson. He made you feel that he himself was
that ideal Englishman, and that in condescending to address you he was imparting to you some of his identity.
When he wrote:

> Oh, East is East, and West is West, and never the twain shall
>     meet,
> Till Earth and Sky stand presently at God's great Judgment
>     Seat.
> But there is Neither East nor West, Border nor Breed, nor
>     Birth,
> When two strong men stand face to face, though they come
>     from the ends of the earth!—

when he wrote that, he meant of course, two Rudyard Kip-
lings, and he made me feel like both of them. And when he

wrote his specifications for the Englishman *in excelsis,* and wound up with the lines:

> *If you can fill the unforgiving minute*
> *With sixty seconds' worth of distance run,*
> *Yours is the Earth and everything that's in it,*
> *And—which is more—you'll be a Man, my son!—*

he meant: "Like me, like grand, tight-lipped old Rudyard Kipling—and like you too, potentially of course."

I was greatly affected by *Gunga Din*—that barroom-version of *Recessional*—and by *On the Road to Mandalay,* and I tingled from head to foot when I read:

> *Though I've belted you and flayed you,*
> *By the livin' Gawd that made you,*
> *You're a better man than I am, Gunga Din!*

But it was only in later years that I was able to paraphrase the lines in a way that brought out the essence of their appeal: "Though I've belted you and flayed you, I'm going to show you that I am, after all, the pukkah Englishman. I'm going to admit that you're a better man than I am, an admission that can only be made by a true sporting Englishman, such as you can never aspire to be. And if it comes to that, I'd belt you and flay you again if I had the chance, and apologize again, so that this fine situation, reflecting such credit on me, might be re-created."

Almost as magical in their effect on me were the lines:

> *Ship me somewhere east of Suez, where the best is like the worst,*
> *Where there aren't no Ten Commandments an' a man can raise*
> *a thirst.*

It did not occur to me in those days—though I had the information—that the Ten Commandments had, curiously enough, been issued just east of Suez. I did not, either,

attach too much weight to the fact that the Ten Commandments were implicitly accepted at St. Jim's. I had before
me one who, in spite of undoubtedly reprehensible leanings,
was after all an English soldier. He was not a St. Jim's man;
it would not be fair to be hard on him; with all his faults,
including his amusing coarseness, he had the right spirit.

There were poems of Tennyson's that were Kiplingesque
in their appeal to the ego. Such were *The Revenge* and *The
Charge of the Light Brigade*, which enabled me to identify
myself with Sir Richard Grenville and the heroes of Bala-
klava. The best of Tennyson, however, or what I then
thought the best, was subtler in its effect. There was a
prickling at the roots of my hair when I read the words of
the dying King Arthur:

> *I think that we*
> *Shall never more, at any future time,*
> *Delight our souls with talk of knightly deeds,*
> *Walking about the gardens and the halls*
> *Of Camelot, as in the days that were.*

Here was a note of modesty and courtliness. It did not invite self-identification so crassly. It waved one to a more
removèd ground. But it was English, through and through.
It summed up quietly the life of the ideal Englishman: combat in youth and memory of combat in old age. Not spiritual
combat of course, but the real thing. As Sir Galahad said:

> *My good blade carves the casques of men,*
> *My tough lance thrusteth sure.*
> *My strength is as the strength of ten,*
> *Because my heart is pure.*

(He is apparently trying to say: "I'm a better killer because
I don't have nocturnal emissions.")

In my boyhood Tennyson was still very popular in England; but Kipling's influence was, and remains, greater. Neither, of course, compares with Shakespeare, who came mightily into my life when I was about fifteen, and who is the supreme formulator of England's Ideal Man and Outlook.

He is much else, for he seems to have been capable of almost anything and everything supremely; and by that token he could express the Tennyson-Kipling ideal with a grace and seductiveness which reduce Tennyson to the level of a rectory-lawn æsthete and Kipling to that of a street-corner entertainer.

And now that I am getting to the heart of my subject I must introduce a few new terms which I hope to justify in the course of my exposition. I shall speak not only of the Tom Merry (or Rover Boy) man, and the Tennyson-Kipling man, but also of the English or Western Gentleman, and of the Renaissance Gentleman or Courtier, also of the classical Pagan Gentleman. All of them are variants of the non-Jewish man of the western world. Outside of the Jewish people there is also a Jewish man of the western world. I shall come to him in due course.

The ideal Western Gentleman appears many times in Shakespeare, and not always as an Englishman; but nowhere, to the best of my recollection, does he appear more completely than in the character of Henry the Fifth. I shall therefore confine my observations to this play, the more readily as I can refer some of my readers to the remarkable interpretation of it given in his famous movie by Sir Laurence Olivier.

Henry the Fifth is Tom Merry, grown up, matured—to the extent that an adult Tom Merry can be called mature—provided with a regal setting and an unbelievable power of self-expression (nobody but Shakespeare ever spoke like Shakespeare's characters—and not even he), and

put through his paces by the greatest of all poets and drama-
tists. He is also Kipling's If man, and Newbolt's unran-
corous, respectful killer. Like these and Sir Galahad he is,
incidentally, almost without sex. So is the whole play,
organically. The bawdy touches on the lowest social level,
like the romantic touch on the highest, are not part of the
essential theme, which is the presentation of the highest
type of noble; that is, of the fighting gentleman, the courtly
and winning adventurer, the laughing, democratic, and
fearless prince, the supremely English achievement of
western manhood's perfection.

For a brief review of the moral and ethical substance of
this perfection, we can begin with the famous oration to the
army before the storming of Harfleur:

> . . . *In peace there's nothing so becomes a man*
> *As modest stillness and humility:*
> *But when the blast of war blows in our ears,*
> *Then imitate the action of the tiger.* . . .

That is, when nothing important is afoot, when no fundamental values are at stake, the daily intercourse of gentlemen should be rendered graceful and gracious with the
choreography of Christian deportment. But the moment
you get down to essentials:

> . . . *Stiffen the sinews, summon up the blood,*
> *Disguise fair nature with hard-favour'd rage;*
> *Then lend the eye a terrible aspect.* . . .

This would seem to contradict the first principle of
knighthood, which forbids the killing of human beings in
anger. We are, however, reassured a little further on in the
play. It is only after the baggage boys have been slaughtered
by the French soldiers that the King lets us into the secret:

## TENNYSON, KIPLING, SHAKESPEARE

> *I was not angry since I came to France*
> *Until this instant.*

So he had been fighting like a true Englishman and knight after all, and slaughtering human beings in the spirit of clean fun.

Thence, again, we might suspect that war is not the one serious business of life, the ultimate purpose of our being, or, in the words of the ancient pagan philosopher, "the father of all things." We should be wrong. The definitive statement on the subject is made by Henry in another pre-battle oration:

> *Nor care I who doth feed upon my cost;*
> *It yearns me not that men my garments wear;*
> *Such outward things dwell not in my desires:*
> *But if it be a sin to covet honour,*
> *I am the most offending soul alive.*

At this point I find a short digression necessary. It is in the light of later understanding that I record what happened to me in my teen years, what forces acted on me and how I responded. I give the story both "from the inside" and in perspective. On these grounds it may be objected that I should not blame Tennyson, Kipling, and Shakespeare (let alone the Harmsworth juvenile writers) for my early over-susceptibility to them. These men were entertainers. If they were also protagonists of a life philosophy, they were not to be taken too seriously in that capacity. This demurrer must be summarily rejected. Entertainers or not, they wanted to be and always were taken seriously; what is more, they merit to be so taken. They are not flippant in their ethics, and they do not write more or less tongue-in-cheek; they mean business—even if, as I shall show, their "business" has its own ghastly flippancy. They are, moreover, the true representatives of the inmost sense of a civilization. If the reader wishes to dismiss the Harmsworth juvenile books and their American equivalents as irrelevant, let him first compare them with the standard Boy Scout Guides and observe how faithfully, and with how much more skill, they inculcate the same values; and of the representative pedagogic character of the Boy Scout Guides it is surely not necessary to say anything. Nor is the depiction of the ideal man as a sporting killer just an exciting fictional or poetical device, a symbolism or sublimation. Recently I came across this observation by Oliver Wendell Holmes (the great jurist, not the minor poet): "I believe that the struggle for life is the order of the world, at which it is vain to repine." And that we may not misconstrue his meaning, and think of spiritual and intellectual struggles, he adds: "I rejoice at every dangerous sport which I see pursued. The students at Heidelberg with their sword-slashed faces inspire me with sincere respect." And elsewhere, speaking *On the Love of Honor*, he says: "Why should you row in a boatrace? Why endure long months of pain in preparation for a fierce half hour that will leave you all but dead? Does anyone ask the question? Is there anyone who would not go through all its costs, and more, for the moment when anguish breaks into triumph—or even for the glory of having nobly lost?"

Quotations from serious pedagogues could be multiplied indefinitely. The one just given suffices to indicate their tenor in this field, and to absolve me from the charge of writing a caricature of the forces that influenced me in my boyhood.

To return to King Henry's oration. The key to the passage under consideration is in the last two lines quoted:

> *But if it be a sin to covet honour,*
> *I am the most offending soul alive.*

I already knew, in my youth, that from a certain point of view—the religious-moral, which then meant mostly the Jewish for me—it was indeed a sin to covet honor; I even suspected what I now know to be true, that it is the essential sin, the father of most sins, and certainly of the most horrible ones, the deep wound in our natures out of which have flowed the blood and decency of countless generations. But King Henry's defiance of God and prophet thrilled me, just as Falstaff's Sancho Panza satire on honor, in the second part of *King Henry the Fourth*, amused me with its coarse obtuseness. Yes, love of honor, and not a plausible claim to the throne, not a misconceived sense of injury, drove Henry to invade France; love of honor impelled him to commit the crimes from which he hypocritically begged the Archbishop of Canterbury to guard him. But there is something exhilarating, a *sursum corda*, in Henry's very acknowledgment of his sinfulness; it lifts us beyond sin; and that is how a person of quality talks to God.

What I would like to emphasize here is not the immorality of the thesis of the play but rather—and I deliberately use the jarring word—the hokum. An intellectual debasement and evasiveness at least as significant as the moral runs through all the play. There is obvious theatrical hokum ("good theater") in Henry's incognito visit to the simple soldiers Bates, Court, and William, sitting round the campfire the night before the battle; hokum in his manly heart-to-heart talk with them, for they, poor souls, are concerned with their obscure lives, and he with honor and the stage of history: his concern for them is as empty a gesture as the rage he summons up against his enemies. He has no relationship to anybody and anything except as the instrument of honor; he neither loves nor hates except to serve his reputation in his own eyes and in the eyes of others. He plays with lives as he plays with his own emotions. But the

supreme hokum is in his prayers to God, and in his philosophical soliloquy:

> And what have kings, that privates have not too,
> Save ceremony, save general ceremony?
> And what art thou, thou idol ceremony?
> What kind of god art thou, that suffer'st more
> Of mortal griefs than do thy worshippers?
> What are thy rents? what are thy comings in?
> O ceremony, show me but thy worth!
> What is thy soul of adoration?
> Art thou aught else but place, degree and form,
> Creating awe and fear in other men?

The peculiar horror of these lines, and of the more magnificent ones that follow, lies in this: that they penetrate
with the insight of the highest moral and philosophic
genius, and with incomparable vividness of imagery, to the
very nature of honor, or, as we should say, of honors, exhibitionism, public prominence, public approbation, the
things we strive for more bitterly than for food and shelter,
the things that poison and distort the comparatively simple
problem of subsistence for the whole human species. These
are the things that add up, in short, to the lust for power,
which is not, as some urge, a form of the hunger for security,
but a frightful impulse to extort applause, "creating fear
and awe in other men."

And these things are suddenly perceived in Henry's
soliloquy to be a terrifying emptiness! They are metaphysical abstractions; they are "place, degree, and form." They
are not substance, though they use substance; they are not
processes, though they use processes. They are a primordial
principle, they are bodiless evil itself.

Thus, precisely as he makes the religious gesture in order
to transcend it, so Henry makes the gentlemanly and cul-

tured gesture of philosophical-moral understanding likewise in order to transcend it; and he does it with such genius that we are shaken, almost as by a prophet. Then it occurs to us to ask: "Does he for a moment contemplate giving up this pursuit of honor?" And at once we recover our balance. Not in the slightest! He is just being philosophic, tolerant, and self-depreciatory, the way a gentleman is supposed to be now and again—even as a gentleman is also supposed to pray now and again. But the prayers and the philosophizing are only ornaments; he rises above them; he rises to honor.

And it is borne in upon us that the gentleman, the lover of honor, is essentially a killer! He must kill because in the last analysis "creating awe and fear in other men" calls for control over their lives, and this control must be demonstrated from time to time in its ultimate form—the taking of life.

Behind the attractive hokum, then, behind the gallantry, the gentleness, the democracy, the modesty, behind all these things, looms in control the ancient abomination. And this ancient abomination we must not confront, because if we do confront it—and I do not mean just intellectually and philosophically, but in a naked *corps à corps* confrontation of complete, horrified understanding—all our world comes tumbling about our ears.

The greatest of all masters of hokum—as he was of the elfin and the lyric, of somber moral discourse, and of many other forms—Shakespeare found, in respect of this play, a gifted interpreter in Laurence Olivier. I do not remember another theatrical performance that satisfied so deeply my inmost convictions about the purpose, conscious or unconscious, of the author. From the opening—the charming and so obviously faked model of Elizabethan London, which is an intimation of the deeper charm and fake of the play—to the climax (as it is for me)—the man of blood in a trance of noble meditation, clowning with profound thoughts before God and his own secret soul—the movie maintains this level of penetration, emphasizing at every point what I conceive Shakespeare to have intended.

I will give a final instance by way of additional illustration. Shakespeare opens the play with the setting up of the pretext for the invasion of France. To the Archbishop of Canterbury and the Bishop of Ely this military adventure is the means of diverting the King's attention from the planned seizure of the Church's property. And to King Henry the long and windy argument in defense of his hereditary claim to the crown of France means nothing. It is true that he warns the Archbishop:

> *And God forbid, my dear and faithful lord,*
> *That you should fashion, wrest, or bow your reading*
> *Or nicely charge your understanding soul*
> *With opening titles miscreate . . .*
> *For God doth know how many now in health*
> *Shall drop their blood in approbation*
> *Of what your reverence shall incite us to. . . .*
> *We charge you, in the name of God, take heed.*

But we learn soon after that Henry is concerned with honor, with honor only, wherein he is ready to be the most offending soul alive. And if forbidden to make war on France, and to kill people, how shall he acquire honor? So the admonition to the Archbishop is just a necessary piece of cant, and the Archbishop himself is only a propaganda stooge. And the dishonesty of the Archbishop fits in neatly with the King's dishonesty, so that both can grin contentedly at their private successes. Olivier, catching instinctively at the spirit of this immoral farce, turns the Archbishop of Canterbury and the Bishop of Ely into two

46

cunning zanies, and the scene before the King into a piece of buffoonery. Like the wooden model of London, this is part of the prelude to the interpretation.

In passing, I cannot help adding a comment as to the queer "timeliness" of the Olivier production. It came just after the democracies had emerged from the struggle with Nazi Germany; it was intended to strengthen and freshen England's morale; and the play has as its theme England's successful waging of a war on grounds so immoral, with justifications so flimsy and cynical, that the ghosts of Hitler and Goebbels might have applauded enviously.

The view I have here set forth concerning the Tennyson-Kipling-Shakespeare gentleman I could not of course have had at the age of fifteen or sixteen, even though I already suspected the basic immorality of the outlook. However, I was becoming an avid reader of Shaw and Wells—the latter was just emerging from the story-telling into the social-program phase. I remember, in fact, already reading at the age of twelve Robert Blatchford, a popular socialist journalist. He must have planted in me the seed that blossomed under the ministrations of Shaw and Wells, the seed of an outlook which led me to challenge the Tom Merry and Henry the Fifth ideal man. But the challenge was, as I shall tell, of a different order from the one I have formulated in this chapter. It was not until my twentieth year or so that I began to get glimpses of my present philosophy, in which Shaw and Wells are seen under the same aspect as Tennyson, Kipling, and the Shakespeare of *King Henry the Fifth*.

# CHAPTER V

## *Genealogy of the Gentleman*

❀

I F THE gentleman as an ideal type had been a mere literary invention, a plaything of writers and readers, I might not have been so fascinated by him in later years, and might not have been so curious about his origin and descent. But as I grew older, and became more interested in the everyday thoughts of people, and in their notions of right and wrong, it came home to me that the gentlemanly ideal was a dynamic psychological force. Nor, of course, was it either peculiarly English or confined anywhere to an aristocratic class. It was, as far as my reading and contacts in many countries went, a universal type. When the lower-class Englishman said "A decent fellow," the American "A swell guy," the Frenchman "*Un bon type*," they meant the same thing—the Tom Merry and Kipling man on his various levels. There were minor variations as between countries, and shocking misunderstandings because of such trivialities as differences in favorite sports, but very clearly there was such a thing as a general western picture of the ideal man.

My interest in the subject deepened as I became convinced that the phrase "Christian gentleman" is a contradiction in terms, that one can be a Christian or a gentleman, but not both. Finally, as I became aware of the historical substance of the contradiction, I came to the conclusion that this is the center of the moral pathology of the western world.

I have said that the Shakespearian or Elizabethan gentleman is the English version of the Italian Renaissance gentleman. This is not to imply that the surface villainies of the latter were transplanted to the former, though if I insist (as I will over and over again) that the gentleman is a killer, the distinction may seem unimportant. For what do kindness, forbearance, courtesy, courage, self-sacrifice—all the highest gentlemanly virtues—mean, if in the final account the gentleman must acquire honor? That is to say, he *must* find an enemy, so that he may display his physical courage in combat, that highest virtue of a gentleman. The virtues become the bawds of evil; they exist to give spice to the adventure; the demand for fairness in a fight is a demand not for goodness, but for more exciting conditions; the pretense at goodness helps to conceal the evil. And as to the maintenance of the Christian virtues in peacetime, what do these become but interim exercises, muscular flexions, between the essential occasions when the gentleman must kill? Must kill for honor, and must kill because life is combat.

It is not, I think, captious to suggest that under these circumstances the virtues of the gentleman are all the more dangerous, like the recurrent religious seizures of an insincere penitent, who emerges from each confession refreshed for his next indulgence. But putting this on one side, we may note with profit how many of the gentlemanly virtues the Italian ruling classes of the Renaissance managed to combine organically with the boundless criminality for which they are justly notorious. Symonds says of them: "As a correlative of their depravity, we find a sobriety of appetite, a courtesy of behaviour, a mildness and cheerfulness of disposition, a widely diffused refinement of sentiment and manners, a liberal spirit of toleration, which can nowhere else be paralleled in Europe at that period." I have tried in my novel, *Web of Lucifer*, to recapture the exquisite manners and revolting villainy which were fused in the characters of a Cesare Borgia and a Katerina Sforza, and I refer the reader to Quiller-Couch's *The Art of Reading* for an attractive account of the influence that the Italians, via their writings, exercised on the mind of the western world, and particularly of England.

Via that Renaissance song of courtliness, with its captivating burden of

*Le donne, i cavaliere, l'armi, gli amori,*

has come down to us the splendor and charm of the Greek concept of the ideal man, tinged with the intervening episode of chivalry and cleansed in part of its homosexuality, but substantially true to character. And we note with satisfaction that one of the most seductive descriptions of the gentleman, Castiglione's *The Courtier*, was written in the high noon of Italian upper-class corruption, written, in fact—and here astonishment must give way to serious inquiry—at the same time as Machiavelli's infamous and pitiful *The Prince* and *The Discourses*.

One might misinterpret the fact that the loftiest and most attractive formulation of the gentlemanly ideal coincided with one of the most corrupt manifestations of western man. It might be regarded as a moral reaction. That this is not the case is clear from the first reading of *The Courtier* and a brief acquaintance with the members of the symposium, who were not fictional characters, but prominent contemporaries. They were of the Italian upper class of which I speak; most of them were of the Borgia-Sforza type; *they* are made, by Castiglione, the protagonists of the

ideal of the gentleman! There is an organic relation between their ideal and their villainy, and it is my purpose to
show that the gentleman as such is an immoral conception.

It might be put thus: the gentleman is the noblest ideal
of man possible in a society that immorally accepts competition and rivalry as the basis of life. For the acceptance
of this view is an initial denial of the validity of goodness;
it is—as I shall show—the contradiction of the prophetic
and Christian (or at any Christ) morality. Gentlemanliness
is a device of the spirit for being immoral without losing
one's self-respect; or rather, a device for heightening one's
self-respect while being immoral. It is, from another point
of view, the idealization or exaltation of immorality—what
the orthodox Jews call "idol-worship."

Because Castiglione's *The Courtier* has been one of the
most influential books in the western world, and because it
is one of the most instructive both intrinsically and historically, I feel it necessary here to give a description of
its contents. But *The Courtier* is also one of the most graceful
books in world literature. It has much of the charm of
Plato at his best; and like most of Plato's essays it is written
in the form of a symposium. A group of highborn ladies and
gentlemen is gathered in the drawing-room of the widowed
Duchess Elizabetta Gonzaga, in the famous castle of the
Montefeltros at Urbino. The conversation turns on the
subject of the ideal gentleman, or courtier, and in the course
of it many subsidiary subjects are touched on, such as love,
the education of ladies, the soul of man, the Platonic philosophy. But principally we are concerned with the highest
pattern of human personality and behavior, that starlike
ideal which should be fixed in the heart of every gentleman.

It is a great advantage, the courteous disputants agree
at the beginning, for a man to be nobly born. In the low-
born and the obscurely born there is an absence of challenge

or provocation to honor; also less fear of besmirching their name. However, to the credit of the Duchess and her guests, it is also agreed that the handicap of obscure or humble birth is not a fatal one. But whether by birth or breeding, or by happy accident, a gentleman must be of comely shape of person and countenance (the American movie gentleman has a tradition behind him); and whether by natural endowment or self-improvement, he must have "a wit, and a certain grace and air." This, however, is background. "The principal and true profession of a courtier ought to be in feats of arms." Constant practice and exercise are requisite to this end; and high physical courage is taken for granted. "As a woman once stained never returns to her former estate," so a gentleman once caught in cowardice "continues evermore shameful and ignominious" in the world's regard.

Courage and daring in his "principal and true profession" must be offset in the gentleman by a modest bearing out of business hours. "He that we seek for [that is, the perfect gentleman] where the enemies are, shall show himself most fierce, bitter, and evermore with the first. In every other place he shall be lowly, sober, and considerate, fleeing, above all things, bragging and shameful praising of himself." (See Henry the Fifth's oration before Harfleur, and many other passages in Shakespeare, such as Ophelia's description of Hamlet as the perfect courtier, the discussion of Platonic love in *The Taming of the Shrew*, and so on, for Castiglione's direct influence on Shakespeare.)

The perfect gentleman is an adept in the sports that are becoming to a gentleman. Such are tennis and high-jumping; but acrobatics and tightrope walking are touched with clownishness and should be avoided. The perfect gentleman should have a good education. A knowledge of languages is to be commended, also a habit of reading, particularly of books that inspire to great deeds; and Alexander the Great is cited as always having by him a copy of Homer, placing it under his pillow when he slept; Alcibiades, likewise, was diligent in the study of Socrates. Whether the gentleman should improve himself by developing an artistic bent is a moot point, and one of the most distinguished guests apologizes for suggesting it, inasmuch as painting is perhaps nothing more than "a handicraft, and hardly becoming to a gentleman." The problem may be considered as having been resolved recently, by Mr. Churchill.

The perfect gentleman, though witty and gay, must "take heed that his jesting be not wicked." He must be reverent toward religion, averse to bawdy conversation, especially in the presence of women—that is, in the presence of ladies; for one of the disputants objects that he hears more smutty talk from women than from men. Likewise the perfect courtier must try not to enter the service of a vicious and wicked prince; and one of the courtiers, a certain humanist called Calmeta, adds: "We must pray unto God to help us toward goodness, for once we are with a wicked prince we must take him with all his faults; for there are infinite reasons why a gentleman, once he is entered into service with a Lord, shall not forsake him." Signor Calmeta may have been remembering, in this little apologia, the days when he served the vilest of Italy's rulers, Cesare Borgia, whom he did in the end forsake—not for his wickedness, but for his failure. But he need not have been so squeamish. Among the cultivated courtiers and gentlemen who made up half the symposium—the other half being made up of ladies—there were few who had not in the course of their careers been in the service of a princely scoundrel. But since the gentleman was essentially the contender, or competitor, or fighter, the man of high emprise, of adventure, of courage which must be regularly displayed, of daring which must find occasion, he was compelled, in the dearth of good princes, to make shift with bad ones. Anything rather than forfeit one's gentlemanliness by rusting in obscure unemployment—a bucolic clown, or an unambitious scholar, or a suffering saint. We have touched again on the structural immorality of the gentleman.

The problem of honorable employment as a gentleman is mentioned only fleetingly in *The Courtier;* it could not have been scrutinized seriously without disrupting the book. But while fundamental morality is lightly bypassed, the role of philosophy as a spiritual adornment for a gentleman is next only to that of physical courage. And there is, at the end of the book, a Platonic sublimation of the conversation which is fragrant with the authentic breath of the classical days of Greece. However, this closing chord, dying out sweetly against the springing light of an Umbrian dawn, cannot make us forget the merry music of the earlier pages. In those we have learned that not only is the gentleman a philosopher; he is also a high-spirited prankster. In *The Courtier* we find the tradition of the unmalicious practical joke, which descends through *Henry the Fifth* (cf. Henry's trick on Bates, the simple soldier) to Kipling's *Stalky & Co.*, and to Tom Merry, in whose annals the "jape" is both a source of amusement and a folkloristic pattern.

Let me, before I leave the Italian Renaissance gentleman, revert once more to his inimitable charm. The little quotation from Symonds barely hints at the winningness of the courtier's presence and deportment. He moves in a play of lovely colors, as if his very spirit were sheathed in shot silk. The changing sheen runs across the pages of Boccaccio and Castiglione and Ariosto. But one need not go to the Italians to get a glimpse of the magic light. Shakespeare has caught it perfectly. It surrounds the Orlandos and Antonios and Orsinos of a dozen plays. It breaks out in a hundred casual

passages which bring an involuntary smile of delight and
recognition to the lips of the reader. There would be no
point in heaping up quotations; and if I offer one it is because it is so unexpected, so casual and gratuitous, yet so
flawlessly true to archetype. In *As You Like It*, Le Beau,
gentleman at the court of the usurping Duke Frederick,
comes up to Orlando, who has just defeated the wrestler
Charles. "Good sir," he says, "I do in friendship counsel
you to leave this place." Then, after lamenting the wickedness and capriciousness of the Duke and the misfortunes of
Rosalind, he closes with these witching lines:

> *Sir, fare you well:*
> *Hereafter, in a better world than this,*
> *I shall desire more love and knowledge of you.*

Can heart of man resist it? Could frankness, manliness, and
polished affability find more seductive expression? And yet
—it is no more than polished affability. Phrases like these
abound in the correspondence of the charming Renaissance assassins. In the very midst of our surrender we know
that it is a simulacrum. It is a *moresco* in perfect step.

Moving backward through history, past the beginnings
of the Renaissance, we shall not find this gentleman's
world again, glittering on such a high level, until we reach
the classical Greeks. And for this ideal of man (it was not
the only one among the Greeks; I have yet to speak of the
Stoics) there is no one who can be read to better advantage
than Plato. Hence, indeed, the canonization of him by the
Italian Renaissance. It seems to me that if no other author
of classical Greek civilization had been preserved, we should
be able to reconstruct from Plato alone the antique ideal of
the gentleman: the grace, the cultivation of manners, the
decorative attachment to intellectual values, the adoration
of the physical, the worship of the combative and competi-

55

tive—all that characterized the well-bred aristocrat of the golden age of Athens. To put it in a phrase: the glorification of the palæstra and the symposium. It was not an accident that these Greeks should have imparted to their games more than a suggestion of divine purpose, and to their discussions more than a suggestion of a game; the mental playfulness of Plato's subtle investigation of man's function on earth, hence his relation to the gods, is the natural complement of the muscular playfulness of the antagonists in the arena. But there is also a mortal seriousness in both: men dedicate their highest capacities to both, and resist to the death any effort to remove their preoccupation to a profounder spiritual level; and in both activities they will display the most brilliant inventiveness and the extremest courage to prevent the intrusion of God.

We must not be confused by the differences between the ideal gentleman of the upper classes (of writers and the public) and the ideal man of the lower classes. The first stands in the same relation to the second as the pious man to the pietist. Certainly these contradict each other in a certain sense, as a caricature contradicts an original. The Harmsworth writers and Kipling produce a caricature of the "real" gentleman. But the caricature and contradiction take point from the resemblance. If I began, in this exposition, by examining the popularization of the gentleman, it was for two reasons: I am describing the growth of my views; and, the popularization being a parody or caricature, the salient points are more easily seized.

I have said that the gentleman is the noblest ideal of man in a society which immorally accepts competition and rivalry as the basis and meaning of life. The gentleman is supposed to be able to kill his enemy without rancor, and honor him while he kills him, or shake hands with him cordially if he has failed to kill him for the nonce; and this,

56

further, is perhaps intended to convey the following notion: "Life is competitive; you and I are competitors, primarily for honor. This is the cosmic law from which there is no escape, and at which 'it is vain to repine.' Let us therefore accept the struggle without descending to the level of snarling beasts (except in pretense). Let us remain human and cultivated, and let us retain our gentlemanly poise in the face of cosmic necessity." Such a declaration, if honestly meant, seems to represent a considerable spiritual achievement. But its honesty is open to challenge on several counts.

First, it is a dishonesty to call the struggle a cosmic necessity when it is a man-made convention. And if the struggle for "honor" conceals a struggle for the means of subsistence, if there is a disguised and transposed "cosmic necessity," there is a second dishonesty. Shakespeare's and Castiglione's advice to the gentleman in the heat of battle, to *put on* fierceness and animality, is a rationalization: men become beasts in battle, however they may pretend afterwards that the transformation was contrived and controlled. That one man can kill another man in combat on a high level of mutual regard is perhaps the most fantastic and perverse notion that has ever sprung from the human brain; and this third dishonesty is especially repulsive.

The theory of the inevitability of war—between groups or individuals—has, as its unadmitted but inescapable corollary, the view that life is an immoral thing. And if life is an immoral thing, the preservation of it is immoral—for it is immoral to breed killers, even if they are intended to destroy an immoral world. The preservation of it by combat, with flourishes and graces, is a hideous farce, which can only be sustained as long as we make of our thinking an instrument of evasion rather than one of search and self-searching.

Finally, if life is immoral, and its preservation therefore immoral, it does not matter whether you kill me or I kill you, though it would be best if we killed each other. And this, oddly and logically enough, is what we of the modern world are preparing to do, on a universal scale, precisely because we have an immoral evaluation of life even though we do not admit it and do not perceive the logic of our development. The line by which the acceptance of the competitive-combative code must lead to the self-destruction of humanity will be traced in a later chapter. Here, closing this hasty summary of the Greek philosophy of the gentleman, I would add that its gamesome view of life leads quite naturally to Greek tragedy, with its frightful burden of inexorable destruction, its disassociation of man's destiny from man's intentions.

In a thinking person frivolity and despair are complementary, and one cannot say which comes first. In the public games and the philosophic drinking parties of the Greeks we have essential frivolity; in *Œdipus*, *The Choephoroe*, *The Eumenides*, we have essential despair. Greek tragedy may fairly be summed up in the little speech that I put into the mouth of the thinking gentleman: "Life is competitive. . . . This is the cosmic law from which there is no escape." The foreground is gay and gamesome, the backdrop gruesome. A marvelous little vignette of this organic balance, a parable of Biblical power, has been drawn for us by Thomas Mann: Hans Castorp's dream in the snow, in *The Magic Mountain*. To the lovely panorama in the sunlight, infinitely seductive, succeeds the vision of the obscene, cannibalistic old hags in the shadowy temple precinct. Life as a game and life as pure horror belong to each other. Despite all that the gentleman can say or do, the gallantry of the competitive life implies that life is, *au fond*, an unspeakable abomination.

58

How it came to pass that the pagan competitive code (hate) and the prophetic co-operative code (love) found separate and almost exclusive expression in the Greek and Jewish peoples we cannot explain; and when we find a thing inexplicable, we incline to deny its existence. We are reluctant to acknowledge this deep distinction between the Greeks and Hebrews. Many readers will suspect that I have rigged my quotations to suit my thesis. But my quotations are intended to illustrate, not to prove. I reached the thesis from continuous reading and thinking, and I have chosen quotations and instances only as being representative. The interested reader must check against his own body of reading. I shall, in later chapters, point to the pagan element which, it seems to me, exists in the Jewish writings; and I shall refer to the element of God-insight among the pagans. But I do not remember encountering, in forty years of interested reading, one prophetic figure of the western world (the prophet is defined in later chapters), whether among the Greeks or northerners, before Christianity—that is, before the spread of the Jewish influence. And I do not know of one Jewish book which is authentically pagan—that is, which presents man under the aspect of the competitive gentleman, and life under the aspect of a game.

# CHAPTER VI

## *The Heritage of Paganism*

❀

Machiavelli's *The Prince* is the twin brother of Castiglione's *The Courtier*. They were born at the same hour, the high noon of the Italian Renaissance, begotten and conceived by the same spirit and flesh. They are, taken together, the essence of that pagan world which is represented by Plato's *Republic*.

It does not matter that Machiavelli knew no Greek; he must certainly have read Plato in Marsilio Ficino's Latin translation. The Florence in which Machiavelli grew up, the Florence of Lorenzo the Magnificent and the Platonic Academy, was drenched in Platonism. It was impossible for a quick-minded, inquiring, and reflective person to live in the city without coming under the influence of the Platonic system. But we do not need even this external evidence. If one reads *The Prince* and *The Discourses* attentively—the two books form a single thesis—the identity with the political-philosophical spirit of *The Republic* leaps to the eye.

Fundamental to Plato and Machiavelli is the concept of the state as the ultimate unit of human organization, and the absolute frame of reference for the individual. It might be the city state of Athens or of Florence, or the unified state of Italy as dreamed of by Machiavelli: mankind is conceived of as being eternally divided, by constitution, destiny, natural law—call it what you will—into competitive units. The highest possibilities of man are envisaged in this framework.

In such a competitive world the first business of the state is to be strong, in the combative sense. Therefore as long as he inhabits the planet, man must subordinate himself to the conditions that produce the strong state. His faculties, dreams, potentialities, God-visions, must serve that purpose; at worst, they must not interfere with it.

From this fundamental concept flow certain evaluations of man. Plato's approach is functional. A man is primarily a shoemaker, a farmer, a tailor, a soldier—or a ruler; and a man only by virtue of what is left over. This residual humanity of man may of course be troublesome, may interfere with efficiency. But it is apparently indestructible and must therefore be taken carefully into account, lest it get out of hand. That is why poets must be excluded from Plato's Republic; that is why the lie is a proper instrument of state policy.

Machiavelli's approach is "moral," but leads to similar conclusions. Man is bad, therefore he must be dictated to, for his own good and the good of the state. The Prince, or dictator, or supreme manager, must use all means—the lie, the threat, calculated kindness, assassination, justice, injustice—in order to hold the state together and strengthen it. Plato and Machiavelli both make the assumption that man is unchangeable.

Neither of them discusses the problem of how the liar and the lied-to, the manager and the managed, establish their relationship, how it is decided which men are fit to be the beneficent deceivers, which must be the deceived beneficiaries. Machiavelli simply assumes that the Prince who achieves and maintains power has proved himself, *ipso*

61

*facto*, fit to be the ruler. The approval of the masses, obtained by force, fraud, kindness, propaganda, display, personal charm, is not an intelligent judgment on the Prince's
fitness. The question of some principle of election does not
arise. The masses must not be permitted to assume any responsibility, in the hope that they will learn, for man, being
static, cannot learn from experience. If the Prince leads his
state into disaster (as Cesare Borgia, Machiavelli's flesh-
and-blood incorporation of the ideal Prince, did with his
state, the Romagna), it proves either that he was not fit to
be the Prince or that *Fortuna* was against him. The event
itself is the judgment, and the next cycle begins. In Plato's
Republic the power is vested in an aristocracy; again it is
implied that its fitness to rule does not have to and cannot
be examined by the ruled. Here too the event judges. Both
cases, Machiavelli's and Plato's, are magnificent instances
of question-begging.

We are compelled to assume that Plato's discussion of
the nature of justice, which leads off into *The Republic*, and
Machiavelli's frequent references to honor and liberty, are
so much eyewash; they are part of the system of deception
that is essential to the larger system of the state. If they are
more than that, they are self-contradictory. It is a confusing
thesis, and is intended to be so. Hitler, too, insists in *Mein
Kampf* that the masses shall not be told the truth, and yet
peppers the book with the oft-reiterated phrase: "the truth
is . . ."

I do not see how they can be extricated from the dilemma.
But this dilemma, in one form or another, confronts all men
who believe that mankind must be served by immoral or
amoral means. They are the queer species, sentimental cyn-
ics or cynical sentimentalists, who labor under a compulsion
to "better" the lot of man on condition that he be regarded
as amoral by nature. They will even sacrifice all prospects

of worldly success in order to establish the eternal truth that there is no such thing as self-sacrifice.

The Platonic-Machiavellian concept of the state provides for three types of men: the masses, the gentleman or courtier, the Prince or ruler. These are the classical Three Estates generally called commons, nobility, and royalty. The Prince commands, the masses obey; the Prince is above morality, the masses are below it. The Prince understands everything, the masses acquiesce in everything. It is true that the ruler, who is above morality, must submit to the laws which govern the "well-being" of the state; but this is a discipline of self-preservation, not of morality. The Prince is the great, beneficent deceiver, the masses are the fortunate beneficiaries of the deception. The Prince is the maximum man, of all-embracing intelligence; the masses are the minimum man, with (ideally) only enough intelligence to be capable of being deceived. (One cannot, of course, "deceive" an automaton.) The Prince is the sum of all faculties; the man of the mass is a single faculty, in which he is functionalized.

What, then, is the gentleman? He is the paradoxical thing which can only be called the morality of that amoral system. The paradox is diminished if we substitute "morale" for "morality." The gentleman, then, is also functionalized in the state, though his function calls for a much higher degree of intelligence, ability, character, and range of activity than does that of the commoner. He is, however, also a victim of the deception, like the masses. Yet he is granted the privilege of examining the deception, if he wishes, because he can be trusted. As a gentleman, he will do it in the right spirit (which in a sense means that he will not really do it), and will not let it go any further. In Plato's *Republic* the discussion on the character of the state is carried on by gentlemen. In *The Courtier* it is not the character of the state that is discussed, but that of the gentleman—by gentlemen.

63

In the first it is agreed that the state must practice deception on its commoners; in the second it is agreed that though it is better to serve a good Prince, a gentleman who has entered the service of a bad Prince must never let his employer down. In both cases there is no harm in the discussion. Besides, the function of the gentleman calls for so much intelligence that it would be futile to forbid him to look below the surface of things.

(Sometimes there *is* harm in the discussion. Gentlemen have been known to take the discussion seriously and desert their class.)

The business of the gentleman, as morale-creator and stabilizer, consists in spreading a cover of glittering illusion over the moral sickness of the society he serves. His charm, grace, attractiveness, loyalty, courage, skill, intelligence, good humor, playfulness, distract the masses from the occasional impulse to ask serious questions about the happiness of their lot, the omniscience of the ruler, or the destiny of man. Although the gentleman is permitted to discuss—strictly in his own circle—some of the somber realities of man's destiny, he seldom does so. Still less frequently will he challenge the omniscience of the Prince or inquire into the happiness of the masses. For the most part he works at being a gentleman, and is at one with his role and function. He knows that he is a pillar of the existing order, and that if he fails in his function, the masses will have no one else to look to. To disturb the faith of the masses is the action of a cad.

Among the classical Greeks Machiavelli's Prince would have been called a Tyrant, which was not necessarily a term of opprobrium; and there is an important technical difference between a tyranny and an oligarchy. The basic attitude toward man remains the same. The Prince and the courtier, the ruler and his entourage, are heritages of paganism, and when paganism came to new and brilliant expression in the Italian Renaissance, the two figures were bound to reappear side by side. But this is fortunately not the whole story. There was a more penetrating concept of man among the pagans, one which seems on the surface to rank with that which was created by the Hebrew prophets. Here we will not find the fusion of the palæstra and the symposium, the athlete-philosopher who can run a mile in four minutes and sit up all night getting drunk and talking intelligently. He is replaced by a more sensitive and serious type. I am speaking, of course, of the Stoics.

At this point I must anticipate both the next chapter and Book Two of this volume. In the next chapter I speak of my revolt from the Tom Merry-Kipling-*Henry the Fifth*-Machiavelli-Plato man, and my transition to a more sober ideal rooted in the laws of nature. It may be called modern Stoicism. In Book Two I return to the subject in order to discuss once more the shortcomings of the Stoic ideal—it also penetrated the Bible—in the light of what I have to say about the prophets.

There was in the best Stoic thinkers—for me they are Epictetus and Marcus Aurelius—something that resembled the prophetic power of the word, a power of a very special kind, which I discuss at length in Book Two. The resemblance issues from an apparent appeal (only apparent, as we shall see) to the same source of morality: the divinity. Marcus Aurelius says: "The poets cry, 'O city of Cecrops, land beloved'; and canst thou not say: 'O city of God, O land of love'?" And Epictetus: "If you were Cæsar's son you would be proud; but you are God's son, and forgetful of it." From this fatherhood of God flows, as in the prophets, the brotherhood of man, and from this brotherhood, the law of love, which was partially understood by the Stoics. They knew there is only one kind of love, that which expresses itself in the desire to see the beloved person filled with goodness, all other forms of love being only alter-egotism, the projection into the loved one of one's own frustrated ambitions. Such alter-egotism is what commonly passes for love, between parents and children, between man and woman, between friends. "What an inhuman thing," says Marcus Aurelius, "it is to forbid men to strive after what they consider suitable and beneficial to themselves! Yet it is precisely this privilege that you refuse them when you wax indignant at their sins. For certainly they are merely pursuing these so-called 'suitable and beneficial' objects. 'Yes,' you say, 'but it is a mistaken quest.'—Very true: then instruct them and point out their error, instead of falling into a passion over it."

A continuous theme with the Stoics is, in fact, this view that sin is error or sickness, and calls for clarification or cure; and a corollary of this theme is the sinfulness of the self-righteous. Epictetus has an illuminating passage on this subject:

"Ought not then this robber and this adulterer to be destroyed? Do not say it thus, but rather thus: 'This man, who has been mistaken and deceived about the most important things, and blinded, not in the faculty of vision which distinguishes white and black, but in the faculty which distinguishes good and bad, should we not destroy him?' If you put it thus, you will see how inhuman it is. It is just as inhuman as if you would say: 'Ought we not to destroy this blind and deaf man?' [1] . . . Man, you ought not to be affected contrary to nature by the bad things of another. Pity him, rather; drop this readiness to be offended and to hate, and those words which the many utter: 'These odious and accursed fellows.' How have you been made so wise all at once? And how are you so peevish?

"Why then are we angry? Is it because we value so much

[1] A brilliant anticipation of the Nazi evaluation, and a reflection on the Spartan.

66

the things of which these men rob us? Do not admire your clothes, and then you will not be angry with the thief.

"Consider the matter thus: you have fine clothes, your neighbor has not; you have a window; you wish to air the clothes. The thief does not know wherein man's good consists; he thinks that it consists in having fine clothes, the very thing which you also think. Must he then not come and take them away?

"When you show a cake to greedy persons, and swallow it all yourself, do you expect them not to snatch it from you? . . .

"I also lately had an iron lamp placed at the door by the side of my household gods; hearing a noise at the door, I ran down, and found that the lamp had been carried off. I reflected that he who had taken the lamp had done nothing strange. What, then? Tomorrow, I said, you will find an earthen lamp, for a man loses only that which he has. You have lost your garment? The reason is that you had a garment."

William Wallace thus summarizes Epictetus' vision of the ideal Stoic:

"He has neither country nor home nor land nor slave; his bed is the ground; he is without wife or child; his only mansion is the earth and sky and a shabby cloak. He must suffer stripes, and must love those who beat him as if he were a father or a brother. He must be perfectly unembarrassed in the service of God, not bound by the common ties of life, nor entangled by relationships, which if he transgresses he will lose the character of a man of honour, while if he upholds them he will cease to be the messenger, watchman, and herald of the gods. The perfect man thus described will not be angry with the wrong-doer; he will only pity his erring brother; for anger in such a case would only betray that he too thought the wrong-doer gained a substantial blessing by his wrongful act, instead of being, as he is, utterly ruined."

Again and again we encounter in the Stoics the note that is so often sounded in the section of the Mishnah called *The Ethics of the Fathers*. "Let death and exile and every other

67

thing which appears dreadful be daily before your eyes; but most of all death: and you will never think of anything mean nor will you desire anything extravagantly." (Epictetus.) "Let thy thoughts dwell on the infinity of men, on the infinite processions and infinite nations, who have passed away. . . . So many heroes of old, so many captains and kings thereafter. . . . Bethink thee, all these have long ago come to dust. . . . In sum, in this life there is but one possession of great price—to pass thy days with truth and justice, showing kindness to those who know neither truth nor justice." (Marcus Aurelius).

The reader may wonder why I have not chosen to dwell on Socrates, the most moving of all the moral figures of pagan antiquity. His life was that of a prophet moralist and teacher; his death, too, was in the prophetic tradition. He was, in all his being, the denial of the worldliness of the Greek civilization, though he conformed to part of its routine; in essence he was contumaciously indifferent to its values; the system of ruler and ruled, the whole game which is the substance of that system, turned into dust before his gaze; he was a discomfort, a troubling of the spirit.

Yet I have not taken him as an exemplar because he has become inextricably intertwined with Plato, who to me is his very opposite. Socrates left no writing behind him, even as Zeno—and Jesus—did not. Epictetus too is reported. But as Jesus had his Paul, so Socrates had his Plato. We would find it difficult to get a glimpse of the authentic Jesus if the gospels had been lost and we had only St. Paul's account of him: this irrespective of the question as to which was written first, and what the gospels, too, contain of alien interpretation. It so happens that there is an account of Socrates by a simpler, less gifted, and therefore more reliable contemporary—Xenophon; and in his description we see a person profoundly different from the one who alternately moves and dazzles us in the pages of *The Republic*. Plato has turned him into the advocate of a completely godless vision of the political state; and it is done so cleverly, with such subtle glossing over of fundamental moral issues, that the Socrates of Xenophon, and for that matter of Plato's own *Phædo*, undergoes a Jekyll-Hyde transformation before we are aware of it. It is a most extraordinary betrayal.

The Stoic morality sometimes declines into affectation and pomposity, and we often find an instructive congruence with what I have yet to describe—the stuffed-shirt philosophy of parts of Proverbs and Ecclesiasticus. Epictetus says: "If a man has reported to you that a certain person spoke ill of you, do not defend yourself, but reply: 'The man did not know the rest of my faults, for he would not have mentioned these only.' " This is stilted and false. Or: "When you are going to meet any person, and particularly one of those who are considered to be in a superior condition, place before yourself what Socrates or Zeno would have done in such circumstances, and you will have no difficulty in making proper use of the occasion." Passages like these are often quoted to show that the Stoic philosophy did not reach deep into the soul of man; it was a system, a set of regulations, a self-serving outlook, in which a man did what was becoming to his noble character, not what sprang from love of his neighbor. Certainly this was what Stoicism became when the inspiration went out of it; and we shall encounter this deterioration again in certain parts of the Bible. But not in this lies the organic defect, which we must seek in Stoicism at its best.

Stoicism assumed—and herein it is, in spite of references to God and gods, the father of rationalist and mechanistic moralities and systems of society—that in being good man was in harmony with nature; and, at times, that the moral incentive comes from study of natural law. If this is so, the appeal to God is formal, because God is only a part of nature. The rules of goodness are equated with the rules of health. We are told that the more we know about nature and natural law, the better we shall be able to manage our souls. But the truth is otherwise; there is nothing in the study of nature which leads to goodness. The Stoics tried to integrate goodness with atomic law; but our immense advances in the study of the internal structure of the atom have not shed the faintest light on the moral problem.

Because the Stoic view of goodness is that of a naturally healthy condition, it lacks a vision of mankind moving Godward; for health is a static concept. We find many passages in the Stoics which speak of men as children of God; I cannot recall a passage that reflects, and is part of, the striving of divinity within man. Marcus Aurelius speaks, as we have seen, of "the city of God." Probably he does mean, there, the ideal moral condition of mankind. But neither in him nor in any other moralist of pagan antiquity that I remember, do I find the idea of goodness *as a national policy*. This drive toward the sanctification of the corporate life, which impelled the Hebrew prophets to tell the Jewish nation that it was not fit to live if it did not live in goodness, is alien to the Stoics. The Stoics plead with individuals, the prophets plead with peoples as well as with individuals. At most the Stoics and their related schools could think only of fellowships in goodness, which is a kind of monasticism.

Therefore we sense a touch of despair in the goodness of the individual Stoic; he does not feel that there is an active, insistent, driving universal force on the side of man's goodness; the Stoic's admonitions, and his loving ministrations, are not carried by the same tide as prophetic exhortation. The Stoic fights a lone battle. And because he is sometimes aware of this, a note of gallantry creeps into his utterances, a pose, a suggestion of defiance. Nature would not come out to meet him and help him along. He had to scrutinize nature, deduce from his scrutiny the laws of human spiritual well-being, and apply these laws without encouragement from anywhere. The fatherhood of God was a very frosty thing, devoid of immediacy and urgency, and not much more helpful than our awareness of our common atomic origins.

There cannot be any doubt that the Stoics had genuine glimpses of goodness; they were far in advance of the Platonic-Machiavellian concept of man and society. But they paralyzed themselves by assimilating the living thing to the dead thing, the soul of man to the law of nature. The morality of determinism (a self-contradiction) which this finally implies colored my thinking strongly during my middle and late teens, and, less strongly, for some time after.

# CHAPTER VII

## *The Mechanist-Moralist*

❀

FROM my thirteenth or fourteenth year on I was shifting gradually from romanticism to rationalism, from the personal view of man to the mechanistic, from patriotism to socialism. My progress did not have the same speed on all planes, but by the time I was sixteen my ideal was no longer the gentleman; he was replaced by the scientific world-improver. I took to Shaw, Wells, Haeckel, Spencer, the Sixpenny Rationalist Reprints, Joseph McCabe, and Karl Marx. For a time I was an extraordinary mixture of attitudes and responses. I despised empire, militarism, Kipling, and Tom Merrydom; but I enjoyed belonging to the Jewish Lads' Brigade, a boy-scoutish organization that went in for uniforms, route marches, camp life, bugles, and reverence for royalty. I looked with a cold, detached eye on the dance of atoms which was the be-all and the end-all of the universe; but I was shaken by the spiritual appeal of Francis Thompson's *To a Dead Cardinal* and *The Hound of Heaven*.

Even when the transition had been completed on all the levels, I was not much less muddled. Just as I do not remember how, in earlier years, I managed to be simultaneously the serious little Jew and the cricket-spirited English schoolboy, so I do not remember how I accommodated myself later to the contradictions and confusions of the mechanistic-socialistic outlook. As a mechanist I "saw" that the laws which had shaped the galactic system were also shaping the course of history: feudalism had developed into mercantilism, mercantilism into industrialism, industrialism into finance capitalism as simply and as ineluctably as the solar system had evolved from a nebula, as life had evolved from the interplay of atoms and molecules in the early days of the planet. By the same inexorable process capitalism would develop into socialism. What the individual human being wanted had as little to do with the grand process of social evolution as it had to do with Kepler's laws of planetary motion. And yet—my socialism was an immensely emotional thing. I loved humanity and I hated anti-socialists (that is, most human beings).

Love and hate were, I could see, quite inadmissible in a universe that consisted throughout of nothing but jigging atoms. But at least the love was a pleasant feeling. Intellectually it was just as contemptible as the hate, and I did make some sort of effort to water it down. Hate, however, was unpleasant; and it was a shade more illogical than love, because it impelled me toward those ridiculous things called moral evaluations. After all, anti-socialists could not help talking as they did; the capitalist system had made of them exploiters and oppressors, or the dupes of exploiters and oppressors. A time would come when, born into a socialist society, human beings would be incapable of anti-historical attitudes. I had read in Engels (I think in his *Anti-Dühring*) that this was the way to look at opponents of socialism and historical materialism. On the other hand, I also read in Marx some wondrously satisfying abuse of opponents. He even stooped, in talking of Napoleon III, to insults about the man's features, which he found loathsome. I felt comforted. If Marx rushed in where Engels feared to tread, it could not be too reprehensible of me to follow.

73

There were other contradictions, to which I shall return. Meanwhile the English gentleman had forfeited all my adoration—which did not prevent him, however, from occasionally getting under my skin and touching off the old emotions. As I read history, and particularly English history, I looked behind the façade of aristocratic highmindedness at the ruthless purpose of empire and government: Ireland, India, colonial America; nearer home, the story of child labor, the closing of the commons, all the savageries that Marx exposed with such relentless fury. *These* were empire and capitalism; and the gentleman was the supreme propagandist of the system.

With the gentleman were associated the priest, the minister, and the rabbi. I knew no priests or ministers; the one or two rabbis who belonged to our Roumanian-Jewish subcommunity in Manchester were peculiarly disassociated in my mind from gentlemen and empire. However, contemporaries of mine may remember a cartoon that was widely disseminated by socialists some forty years ago. It came from Russia, and it showed three platforms, arranged one above the other—the smallest at the top, the largest at the bottom —to form a pyramid. On the top platform stood the Czar and his family and the nobles, saying: "We rule you." On the middle platform below stood the priests and rabbis, saying: "We fool you." On the third platform stood the landowners and capitalists, saying: "We exploit you." On the ground, supporting the bottom platform and the whole structure, stood the masses, saying: "We work for everybody." It made a deep and, as we see, an ineradicable impression on me.

I shall always remain grateful to this socialist propaganda for the information it gave me on the condition of the masses of mankind, and for exposing before me, in my impressionable years, the wrongs which human beings inflict on each

74

other in the name of religion and patriotism. It is a pity
that the revolutionary social movement should have entered
into partnership with a mechanistic view of life. I have suggested that there is a line of descent from the mechanistic
background of Stoicism to the historical and materialistic
determinism of the socialist and communist movements.
These last fell into a trap; the opposition of entrenched
religion to social progress pushed them into the unnatural
alliance. The result was inner contradiction and intellectual,
spiritual paralysis.

As a mechanist I could see that freewill was an illusion.
(That blessed word "illusion"! I did not feel myself called
upon to explain an illusion; it did not have full status in
existence.) In practice I behaved, like everyone else, as if
I believed in freewill. I had to justify my actions in terms of
choice; and here I encountered contradictions within contradictions.

First I had to find a reason for accepting the personal
sacrifices that socialist activity entailed. Then I had to convince myself that these sacrifices were not wasted. I could
not speak of a moral imperative, because there is no such
thing in a mechanistic universe. I was therefore driven back
to the argument from prudence. But the argument from
prudence turned out to be a fraud. Condensed from hundreds of rehearsals between me and my early socialist
teachers, and stripped of digressions and insults, the discussion ran as follows:

Teacher: "You do not make any sacrifices in working for
the socialist cause; you are only practicing enlightened
selfishness. The intelligence, not the superstitious thing
called morality, must spur you on. The more clearly you
see that capitalism makes for war, and for universal ruin, in
which you will be involved, the harder you work for the
cause. It is a matter of self-preservation."

75

I: "Capitalism undoubtedly makes for war and universal ruin. I couldn't see it more clearly than I do. But something else bothers me, and that is my role in saving the world. Is it of crucial importance? If it is not, if the world can be saved without me, I am throwing away my life, which is my all, in a futile and disagreeable sacrifice."

Teacher: "What is going to happen if everyone talks like you?"

I: "The world will obviously be ruined. But if everyone talks like me, what difference will it make if I start talking otherwise?"

Teacher: "You are not alone. What you say and do influences others."

I: "Undoubtedly. But I must stick to my point. Do you suggest that my influence will have a decisive effect on the outcome?"

Teacher: "Why do you insist on a decisive influence? Is it not enough for you to exert *some* influence?"

I: "It is not. We are talking of 'enlightened selfishness.' I want to have a good time in this one brief life of mine. Being a socialist is not my idea of having a good time. If, however, you can show me that if I don't turn socialist the world will be ruined, and I with it, I have no intelligent choice but to turn socialist. If on the other hand the world will go socialist without me, or go to hell in spite of me, I cannot see what 'enlightened selfishness' leads to but my continuing to have a good time."

The teacher is at an impasse. Either he has to appeal to my moral impulse, and abuse me for being ready to let others save my world; or else he must concede that my role in saving the world is absolutely essential—that is, decisive. He cannot do the first, since he does not believe in a moral law; he cannot do the second, since he does not believe in the decisive role of the individual in history. And if he did believe in the indispensability of the individual, he would be that individual, not I. As a matter of fact, he uses both arguments, alternately. But first he hedges.

Teacher: "You cannot tell what your influence is."

I: "No. But we will look at it mathematically. In order that my influence in world history shall be decisive, the forces for and against socialism must reach a condition of finest balance, with myself holding the deciding vote. Do you seriously suggest that I ought to throw my life away on this one-in-a-billion chance? I mean, as a matter of prudence, of enlightened selfishness."

Teacher: "If you were in a boat would you, for your personal pleasure, bore a hole under your seat?"

This argument was supposed to be a clincher. The answer, when you found it, was astonishingly simple.

I: "How big is the boat, and how big is the hole I am boring?"

We are back at the question of "decisiveness." The teacher hedges again.

Teacher: "If there's only a one-in-a-billion chance that your sacrifice can be decisive, isn't it worth taking, since the only alternative is ruin for all—including you?"

I: "No. Boring a hole in the bottom of the boat—by which you mean pursuing my selfish interests—is the only thing I live for. Throw it away on a one-in-a-billion chance that I am saving the world and myself? Ridiculous!"

So far the argument from prudence and enlightened selfishness. Now the rationalist teacher usually shifts his ground and tries to appeal to something that is neither strictly reason nor overtly moralistic. He observes that the pupil is a megalomaniac for demanding a better than a one-in-a-billion chance to save the world. He also asks despairingly whether there isn't more pleasure in stopping up holes and getting others to do so than in boring them. Is the pupil so made that his pleasure—which is a mad one anyway—is not poisoned by the thought of impending world destruction? All this, however, though it uses pseudo-psychological and social terms, is only old-fashioned moral exhortation, disguised and crippled.

These last few pages may well have bored the reader, too. The argument is jejune, witless. But one thing it is not— and that is, irrelevant. I have heard it repeated literally hundreds of times throughout the years. It is the substance of that moral condition which leads thousands, hundreds of thousands, into the corruption of falsely motivated public action, but falsely motivated in a specially vicious and dangerous sense. The conclusion to which the teacher is driven may be briefly put as follows: "If you cannot convince him, fool him into co-operation. If you cannot do either, overwhelm him by force." If we expand the conclusion and its effects, we find ourselves in the midst of the ultimate problems of our day. Between those alternatives, "If you cannot convince him" and "fool him into co-operation," there is room for infinite moral deterioration: there issues a contempt for the "beneficiary" of the deception which reacts in self-contempt on the part of the deceiver. The concept of the human being undergoes a revolting change. The teacher thinks that the intelligence of the pupil is *in its essence* something to be distorted by misinformation and ingeniously implanted fallacies. If this cannot be done, force must be used. "If you can neither convince nor fool him, kill him." That is not all. A pupil who has once shown obduracy, whom it was difficult to convince or fool, is forever after suspect; the more so because he has touched, somewhere in the teacher, unresolved, suppressed problems. Hence the malevolence that accompanies the cold advice.

I was for some time involved—not too deeply, I recall with gratitude—in that hideous complex. However, besides being dissatisfied with the slickness of the mechanistic and materialist view, besides growing weary with the bright, extraverted self-assurance (in some cases forced) of the rationalists, I found amoralist idealism sickening in itself. I was, without knowing it, looking for a faith.

Years later something became very clear to me. I was not getting in those days, from the contemporaneous writers I was most attached to, the intellectual and spiritual nourishment I needed. Those writers—Shaw, Wells, Somerset Maugham, Arnold Bennett—were to me the representatives of the modern mind. My response to a poet like Francis Thompson I felt to be a reversion to an early condition, like my recurrent twinges of admiration for the gentleman type. But the representatives of the modern mind let me down. I did not discover the nature of the let-down until long afterwards, and when I did, many of my early struggles were clarified for me. These men were careerists, spiritually unfit to serve a young generation. They were devoid of moral seriousness. When I sum up, after this interval of nearly four decades, the total achievement of these men, I have a picture of misspent lives and abused talents.

They have given us, in the course of the years, their confessions, sometimes conscious, sometimes unconscious. Shaw has tried to make a great joke of his passion for success, but his engaging frankness is only intended to deflect our attention from his deeper dishonesty. The gap between Shaw's promise and his fulfillment has been well described by John Strachey, and rightly written down by him to Shaw's voracious enjoyment of fame. Bennett has been more open than Shaw. He never tried to make a cheap joke of the careerism that marred his work. Not long before his death, in a moment of self-realization and self-exposure rare among such men, he had this to say about his early betrayal of his responsibilities as an artist: "My soul glances

79

back furtively, and with loathing, at that time of emotional and intellectual dishonour."

Somerset Maugham has also made his confession, but in his characteristic way, by a blustering denial of the moral responsibility and significance of the artist. This man, who wrote one near-great book, *Of Human Bondage*, has devoted all his considerable ability to the systematic production of second-rate entertainment. He explained himself in his later years in these words:

"I am a professional writer. I have read a great deal, sometimes for instruction, sometimes for pleasure, but never since I was a small boy without an eye on the relation between what I was reading and my professional interests. . . . The ablest editor I know is accustomed to say: 'I am the average American, and what interests me will interest my readers.' The event proved him right. Now I have most of my life been miserably conscious that I am not the average Englishman. Let no one think I say this with self-satisfaction, for I think there is nothing better than to be like everyone else. It is the only way to be happy, and it is with but a wry face that one tells oneself that happiness is not everything."

I suspect that it was but a wry face (or as much of it as his tired soul permitted) that Maugham wrote this passage, his nearest approach to self-exposure. It is the "average" British "No-damned-nonsense-about-me-sir" line, like Samuel Johnson's utterly silly: "No one but a blockhead ever wrote except for money."

H. G. Wells, one of the superior deities in the pantheon of my adolescence, has revealed himself with a naïveté, almost a shamelessness, that makes the reader uncomfortable. The following passages, which deal with his early years and his friendship with Arnold Bennett, are taken from his autobiography, written in late maturity: "He [Bennett] was friendly and self-assured; he knew quite clearly that we were both on our way to social distinction and incomes of several thousand a year. I had not thought of it quite like that. I was still only getting something between one and two thousand a year, and I did not feel at all secure about getting more. But Bennett knew we wouldn't stop there. . . . In 1894 I earned £383/7/7, in 1895 £792/2/5, and in 1896 £1,056/7/9." Farther on he tells us that he had long planned to write something which might not bring him money, but would satisfy his intellectual cravings. (One wonders how strong they were, to endure such disciplined frustration.) But he did not feel it safe to do so until he had saved up thirty thousand pounds—and a house! This about thirty years ago, when thirty thousand pounds in England was about the equivalent of close on half a million dollars in America today. It was then that he wrote his *History of the World*, which, commercially, turned out to be his most successful book; intellectually it made no higher demands on his readers than his previous books.

All these things about my boyhood teachers I did not find out until I was in my forties. They explained to me part of the troubles of my teens. The leadership of my boyhood world was composed óf success-hunters, which means in general power-hunters; the men I looked up to were primarily concerned with personal self-advancement. They were intelligent enough, but they were cagey—and on the make. Popularity was a condition in their contract with humanity. They would not, therefore, take up themes and problems for which there was no large audience. And when they thought they did, they got themselves large audiences anyhow by misrepresenting the real intellectual and spiritual difficulties of their subjects. Their inborn craftsmanship generally prevented them from playing down to the lowest reading mob, but Wells and Bennett did for a time contribute to *Titbits* and other guttersheets. Their higher

aim was to ingratiate themselves with the large and growing upper-level audience that considered itself spiritually
emancipated.

That emancipation consisted in the materialist outlook
which I have touched on. It did not always have to be extreme. In its milder form it veered away from Marxism and
socialism, and was content to affirm that human "progress"
was a thing which "made itself." Humanity was getting
better and better inevitably. It was not necessary to moti-
vate the ethical improvement of individuals; they were
caught up in it incidentally and despite themselves. Super-
stition, privilege, intolerance, jingoism, the lust for power,
were not things that one argued out of people; you simply
taught them biology, mathematics, economics, Darwinism;
and the natural result was an improvement in human relations.

It was altogether unprofitable, from both the careerist
and the public point of view, to concern oneself with the
metaphysical problem of good and evil. Good behavior
and bad behavior were by-products of social conditions.
Improve social conditions—and that also meant raise the
scientific-educational level of the public—and bad behavior
would diminish without further ado. Make social conditions
perfect and bad behavior would disappear completely,
would become a sociological impossibility. There was nothing to invoke in the individual, nothing to appeal to, nothing even to examine, anywhere outside this basic social
reality. This argument in a circle, this begging of the question, is best expressed in the sentence: "Make social conditions perfect and bad behavior will disappear completely."
Communism presupposes a state of mind without which
communism is impossible and with which it is unnecessary.

This was the "liberal" outlook which Shaw and Wells
and others (I am not speaking now of the unpolitical artists,

like Bennett and Maugham) played up to. It is still the liberal outlook. I know now where and why and to what extent I part company with it. I did not know it when I was nineteen or twenty. I was asphyxiated by it for a time. It did not permit me to look deep into the springs of human action. It told me that any preoccupation with spiritual problems was a hangover from my childhood miseducation. But I could not suppress the feeling that I was being bullied out of a basic and essential intellectual and spiritual experience.

||||||||||||||||||||||||||||||||||||||||||||||||||||||||||||||||||||||||||||||||||||||||

# CHAPTER VIII

## *The Evasion*

❄

||||||||||||||||||||||||||||||||||||||||||||||||||||||||||||||||||||||||||||||||||||||||

T HAT intellectual and spiritual experience was the study of the ideas which accompany individual human motivation. Instead of being encouraged toward it, I was fobbed off with a number of formulas that were built up into a system of evasion.

The three principal formulas were: "The Struggle for Survival," "The Economic Struggle," and "The Will to Power." They were, in fact, almost sufficient to explain the human problem.

The struggle for survival was the brute fact of life; the economic struggle was the form taken by the struggle for survival in an organized society; the will to power was the will to the means for carrying on the struggle. Thus the will to power was a form of the will to survival, and therefore a reasonable thing. If in an organized society you took away the economic struggle and substituted economic co-operation, there would be no more struggle for survival; with both of them gone, the will to power would also disappear. It was all very simple.

It was still very simple even if you admitted that the struggle for survival meant something more than the struggle to prolong one's life. True, man wants to live, but he also wants to play, love, laugh, and create. Above all, he wants the approval of his kind, a little bit of importance and a little bit of applause. To these things he is entitled, and they do not call for a struggle, except in a playful way. Their satisfaction is not connected with the will to power.

At the time of which I am speaking—my nineteenth or twentieth year—I was beginning to suspect this outlook. It seemed to me, obscurely, that the will to power was a much more basic thing than a by-product of the economic struggle; it was, perhaps, more basic even than the struggle for survival! I also suspected that the phrases "approval of his kind," "a little bit of importance," "a little bit of applause," were the masks of something darker and much less manageable than appeared on the surface. To clarify my perplexities of that time, I shall again go forward to my maturer years.

The following passage occurs in Professor Harold Laski's book, *Where Do We Go from Here?* "The only values which they [the Nazi and Fascist leaders of Germany and Italy] understood, the only values, indeed, which had any meaning for them, were those which consisted in the exercise of power by themselves. If it be asked for what end they proposed to exercise power, the answer is, for the sake of power itself. Any other answer would have involved them in subjection to rules which made power the recognized servant of an end beyond itself, and that recognition would have been a denial of their own nature as outlaws."

This reaches toward the heart of the difficulties which I struggled with long ago. But it is an extraordinary fact that, having made this shattering analysis of the will to power, Professor Laski ignores all its implications. In this book, as nearly everywhere else in his other books, he sticks to the classical analysis of the economic struggle, making it appear—as nearly all leftists do—identical with the struggle for survival. Like the teachers of my boyhood, he analyzes

85

the social struggle in terms of economic rivalries between men and groups, implying that the problems of war, exploitation, mass hatreds, can be solved on the primary basis of wages, markets, colonies. I shall attempt to show how fatal this evasion is to a genuine understanding of the problems of man.

What Professor Laski says in the quoted statement is that for "these men" there was no substitute for power, and no purpose in possessing it beyond perpetuating their possession of it. But to perpetuate one's possession of power is to perpetuate one's life in the same degree. Why, then, does not Professor Laski say that these men proposed to exercise power as a means of survival? I do not know. But for me the obvious answer is that the path to power is not identical with the path to survival. A cunning member of the obscure masses has a better chance of survival than a cunning power-seeker on the grand scale. In any case, the survival value of power is not its rationale.

But "these men" were not members of a peculiar human species; they were only extreme examples of the ordinary species. Nor were they spoken of as madmen, except figuratively. And yet "power for power's sake" is, as we shall see, so mad a principle of action that he who adopts it should be regarded as a technical lunatic; and if he is not, it must surely be because all of us are tainted with the same lunacy.

Let us look into the operation of the will to power. Do men, having acquired a certain amount of power, say, of their own volition: "This is enough"? Hardly ever. They want at least just a little bit more. To the power impulse may be applied Punch's remark about the drunkard in the gutter: "He's had a bit too much of what he hasn't had enough of." It is a common observation that men who have acquired power are not satisfied with their position or convinced that they have received their due. The classical symbol of the contented human being is not drawn from the arena of the power struggle. It is not Henry the Fifth on his throne, but Paddy-without-a-shirt-to-his-back; not Alexander, sighing for more worlds to conquer (what a revealing phrase!), but St. Francis of Assissi, begging his meals from door to door.

What are the apparent uses of power? How do I exercise power over you? Obviously by making you act (or feel) as I want you to act. If you are already acting the way I want you to act, without any intervention on my part, I am not exercising power over you. To exercise power I must influence your choice of action. I may do this by what we call physical compulsion; that is, I may confront you with such discomforts and dangers that you do what I want you to do. This is the simplest exercise of power. Its satisfactions are narrow, and therefore its term is short. Since I want "real" power over you—that is, I want your will to conform to my will—I want you to *want* to do that which I want you to do.

Therefore a higher form of power is persuading you to act as I want you to. *This does not mean teaching you*, which is an act of love, not a search for power. Teaching you means helping you to develop your own mind, making you independent of me, which is the opposite of what I seek in the quest for power. It means, instead, propagandizing you, hypnotizing you, misleading you. (Not bribing you: for then you will not be wanting what I want you to want; you will be wanting only the reward.) I shall prevent you from developing freely by withholding information from you, by blocking your inquiries, using derision and mass pressure to discourage your inquiries (as my teachers did). I shall guide you into certain channels of belief so that, acting under dictated and implanted error, you will yourself choose the line of action I want you to choose. Then you will be wanting what I want you to want, and that is more satisfactory.

But I have implied that the lust for power is insatiable. What, then, is the next stage? At the next stage I become dissatisfied with your robot-like acquiescence. I am cloyed and irked. At first I became weary of your obedience to my will because you offered it under physical compulsion, while cursing me under your breath, or to win a bribe, while despising me. Now I am weary of it because you offer it under psychic compulsion or fraud. In neither instance did you have a real choice. Now I want from you that impossible thing, the unquestioning obedience and acquiescence of a free man! And here we reach the final and ghastly self-contradiction of the power drive. If I make you capable of a free choice, you will not be obeying me; at best you will be co-operating with me, which admits you to equality with me and is an affront to my will to power. So I must either abdicate or put up with the progressive boredom of your *golem*-obedience and *golem*-applause. Abdication is extremely difficult, though it has been achieved. I have, in the process of acquiring power over you, become so necessary to your life that if I try to withdraw from it you will tear me to pieces for disappointing you. But if I go on listening to your hideous, mechanical ovations, I shall go mad. I am at the impasse of power; the nemesis of the process has overtaken me. When Alexander sighed for more worlds to conquer, he meant—whether he knew it or not—different worlds, in which this nemesis did not exist.

What, meanwhile, has happened to you and *your* will to power. The answer is familiar to all of us. When the will to power cannot express itself in mastery, it finds satisfaction in subjection—that is, in self-indentification with the powerful. Every Hitler-worshipper sees his ideal self in Hitler, and is a little Hitler-image; every Stalin-worshipper is a little Stalin. Nor need we confine ourselves to notorious instances of power-wielders. The worship of *any* man is an inversion of the will to power, and a self-identification with the worshipped. The truth of this betrays itself in a curious way. If you want to drive a man-worshipper mad with rage, you must insult not him, but his idol. He will then say: "An insult to So-and-so is an insult to me!" How much truer that is than he realizes!

The exercise of economic control is not the *reason* for wanting power; it is one of the forms of power itself. It is an instrument for putting physical and psychic compulsions on others. We want money for the power it confers, not power for the money it brings. Some of that power we will of course use in order to get more money, as the farmer uses some of his crop as seed. But as the farmer sows for the crop, so we labor for power, which in a civilized society is most easily exercised through economic control.

But what satisfaction does power seek? Its satisfaction lies in the acknowledgment by others of its existence. We want power for the sole purpose of having people testify to our power. As our power increases, we shall demand that they gather in crowds and clap their hands when they see us, or hear us, or hear our name mentioned; that they sing laudatory songs about us, or songs indicating their fear of us, their respect for us, or their love of us; that they paint and print pictures of us, and look at these pictures frequently, while experiencing, expressing, and communicating emotions of awe, gratitude, humility, or mere stupefaction; that they engrave our names on public buildings, or bestow them upon cities; that they use our birthday as the beginning of a new calendar; that they deprive themselves of certain comforts in our name (the sacrificial offering); that they deepen and spread their own attitude toward us in various rituals; that they put on uniforms and parade before us; that they feel and express rage when they encounter in others an absence of their emotions toward us; that they commit homicide and suicide in large numbers for our sake—or rather, as extreme evidence of their regard for us; finally, that they follow our corpse in large numbers to the place of interment, or perhaps embalm the corpse and expose it to reverential public view. The last tributes must naturally be savored in advance, and the contemplation of the arrangements, set forth in detail, must suffice us. These and similar actions constitute applause. The more frequently they are directed at us, the greater is our importance, the more ample our power.

To say that the will to power is irrational is beside the point. Love is irrational, so is art; and goodness is the most irrational of all things. The point about the will to power is that it is maniacal and destructive—destructive both of values and of life. It creeps into every human activity and takes away its integrity; our relations to men and things become extrinsic. It infiltrates into the most ingeniously devised social systems and corrupts them to its own purpose. It is by its nature implacable; or rather, it is the embodiment of implacability. You and I may under certain circumstances struggle "reasonably" over food and housing as long as there is not enough for both of us. The moment there is enough, we can presumably stop struggling. But there can never be importance enough for both of us; for if you have as much importance as I, then neither of us has any importance. Neither of us can then extract from the other the gesture of deference which is the tribute to power, or rather the sole object and even substance of power.

I suspected, then, before I was out of my teens, that most of the economic struggle was not a struggle for subsistence, and not even a struggle for appetitional enjoyments. I suspected also that my teachers, the rationalists and historical materialists, were trapped in a dilemma that they refused to acknowledge—or even discuss. But—again—it was not until long afterwards that I was able to formulate the dilemma. I refer to the reading of later years. Sidney Hook, in his *Toward the Understanding of Karl Marx*, has this extraordinary quotation from Marx:

"A house may be large or small, but as long as the surrounding houses are equally small, it satisfies all the social requirements of a dwelling place. But let a palace arise by the side of this small house, and it shrinks from a house to a hut. The smallness of the house indicates that its occupant is permitted very few claims or none at all; *and however high it may shoot up with the progress of civilization, if the neighboring palace shoots up in the same or greater proportion, the occupant of the small house will always find himself more uncomfortable, more discontented.*" (My italics.)

Would one guess, from the vast bulk of Karl Marx's work, that he had thus penetrated to the basic principle of the power relationship? What does he tell us here? That it is no use improving the condition of the poor if, in the process, the rich remain relatively as rich! What avails it, then, to protest against the hunger and nakedness of the dispossessed and exploited if neither food nor clothing nor shelter in abundance will make them happy and contented? Nothing, Marx tells us here, not even the greatest affluence, can reconcile us to the greater affluence of others. Or, to put it another way: Social discontent consists in the envy of the poor, and you will never get rid of social discontent merely by improving the lot of the poor.

And oddly enough this truth, which Marx saw so clearly, and which he and other leftists and revolutionaries ignore, is of great creative value; it gives us a new insight into the psychological side of our social distress. It reveals that the competitive form of society is the natural milieu of the will to power or importance. *The competitive form of society is in fact the organized provocation of envy.*

The desire to be important is, among other things, the desire to have someone envious. It demands that somewhere in the environment of the important man, or man of power, there shall exist inferiority and discontent. Where wealth is the expression or instrument of power, the rich must have the less rich, the less rich must have the poor, below them; there must always be someone who looks up and envies.

What, then, do the rich mean when they say: "Let the poor be content with their lot, and then we shall have no social restlessness"? They mean: "Let the poor be 'content' to envy us and applaud us. Let them feel the distress of inferiority, but let them make their peace with it. Let them be class-conscious—and resigned."

If by some miracle of universal spiritual clarification the poor ceased to envy the rich, the rich would be as miserable as if they had been deprived of their wealth. They would, in fact, have been expropriated by devaluation. The silk toppers, the high-class brands of cigars and wines, the exclusive residential districts, the St. Patrick's Day parades, the Junior Leagues, the gestures of philanthropy, would lose all their flavor, and a frightful *tædium vitæ* would invade the life of the rich: no crowds to stare, no newspapers with pictures of the élite, and—for the more refined—no newspaper publicity to despise; no bank presidents invited to lecture on public duty and patriotism and the right life, no success stories about the rich in the magazines—in a word, no respect for the substantial men of the community.

Then, no doubt, another principle of importance, another expression of power, would begin to push upward—if the clarification did not last. But we are dealing with our society as it is, a society in which economic control is the accepted measure of comparative human importance.

It will perhaps be objected that I have cited extreme cases, that the vast majority of human beings are not the *agents provocateurs* I have painted. The harmless middle classes, for instance, who want to live decently and modestly, those professional people, those amiable families— are they too on the prowl for the less fortunately circumstanced on whom to vent their will to power and importance? I would answer that the will to power and importance runs in practice to the limit of a man's ability, and in fantasy beyond that. There are, thank God (this is meant in a peculiarly literal sense), many exceptions, and they are of two kinds. In some men the addiction to power is really mild; they are good by nature. Others practice self-discipline on moral grounds. But for the most part men sensibly come to terms with their moderate worldly abilities—and then claim the credit for self-discipline. They are "moral" enough not to ask for more power than they can get; then they falsify their morality by mob worship of the powerful. But this too they regard as self-discipline, and give it names like loyalty and idealism.

The best way to measure the deep-rootedness of the power principle in the "little, modest, harmless" people is to see them not when they are stationary in the social scale, and not even on the way up. It is on the way down that they reveal themselves. Who has ever lived among the middle classes and the poor without observing the devastating effect of an economic descent? What physical privations, in contradiction to the survival principle, do they not voluntarily accept—not to mention involuntary psychic suffering, equally dangerous to the health—before they admit their defeat (if they ever do)? We are foolish and wicked according to our abilities, and where these fall short we are cunning enough to call it modesty.

Returning to the story of how my ideas unfolded: I was

beginning to see that the rationalism and materialism of my teachers lacked a metaphysical basis; the element of man's perversity had been left out of the account. My teachers refused to admit that men fought for bread not because they had to, but because they wanted to fight. They wanted to fight because they had the fixation of the competitive principle—that is, of the struggle for power. As soon as the subsistence problem was solved—and even before—they sought "glory," "distinction," "applause," "honor"—in short, power. And the sport cult of the western world, to which I return in the next chapter, is the ritual of this view of life.

# CHAPTER IX

## *The Two Worlds*

❀

$H$AVING ceased to be a romantic, and finding no rest-
ing-point in rationalism, I fell into a period of homelessness. I misunderstood, at the time, the source and character
of this uncomfortable experience. I was distressed, it seemed
to me, by the fact that I was not a native Englishman. I
found something tactless in my self-identification with the
English masses, whose cause I had made my own. The reason, I believed, was that I could not say as an insider:

> *Men of England! who inherit*
> *Rights that cost your sires their blood,*

and:

> *O remember, England gathers*
> *Hence but fruitless wreaths of fame,*
> *If the spirits of your fathers*
> *Beat not in your breast the same.*

My sires had had nothing to do with England; whatever
they had bled for, it had not been the political freedom of
the Englishman. And so I felt that among the Lancashire
weavers whom I addressed at socialist meetings there was a
love of England which was different from mine: not acquired, not self-conscious, not meritorious. I had a great

affection for these people, and still have. But it seemed to me that it was not enough to make me one of them.

The feeling came from within. I was never challenged as a stranger, I was never aware of anti-Semitism or xenophobia. An immigrant Jew, I went through high school and college on scholarships won in competition with unchallengeable Englishmen. Was I afraid, then, that some day they would remember? My thoughts did not run so far ahead. As I piece it together now, I can see that if I had been as Jewish in those days as I have since become, I would have transcended our differences by accepting them creatively. As a self-conscious and informed Jew I would have seen clearly a co-operative relationship with England, as I see one now with America and the world.

I could not transcend the differences because I did not understand them. They were deep differences—far deeper than "the mere accident of birth." My despised Jewish upbringing, the rejected values of my childhood and boyhood environment, were at work in me. I had been touched with the Jewish tradition, the non-combative, non-competitive ideal; this tradition, which I had not acquired from books, but from unbookish people, from parents and relatives and neighbors—this tradition is separated by a tremendous gulf from the tradition of the western world. I was trying to bridge the gulf without knowing how wide and deep it was, without knowing the terrain on either side.

It was not the difference in ancestry that made me uneasy in the company of my English socialist comrades, though I continued to believe so for many years. It was my dawning and confused perception that the combative-competitive philosophy was as deep-rooted in the English masses as it was in the gentlemanly classes. This philosophy, or life-outlook, or life-form, or life-feeling permeated the socialist groups I worked with; it underlay the formal pro-

gram of a co-operative reorganization of society; it deflected the co-operative impulse into competitive expression; it was transferring to the new system of society, even
while this was in the making, the immemorial evil that had
haunted all societies hitherto.

Among these socialist mill hands, bricklayers, tram-
drivers, carters, laborers, and navvies the precepts of socialism were one thing; the daily tenor of thought and feeling
was another. Socialism was to them what Christianity was
to church-goers. The precepts came from the teachers, the
tenor of thought and feeling flowed from daily life, from the
folklore, the tremendous pagan tradition. Daily life, not
precept, dictated the realities.

But most baffling of all was the fact that the teachers too
belonged to the folklore—just as the clergy did. The teachers demanded that co-operation replace competition, but
not only did they fail to correct the competitive bent in the
socialist masses: they shared it and encouraged it! And both
teachers and masses shared with the gentlemanly classes
the civilizational complex that interprets life in terms of
competitive sports.

The difference that I was beginning to perceive between
the Jewish and gentile traditions sets the Jews apart in the
world; the longer I thought about it—and it has been my
chief preoccupation since my boyhood—the clearer and
more meaningful did the division become. Today I would
accept Mordecai M. Kaplan's definition of Judaism as a
civilization if it went further and stated that there are only
two conceivable ideals as civilizations, the Jewish and the
non-Jewish—and I use the word "Jewish" in its widest
sense to include Christianity. The fateful difference lies in
their concept of the moral problem.

The non-Jewish civilization has set up an immense structure of moral substitutions which may best be described as

*the sporting formulation of life.* Life is conceived as a game, and good behavior consists in scrupulously following the rules of the game. Therefore by definition a good man is one who always "plays the game." To find moral guidance, to achieve the right attitude toward his fellow men, to perfect his discipline, a man must go in constantly for games. The purpose of games is only in very small part physical exercise, which is merely athletics. Their essential function is to express and keep alive the combative spirit. They are a moral cult. They are, in fact, *the* moral cult. We are once more in the Tom Merry-Kipling-*Henry the Fifth* world (nor must we forget Oliver Wendell Holmes), but we are looking at it in wider bearings.

Games, as distinguished from exercise, have the following characteristics: they are based on rivalry, *and there must be a winner and a loser;* they involve the honor or status of groups, whom the players represent; the defeat of the players is the defeat of the group, their victory is the victory of the group; the games are played according to rules, the attempted evasion of which is—at least in theory—more disastrous than defeat. The groups represented may be clubs, colleges, cities, nations, or continents. Games, to be spiritually successful, must have large audiences (in proportion to the size of the groups, that is) and arouse deep emotions of loyalty in the spectators, as well as in those who receive the news at a distance. Small or apathetic audiences are evidence of the moral decline of a group.

Games, or public sports, have such a ubiquitous, ancient, and organic part in western civilization that we accept the phenomenon as tacitly as the air we breathe. We must remind ourselves of a few aspects of it before we can take in its crucial cultural and spiritual significance. No unsubsidized newspaper can exist without a large, expertly written, and expertly illustrated sports section. No college of any size, be it secular or denominational, can withdraw from the ritual. No city can remain unrepresented in the field. No king may reign, no president hold office, without periodic attendance at the most important games ceremonies.

The language of games, sports, and contests predominates in our homely descriptions of human situations. A ´man whose plans are blocked is "stymied." If he is in trouble he is "behind the eight ball." If his enterprise is approaching success he is "in the home stretch" or "approaching the goal." A man cheerful in defeat is "a good loser." An American President asks for public consideration by admitting he cannot promise a hit every time he comes to bat. It is, however, for terms of moral approval or disapproval that we draw most heavily on the race-track and the arena. If everyone gets an equal chance in life's struggle, it is "a fair field and no favor." If a man takes advantage of you in a time of distress, he is "hitting below the belt." A man still reclaimable is "down but not out." A narrowly selfish man is one who "won't play ball." The attack on Pearl Harbor is denounced before the Eternal Throne as "a sneak punch." But we must not be surprised to find that in our daily as distinguished from our strictly Sunday language (and that is not spoken all Sunday, either—nor is Sunday language free from weekday admixture) Hoyle and the Marquis of Queensberry have pushed out Isaiah and Jesus. If the true preparation for life is to be found in games or sports, our most important teachers will not be the prophets.

In the classical days of Greece and Rome public games were frankly associated with religion. They were forms of worship, and the attendance of the highest rulers was compulsory. Even Marcus Aurelius, who despised the arena, had to put in an appearance, though he always left the

99

services early. But the formal withdrawal of the religious motif has not diminished the numbers of worshippers at games, or changed the role of the games as expressions and instruments of the moral purpose. The modern Olympiad is a faithful continuation of the ancient, not only in name, but in function and effect. The roar that goes up from Wembley or the Yankee Stadium or the Rose Bowl is the one that went up from the Colosseum, the Circus Maximus, or the racing-track of the New Rome on the Bosporus. Its spiritual content, expressed in universal mob language, is what it has always been: the intoxicating affirmation of the exclusive rightness of the combative ethic; the sublimation of frustrated individual ambition into group assertiveness, focusing in the hero; the surrender or evasion of moral perception in favor of the automatism of a Yes-or-No loyalty; the substitution of a simple functional test for a difficult, thoughtful approach to the meaning of personality. The intelligence is put to rest while the most easily manipulable emotions take charge.

Although sports for youngsters are candidly advocated as character-builders, we rarely give serious thought to the fantastic absorption of our grown-ups in sports. When at certain moments it manifests itself in a kind of national catalepsy, as in a Test Match or a World Series, a few serious people will mention the condition with a deprecatory smile, half of indulgence, half of helplessness. There will also be frequent attempts to find moral justification on high levels. Such, for instance, is the plea for the "unifying" effect of international sports. The Olympiads of ancient Greece are supposed to have contributed to such Hellenic unity as existed; and modern Olympiads are supported as a form of international communion. Or we are told that games serve a unique purpose in sublimating man's natural aggressiveness. Both theses are based on self-deception.

One need not go further than newspaper reports to realize that modern Olympic games are actually international irritants. Behind the standardized gestures of courtesy there is a rancorous and grudging spirit, which festers the more bitterly because of attempted concealment. That the "democratic" nations should have participated in the German Olympic games at Garmisch-Partenkirchen in 1936 proved once for all that the slogan of "international understanding" is in this connection without meaning. And in general we do not find among sports promoters, professional or amateur, what could be called the democratic or internationally minded type. The value ascribed in this sense to the ancient Pan-Hellenic games arises from an optical illusion. The unity of Greek civilization made these games possible, just as the unity of modern science helps in the universal advance in atomic research; but just as it would be absurd to say that the advance in atomic research has (so far, at least) promoted world unity, so there is no evidence that the collapse of Greek civilization was delayed by the Olympic games, or that these helped to unite the Greeks against external threats, like the Persian or Roman.

As to the argument of "harmless sublimation," one might as well affirm that the gladiatorial combats mitigated the savagery of the Roman spectator mob. Machiavelli has with clearer insight praised them for the opposite effect. It might be urged that modern spectacles, being mostly bloodless, have the advantage in this respect; and we are also reminded that the bloody riots that attended many of the contests in ancient times—riots in which thousands were sometimes killed—do not occur today. Modern states are, of course, better organized, and the weapons of a modern police force cannot be matched by those of a mob. But the combative emotions of a crowd at a football match are not sublimated and dissipated; they are stored up. They are incorporated in the national temper, in both senses of this word. They await release in the greatest and grandest and most thrilling of all football games—war.

If we are told that by and large there are fewer wars now than in the past, and that this is somehow connected with the increasing harmlessness of sports, we must ask: "Is there less inter-group hatred in the world today than there was in the past?" We might also find that the proportion of the world's population killed off directly and indirectly by wars (soldiers and civilians, combat and postwar epidemics— not to mention blockades and genocide) has varied little from century to century; or that the variations establish no pattern. On the other hand, we shall not find in the older wars the paroxysms of national fury that are a feature of our wars, total wars. The change, we say, is due to the superior integration of the modern state; also to "better" organiza- tion of public opinion, to superior propaganda technique, itself the result of that superior integration and of scientific progress. But is it not obvious that the superior propaganda technique, whatever it is due to, always plays on the com- bative and competitive mob response, and is only an exten- sion of the games appeal? One of the crimes of psychiatry is to have popularized the notion of "directing" or "subli- mating" the aggressive impulse into "useful" and "con- structive" channels. The result has been that social prob- lems are offered as "challenges," with victory-or-defeat rewards and penalties, while the basic social problem, the existence of the combative impulse, is repressed. In every field, the justification of the games and challenge psychology on social and moral grounds is a trick of the combative ego.

Returning now to my growth: I began to reconsider my rejection of my upbringing and my boyhood Jewish world. The perplexed unresponsiveness to Tom Merrydom and cricket, to football and "play the game," took on a strangely purposeful air—no more than that, at first. It had, apparently, affirmative possibilities. My parents and my *Rebbi* had stumbled on something. They had a kind of case. One had to look into it. And I did so—with all the intellectual snobbery of the rationalist I still was.

The first purpose of my inquiry was to establish that my boyhood world really did not know what it was doing. I therefore found many reasons for the contrast with the sporting psychology of the gentiles; and all these reasons stemmed from the peculiar life of the Jews in exile. Their minority position had always encouraged the mental rather than the physical skills; it would have been suicide for them to have accepted the challenge of the gentile world on the physical plane. Moreover, the very paraphernalia of sports were lacking in their world—physical space in the ghettoes, to begin with; but also spaciousness in the wider sense, the spacious life, armies, navies, tournaments, banners, untroubled assembly in the open, the village green for wrestling, the woods and hills for hunting. Their attitude was the consequence of their inferior and restricted condition; it had not been a free moral choice.

The reader must understand that this last point was of tremendous importance for me. As a rationalist I could not admit that freedom of choice played a role in the life-outlook of a people. Even an individual was chained, in his philosophy, to causal necessity. An individual, however, could not be "controlled," in the laboratory sense, because he was not a statistical mass. A people, *per contra*, was amenable to historical and statistical analysis. Its spirit or philosophy was a function of observable forces.

And then I recalled what my *Rebbi* had taught me concerning Esau and Jacob, the twin sons of Isaac. Esau was a hunter, while Jacob was a studious dweller in tents; Esau was a *goy*, while Jacob was a traditional Jew; Esau rejected the God of his fathers, while Jacob accepted him. My *Rebbi* went on to say that the hairiness of Esau's hands was an indication, indeed part, of his animal nature, while the smoothness of Jacob's hands bespoke the *Talmid chacham*, the scholar. Esau had deserved to lose the blessing not only because he had despised it, not only because he had shown himself to be at the mercy of his animal appetites, but because he had flouted the Jewish decencies: he sat down to eat without washing his hands, he rose from the table without saying grace. Recalling this mixture of exegesis and folklore, I was delighted to see how it fitted into the deterministic argument. How long it was since Jews had been prevented from being hunters and men of the fields! How long since they had been excluded from the crafts, how long since they had had to live by their wits in a world of Esaus. How natural, therefore, that they should despise the huntsman and glorify the smooth hands of the scholar. It was not my *Rebbi* who was speaking, and not even the Jewish people: it was an economic and sociological pattern. A people—any people—exiled, repressed, frustrated, expelled from the fields and the crafts, confined to its ghettoes and its few sedentary occupations, could not respond otherwise.

It did not occur to me, at that time, to inquire why other oppressed minority groups had not developed like the Jews. Why were there not many persecuted and physically helpless minorities surviving across the millennia by the exercise of their wits? I only said: "The Jews could not have survived otherwise." I did not ask: "Why should they have survived at all?" Not that I would have found a satisfying answer: but it would have moved me sooner to look systematically into the history of the group.

When I did, I made an extraordinary discovery. The Jewish aversion to sports long predated the exile of the people and its minority condition. My parents and my

*Rebbi* were *not* the obvious product of the ghettoes. Certainly they had characteristics that only the ghetto could explain; but their total character was something more complex, and had to be explained in terms of a record that went back three thousand years and more. The Jews had *not* evolved their technique of survival under the pressures of the exile; they had brought it with them into the exile! Whatever modifications the ghetto had introduced into it, the substance of it was there long before.

The language that my parents and my *Rebbi* spoke— namely, Yiddish—was altogether free from the sporting expressions that were so thickly distributed, in strategic ideological areas, throughout English. The Yiddish books they read had no sporting coloration, let alone heroes of the arenas. If you had lived out your life in the ghetto of Manchester without discussing any of the affairs of the gentiles, you would never have known that there was such a thing as a football field or a cricket bat, a racing-track or a wrestling-mat. But if you read the Bible and the Jewish Apocrypha, the Mishnah and the Talmud, *and ignored the refer- ences to gentile nations and customs*, you would likewise never suspect that the world of antiquity had been as addicted to sports as is the modern world. None of these books and collections of books—as I know in part from reading and in part from the reports of scholars—contain any reference to sports spectacles among conforming Jews.

It is true that the Mishnah and the Talmud, as we have them, were put together long after the Bible text was fixed, and long after the Jews had lost their independence and ceased to conduct wars. But Mishnah and Talmud alike deal with the laws of the Jews as these were formulated in the Bible (the Pentateuch chiefly) and modified by exegesis to meet the needs of Jewish post-Biblical life in Palestine. The same laws and modifications went with the Jews into the exile. For a score of centuries after the destruction of the Temple, Jews went on studying and clarifying the regulations of the Temple sacrifices; a Jewish education consisted, in large part, in a knowledge of how to live a Jewish life in a Jewish state in ancient Palestine. There are sixty-three tractates in the Mishnah, dealing with an immense range of laws, customs, beliefs, and ethical precepts and quoting the conflicting opinions of various schools. All the exigencies of life are covered. The Talmud has collected the comments and elucidations of hundreds of scholars on these laws, customs, and precepts. There is not one page, not one paragraph, devoted to the management or regulation of public games.

The Bible itself shows no trace of the sports fixation. Here and there we have a fleeting reference to competitive exercises or to contests; nowhere is there a hint of organized spectacles. "Rejoiceth as a strong man to run a race," says the psalmist of the sun's daily course. Joab, David's general, proposes combat between men picked from his army and that of the army of Abner, the rival general, with these words: "Let the young men play before us." There is a section in the Second Book of Samuel listing the heroes of David's army and their most famous deeds, which the Jewish historian Dubnow compares with Homer, pointing out that the two documents are approximately contemporaneous. But whether the Jews had an epic of the Homeric type and "repressed" it, or never had one, the fact remains that the sports type is not a Jewish figure, and the fighter as such is not exalted in the literature that became the national heritage, the expression and the molder of the national character. No Jewish king is remembered as a hunter. David, who solidified the Jewish state and made Jerusalem its capital, is forbidden to build the Temple because he has shed so much blood. Recently, strolling through St. Paul's in London, and pausing before the countless statues and friezes dedicated to England's generals and admirals under the ægis of the Prince of Peace, I contrasted this circumstance with the Jewish penalization of a successful warrior king—one who, moreover, had been represented as a matchless psalmodist.

I will make my point clearer by juxtaposing two texts; not (as I have already remarked) by way of proof, since single texts prove nothing, but by way of exposition.

Solon, wisest of Athens's lawgivers, said to Crœsus that two men, Cleobis and Bito, had been happy, because "they were of Argive race; their fortune was enough for their wants, and they had both gained prizes at the games." Likewise, Herodotus reports the son of Crœsus as saying: "It was deemed the noblest and most suitable thing for me to frequent the wars and hunting parties." Against this I set the opening of the Book of Psalms: "Blessed (happy) is the man that walketh not in the counsel of the ungodly, nor standeth in the way of sinners, nor sitteth in the seat of the scornful. But his delight is in the law of the Lord; and in his law doth he meditate day and night."

Certain Biblical scholars insist that the Old Testament as we now have it was practically all written or rewritten during and after the Babylonian exile. Therefore one could argue that the Jews had already learned from experience that if they were to survive it would be by their wits. I shall show that these Biblical scholars have been misled; but for the moment we remain confronted with the fundamental question already posed: Why did not other small peoples of antiquity hit upon this adaptive technique and thus outlive by a couple of millennia their destroyers and oppressors?

The answer is that we are not dealing with an adaptive technique, or with a product of biological shrewdness. In any case, addiction to sports does not mean atrophy of the wits: the Jews could have been sportive *and* shrewd. As technical thinkers the Greeks were clearly the superiors of the Jews. The rejection of sports was not an ingenious even if unconscious stratagem in the struggle for survival. It was the result of a moral fixation. And it must have been a very early one, for there is no evidence anywhere in the Bible of a Jewish bent toward the sporting expression of life. Nowhere do the prophets and teachers have to prohibit the practice of sports. The sins of the Jews were many, and whether native or imported they were denounced in great detail. Neither of their own accord nor under foreign influence did the Jews in Biblical days ever fall into the error of glorifying and enhancing the competitiveness of life with the symbolism of games, or of refining and idealizing military combat with punctilio.

There was, indeed, a period in Jewish history, post-Biblical but Palestinian, when Jewish rulers made a systematic attempt to instill this philosophy and ritual into the common people. This was in the time of the Hasmonean Princes. The conforming Jews turned in horror upon their rulers; and the tradition of the Jewish people derives, not from the Hasmoneans and their supporters, called the Sadducees, but from the opponents of the Sadducees, the Hasideans and the Pharisees. With this profoundly instructive episode I deal more fully in Book Two.

It was my reading of the Bible and of the Jewish records that gave me the proper perspective on the spiritual position and significance of the humble Jewish world I was born into. The frustrations of poverty, the distractions and displacements of exile, had not obliterated the moral idiosyncrasy of this people; the line went back sixty, seventy, eighty generations to the streets of Jerusalem and the fields of Judea. The pacifist fixation of my boyhood world, expressing itself in abhorrence of violence, and in contempt for the mimicry of violence, was not a stratagem of slaves. It was an ancient tradition which had been born in freedom. What I had once despised as backwardness and obtuseness was a unique utterance concerning man's destiny.

As I went on reading the Jewish records, something in my personal experience rose to sharpen my emerging perceptions. I had known an earlier world than the Manchester ghetto—namely, the Roumanian village of my birth. As I grew older, my first childhood began to shine more clearly in my memory. I saw the synagogue in the fields, the ritual baths, the cemetery; I saw the little village garden (closed to Jews) opposite the town hall; I saw the *tzarani*, or peasants, with whom my father dealt; and I was aware that there, among an earthy, sportive, and hostile people, our contingent of Jews—those who finally settled in Manchester —had clung stubbornly to this way of life and this expression of a way of life which derived from the Biblical setting. Behind these Roumanian Jews were their forefathers, in Poland and Russia; and behind them, generation before generation, other forefathers, in other Roumanias, Polands, and Russias, all of them equally obstinate in their devotion among peoples equally earthy and hostile. These vivid glimpses of my earliest childhood gave tangibility to what I read of the Jewish *galut*, the exile, and made me a kind of first-hand witness of what I had never seen—or hardly seen—in person.

Two obstacles slowed up the process of clarification in me. First, it seemed to me "immoral" to have a special love of my people—I had learned that one must love all peoples equally. Second, I had learned that morals did not exist: there existed only "behavior patterns" (I do not know whether this phrase was current then; I cannot remember its preceding equivalent). Therefore it was *not* immoral for me to have a special love for my people. But my love for my people was rooted in my love of its moral bias. . . .

I came out of this witless dilemma, and out of a growing condition of political and social cynicism, under the influence of the prophets, with whom my Biblical reading began. Because the Bible has shaped my outlook, and because I see it as the great formative influence of the Jewish people, I am compelled, for the completeness of the argument, to devote an entire section to the examination of it. I am aware that to some readers this will seem an unwarrantable digression, but I cannot advise them to skip Book Two and resume with the contemporaneous scene in Book Three. What we think of the Bible today is of deadly import. I cannot permit myself to be frightened off by the complexes that have accumulated round the subject. My picture of man, of Christendom, of Jewry, and of myself has the Biblical experience at its center; the Bible and our view of the Bible must be taken up in detail.

# BOOK TWO

## The Ancient Records

## CHAPTER X

## *The Essence of the Prophets*

❀

Iɴ ᴍʏ first readings of the Hebrew prophets I was re-
pelled chiefly by their furious proclamation of retribution
and reward as the foundation of morality. They did not
seem to look on goodness as a good in itself, on evil as an
evil in itself. And as if this were not repellent enough, the
rewards and punishments were often handed out in bulk
to whole populations, like the bounties and brutalities of
nature, without regard to individual merit: the wicked
shared the general prosperity, the good were overwhelmed
in the general calamity. A third element in my distress was
the obvious practical futility of the retributive theory.

A single passage will illustrate all three perplexities.

Amos thus addresses the sinful people of the Kingdom of
Israel, in the time of Jeroboam the Second: "I have smitten
you with blasting and mildew: when your gardens and your
vineyards and your fig trees and your olive trees increased,
the palmerworm devoured them: yet have ye not returned
unto me, saith the Lord."

I could not then, I do not now, believe that there was
any connection between the sinfulness of the people in-
habiting the northern Kingdom of Israel and the invasion
of the crop-destroying *Ypsolophus pometellus* which—presumably—occurred in that area round the year ʙ.ᴄ. 750. This

difficulty did not haunt me long. I understood that miracles were the language of the time; the moral philosophy of Amos, like the poetical quality of Milton, had to be judged apart from the scientific picture attached to it. But it was precisely his moral philosophy that would not stand up to scrutiny. Amos seems to be wondering whether God should throw good plagues after bad in the effort to get better behavior out of the people of Israel. But if the bad man saw the good man suffering equally with himself, what incentive had he to reform? What incentive had the good man to remain good? And what kind of "reform" would it be anyway which was extracted, like that of Nineveh, under duress?

I found in another prophet, Ezekiel, a repudiation of the corporate system of retribution. He says: "The soul that sinneth, it shall die. The son shall not bear the iniquity of the father, neither shall the father bear the iniquity of the son: the righteousness of the righteous shall be upon him, and the wickedness of the wicked shall be upon him." This was a little better, though basically unsatisfactory. I found other passages, quoted below, which aimed the exhortation at the individual. But the dominant thesis of the prophets was corporate goodness and corporate wickedness, corporate reward and corporate punishment; it was so with Moses when he addressed the Jews on the mounts of blessing and curses, before they entered Canaan, it was so with Jeremiah when he addressed them in the streets of Jerusalem nearly a thousand years later, when they were about to be expelled from Canaan.

A theory of corporate reward and punishment is futile even as policy. You do not improve the moral insight of people by threatening them with public disaster. The approaching destruction of the world, visible to all as the consequence of our viciousness, would not make us "better."

It is not doing so today. You do not even stir people to "intelligent egotism" in this way. It is impossible to convince them that sometimes, at least, their calamities are due to their sins rather than to some error of calculation. This holds both for the individual and for the public. The criminal who has been caught broods on the oversight that betrayed him to the police; the members of a defeated criminal movement like Nazism brood on the strategic mistake that led to their defeat—usually the mistake of having "gone too far" or "chosen the wrong moment."

There is also a psychological difficulty. What sinners remember best is that they were happy while sinning. Surely the prophets had sense enough to see this. I found a beautiful illustration of the axiom in Jeremiah. After the destruction of the Temple by the Babylonians, the unhappy old man assembled the Jewish refugees in Egypt, and in the name of God flung these words at them:

"Ye have seen all the evil that I have brought upon Jerusalem, and upon all the cities of Judah; and, behold, this day they are a desolation, and no man dwelleth therein. Because of their wickedness which they have committed to provoke me to anger, in that they went to burn incense, and to serve other gods."

Jeremiah was referring chiefly to the days of King Manasseh, who, during a peaceful and prosperous reign of over half a century, demoralized beyond repair the structure of the state. He introduced into Judea (he was not the first to do it) the beastly practices of surrounding peoples: the male and female whores in the Temple, the burning of children in sacrifice to Moloch—all the debasements that undermine the vitality of the body politic. In particular the Jews had developed a weakness for "the Queen of Heaven," an Astarte goddess of the usual degenerate oriental type. More than that, the refugees in Egypt were still continuing the enervating cult; so that Jeremiah went on, furiously: "I will punish them that dwell in the land of Egypt, as I have punished Jerusalem, by the sword, by the famine, and by the pestilence."

Thereupon the assembly of sinners answered Jeremiah with these startling words: "We will certainly do whatsoever goeth forth out of our own mouth, to burn incense unto the queen of heaven, and to pour out drink offerings unto her, as we have done, we, and our fathers, our kings, and our princes, in the cities of Judah, and in the streets of Jerusalem: for then we had plenty of victuals, and were well, and saw no evil."

There you have it! Thirty-odd years ago I laughed over this passage, and thought of Napoleon on St. Helena. Disaster had taught him nothing. He spent his time brooding on the happy days that had been, and on his political and military missteps: he should have crossed the Niemen earlier, when invading Russia; he should have destroyed Prussia. That his basic error lay in seeking world power did not to him. Today the passage in Jeremiah puts me in mind of Italian Fascists and German Nazis nostalgic for the happy times of Mussolini and Hitler in their ascent. How good things were then! If they had only been a little cleverer . . .

Yet even the appeal to prudence is unreliable. As a young boy I used to think that most people only pretended to believe in an after-life; their behavior proved that they did not. Later I saw my error. Surely most people outside of lunatic asylums believe in natural cause and effect; but how little their daily behavior testifies to this belief. They know what is bad for their health, unwise for their careers, destructive of their comfort; they know it and ignore it, except in fits and starts. The weakness of the plea for goodness on prudential grounds is that people are not even prudent.

Were the prophets, who give frequent evidence of deep psychological insight, blind to this elementary truth? Amos and Jeremiah themselves confess that threats and promises did not work. What was it, then, that they meant? I was fascinated by the contradiction; and I suspected that beyond it lay the something I was looking for, the authoritative insight.

I do not know how long I read before the contradiction was resolved. I do not remember ever experiencing a "conversion," a sudden illumination, any more than I remember when I acquired the rationalist philosophy, which had promised so much and given so little. I can only say that in time, as I caught the spirit of the Bible, I realized that the prophetic appeals to prudence, individual or corporate, to hope of reward and fear of punishment, were as irrelevant to the essential prophetic utterance as is the belief in miracles. Both in the corporate and in the individual application reward and punishment were forms of expression. Rightly understood, the prophets transcend their own threats and cajoleries to produce an effect that is in no way related to earthly calculation, and in no way commensurate with it. The belief in miracles and the theory of retribution are the stylization of the age; the essence of the utterance is timeless.

Let us reread attentively the rebuke administered by the prophet Nathan to King David for the theft of Bathsheba and the cowardly murder of her husband, Uriah the Hittite:

"And the Lord sent Nathan unto David. And he came unto him, and said unto him, There were two men in one city; the one rich, and the other poor. The rich man had exceeding many flocks and herds: but the poor man had nothing, save one little ewe lamb, which he had bought and nourished up: and it grew up together with him, and with his children; it did eat of his own meat, and drank of his own cup, and lay in his bosom, and was unto him as a daughter. And there came a traveller unto the rich man, and he spared to take of his own flock and of his own herd, to dress for the wayfaring man that was come unto him; but took the poor man's lamb, and dressed it for the man that was come to him. And David's anger was greatly kindled against the man; and he said to Nathan, As the Lord liveth, the man that hath done this thing shall surely die.

"And Nathan said to David, Thou art the man. Thus saith the Lord God of Israel, I anointed thee king over Israel, and I delivered thee out of the hand of Saul; and I gave thee thy master's house, and thy master's wives into thy bosom, and gave thee the house of Israel and of Judah; and if that had been too little, I would moreover have given unto thee such and such things. Wherefore hast thou despised the commandment of the Lord, to do evil in his sight? thou hast killed Uriah the Hittite with the sword, and hast taken his wife to be thy wife, and hast slain him with the sword of the children of Ammon. Now therefore the sword shall never depart from thine house; because thou hast despised me, and hast taken the wife of Uriah the Hittite to be thy wife. Thus saith the Lord, Behold, I will raise up evil against thee out of thine own house, and I will take thy wives before thine eyes, and give them unto thy neighbour, and he shall lie with thy wives in the sight of this sun. For thou didst it secretly: but I will do this thing before all Israel, and before the sun."

And now let us observe, after several readings, the effect and intent of this astounding passage. It is not the punishment meted out to the criminal King (mingled, actually, with visitations on unborn persons) that fills us with horror; that is only a sort of epilogue, a ringing down of the curtain. The story rises toward its climax throughout the parable of the poor man and his little ewe lamb; it pauses sickeningly when David says: "The man that hath done this thing shall surely die," and in a final, half-expected, half-unexpected lightning leap reaches its terrifying peak when Nathan points his finger and says: "Thou art the man!" By comparison with this frightful denouement, this confrontation with the supreme horror of evil, the catalogue of punishments is almost meaningless. I would not say it is anti-climactic. One has to say something, do something, by way of symbolizing gesture, to make the blood return to the heart. And this is the only relationship, in reality and effectiveness, between the crime and the prophecy of punishment.

There is another tremendous story of crime and prophetic denunciation in which the structure and "technique" are the same: that of the weak and vicious hedonist Ahab, the conscienceless power-seeker Jezebel, and the unfortunate Naboth. When Naboth had been put out of the way at the instigation of Jezebel, Ahab went down to take possession of the vineyard.

"And the word of the Lord came to Elijah the Tishbite, saying, Arise, go down to meet Ahab king of Israel, which is in Samaria: behold, he is in the vineyard of Naboth, whither he is gone down to possess it. And thou shalt speak unto him, saying, Thus saith the Lord, Hast thou killed, and also taken possession? And thou shalt speak unto him, saying, Thus saith the Lord, In the place where dogs licked the blood of Naboth shall dogs lick thy blood, even thine. And Ahab said to Elijah, Hast thou found me, O mine enemy? And he answered, I have found thee: because thou hast sold thyself to work evil in the sight of the Lord. Behold, I will bring evil upon thee, and will take away thy posterity. . . ."

Once again, it is not the sentence pronounced on the sinner that makes the blood stand still. It is the abomination of evil which, in a concentrated revelation, stands out

119

from the words: "Hast thou killed, and also taken possession?" It is from their icy fury that we shrink, and not from
the predicted retribution. And we feel also that when Ahab
says helplessly: "Hast thou found me, O mine enemy?" he
means something like: "Hast thou found me, O my conscience?"

The motive of prudence, so feeble as a deterrent from
crime or folly, is also transcended by the prophets when the
drama is not personal but national. Amos thus addresses
the wealthy, luxury-loving women of the northern Kingdom of Israel: "Hear this word, ye kine of Bashan, that are
in the mountains of Samaria, which oppress the poor,
which crush the needy, which say to their masters, Bring,
and let us drink. The Lord God hath sworn by his holiness,
that, lo, the days shall come upon you, that he will take you
away with hooks, and your posterity with fishhooks." The
power of these words certainly does not lie in the threat of
punishment, so cogently and so bitterly expressed; it lies
in the intimation of something unbearable in the evil itself. The heart is constricted by horror and disgust, not
by fear; the sickness of spirit induced by the contemplation
of evil has nothing to do with the prospect of retribution.
For the retribution consists of earthly misfortune, and misfortune may come on a man unmerited, as everyone knows.
The Bible itself is full of references to unmerited personal
calamities. What the prophet does here, despite the stylization, is to remove the problem of good and evil from the
realm of the prudential. It was this that I failed to understand in my first readings; and it was this that I had been
seeking.

As the threat of punishment falls away from the essence
of the prophetic message, so does the promise of reward—
that is, of reward as we generally understand it. What
catches at the heart is not the offer of bountiful harvests

and rich flocks, and not the vision of each man sitting in safety and comfort under his own vine and his own fig tree, but this: "And the earth shall be filled with knowledge of God as the waters cover the sea," and: "I will pour out my spirit upon all flesh; and your sons and your daughters shall prophesy, your old men shall dream dreams, your young men shall see visions."

Here is no suggestion of the practical and calculable, or even of the describable. It cannot be made the basis of a bargain; it empties of all meaning the notion of a bargain. It suggests—and herein it is so alluring—the possibility of an other-being, something we have not known till now, a release from the equivocal, somewhat disreputable concept of prudential goodness. It is a glimpse of something as remote from the life we have known hitherto as this life is from that of the vegetable kingdom. When we have learned to understand this spirit in the prophet we become unfitted for everyday calculation.

We might say, then, that a prophet is one who excises from our system the question: "Why should I be moral?"—the question I had wrestled with futilely among the rationalists and determinists. He does so not by answering it, but by making it unintelligible, not to mention distasteful. Goodness thus becomes incommensurable with any form of worldliness; and when we are thus carried along we do not think of prudence, security, longevity, and honorable estate, and not even of peace of mind, self-esteem, and inner harmony, which are the rewards promised by the Stoic and wisdom morality.

We cannot be argued into this condition; we can only be caught up in it. We cannot, either, be maneuvered into it by social programs. It is not a statistical product, and it is not a policy.

Oddly enough, it is this very incommensurableness of

goodness that is its only appeal. There is no rationale or justification of goodness. I do not mean that it has no practical or social consequences. On the contrary, human life is probably impossible without it; but that is no "reason" for being good. The prophetic utterance makes no argument, except as a matter of style. It is by its nature unchallengeable. An obtuse man may be deaf to it; a half-witted sophisticate may slip away from it; a villain may either outstare it or else pretend (sometimes believe) that he has been carried away by it. And most of us are usually compounded of all three. But one cannot talk back at it intelligibly.

In a true surrender to it, one is aware that a basic paradox has suddenly disappeared. The paradox is contained in the baffling question: How can a human being perform an act that is not derived from the economy of practical, personal, egocentric motivation? The question and the paradox have disappeared because the "why" of goodness has disappeared. "Why should we be moral?" is not an intelligible question in the presence of the prophetic light. We perceive it to be the question of a defective creature.

This is the distinguishing mark of the prophet as individual: that he moves us to a condition in which not to do good seems to be an inexplicable stupidity, a privation, a confinement or unnatural restriction. Goodness has existed, does exist, without the intervention of prophets. The prophet enables us to realize that goodness is a fulfillment or completion.

How does he achieve this effect? By the word. His instrument is the word. Shall we, then, get at the secret of prophetic power by studying prophetic utterance as literature, as style? If we do so, we shall not even learn anything about style, let alone about prophecy. By way of analogy: a scientific essay by Thomas Huxley is usually, in the matter of style, a piece of literature. But if we read Huxley for style alone and obtain from him no science, we do not get the style either. If we read the prophets and obtain from them no moral experience, we do not get from them any literary value.

The word of the prophet is a deed. Statement and act are in his case aspects of the same thing. In general we think of the word as essentially different from the act. Thus, we say that we will do something; then we proceed to do it or we fail to do it. But a kind of language which is simultaneously a saying and a doing, which in fact knows no distinction between the saying and the doing, is precisely what is peculiar to the prophets. It is something like the act of creation as described in Genesis: "God said, Let there be light: and there was light." The fabulist does not mean that an announcement was made and a phenomenon followed, that an order was issued and carried out. God's saying: "Let there be light" was itself the creation of light. The prophet, when successful, does not discourse on goodness, letting conviction follow: he changes the person.

I observed with astonishment that the identity of word and act is also found (at any rate in theory) with the opposite of the prophet: namely, the mechanist, whose theory has no relationship to goodness. For the mechanist, the word is an act or deed exclusively; it is an agitation of certain muscles producing vibrations of air columns in the oral cavity, with consequent communicated activity in the auricular mechanism and the related brain cells of the listener. That which we most intimately associate with a word, meaning, does not exist for the mechanist-behaviorist; at least, not in the sense of being sense. To illustrate, I choose a passage from a recent book by Bertrand Russell.

A man has just received a telegram reading: "All your property has been destroyed by an earthquake." The man exclaims: "Heavens, I am ruined." Russell then goes on:

"It seems probable that if you had a sufficiently minute knowledge of this man's brain structure, and were a sufficiently good mathematician, you could foretell that when the shapes making the message on the telegram came into his field of vision, they would set up a process ending in certain movements in his mouth, to wit, those producing the sounds which we represent in writing as 'I am ruined.' It is assumed that you could make this prophecy without knowing English; it should not be necessary for you to know the meaning either of the telegram or of the exclamation."

In the case offered by Russell, the word is pure act or event; not because word and event coalesce to become one, but because the word lacks that which we think characteristic of the word: meaning. Here the meaning of a word is not merely irrelevant. *It does not exist.* What, then, is our illusion that there is such a thing as meaning? It—the meaning and the meaning-illusion—is an inexplicable superfluity in the cosmic economy, an unplaceable item in the balance book; it does not belong; what its function is, and how the devil it manages to exist—for some sort of existence, however illicit and shady, it certainly has—is beyond conjecture (if one may be permitted such a dubious word as "conjecture" in this argument). But if there is no such thing as meaning, there is no such thing as activating motive or explicable purpose. In the mechanistic concept of the universe all phenomena are accounted for in terms of matter-energy: all physical effects (and there are no others) are locked up in a perfect balance-sheet of measurable or calculable laboratory units; there is not a single erg left anywhere throughout the universe for directive intrusion of a moral (or immoral) intent. Meaning is quite literally squeezed out of the *real* business of the universe.

Philosophic hairsplitting? Not a bit of it. If there is no such thing as meaning, it does not matter what we mean. The use of words as morally neutral instruments of action is a consequence of the mechanistic view.

We might also say of the prophet, then, that he gives meaning to life, thereby illuminating the whole universe. Not all of us, and not any of us at all times, can accept the illumination. For instance, it is useless for the prophet to address himself to the mechanist, for the mechanist will, while he acts as mechanist, only examine the prophet's cranial structure and take measurements, to which he will apply mathematical analysis. In practice the mechanist is compelled to come down; he stoops to bandy words with people. But that, he tells us with an unhappy sigh, is only because of defective intelligence and inadequate information. But why a man with defective intelligence and inadequate information should make such sweeping statements is another of the riddles of the mechanistic philosophy.

If we ask what is the meaning that the prophet pours out on the universe, we are pulled up short; for the word "meaning" can only be described in terms of itself; and this is like using a microscope in order to investigate the principle of the microscope. We can only say what some of the effects of "meaning" are. It releases us from the mechanistic or purely materialistic obsession as a sufficient picture of the universe. In the presence of "meaning" we do not ask why we should be good. We accept the impulse or faculty as being in the nature of things (which does not mean in the things of nature), although we recognize that it faces obstacles. The chief obstacle, as we all know, is the tendency to misuse the prophets for our private ends, making them our sponsors in egotism, exhibitionism, intolerance, and self-righteousness.

This tendency is, in fact, our daily strategy against the prophets. We call it hypocrisy, "the tribute which vice pays to virtue." But the self-identification of the power lust with the moral utterances of the prophets is not hypocrisy. It is a subtle form of self-protection from them, and it is also the most potent form of slander: most potent because it induces well-intentioned and gullible men (and their gullibility is half-willed) to turn from the prophets in disgust. But, as I discovered, there is no one else to turn to. The good intention which rejects the prophets is a refusal to fight out the spiritual battle. The atheistic power-seeker (the openly atheistic—the other may be atheistic too) does not use the prophets as his façade; he plays the prophet himself; and him the well-intentioned ones accept "intelligently" and "rationally." But what this acceptance amounts to, I have already described. Thus, when we leave the prophets in the charge of power-seeking priests and boards of directors, we surrender the field; and when we substitute the rationalist for the prophet, we abandon it altogether.

The ways in which the prophet differs from the moralist I shall consider further on. Here I am concerned only with the essence of the prophetic message to the individual, which I summarize as follows: the prophet makes us see goodness as self-subsistent; he makes us see that life has meaning, that the meaning expresses itself in goodness, and that life is impossible without goodness. Not impossible in the sense that it cannot continue without goodness—though this may also be the case—but rather as we say that so-and-so is an impossible person.

# CHAPTER XI

## *The Prophets and the Nation*

❀

In the last chapter I dealt with the prophet as individual,
and with his effect on the individual. In the present chapter
I deal with Biblical prophetism as a national phenomenon.
The subject is a touchy one: it offends us to think that the
overwhelming gift of clarification, such as I described in the
last chapter, is tied up with nationhood or peoplehood. Yet
it will be seen that there is a curious connection between
prophetism and the Jewish *people*. Unless we realize this, we
shall not reach an understanding of the Jewish character
throughout the ages, the Jewish position in the world today, the relationship between Christendom and Jewry,
the origins and purpose of the State of Israel. For my personal thesis, this connection explains how my parents and
my *Rebbi* came to be what they were, and how I came to
be what I am.

After a number of readings of the prophets, and of the
historical Biblical books from Judges to Kings, prophetism
begins to take on an undeniable pattern. We perceive, to
our astonishment, that the prophets are not random erup-
tions of the spirit. What lies before us is an organic historical
episode with a clear trajectory of development.

The prophets begin dimly. We read first of magicians,
medicine-men, dervishes, augurs, manipulators of divin-

ing-bones and sacred figurines. They seem to be part of the general picture of the east where—as elsewhere but more markedly—magic exertion (the strategy of animism, as Reinach calls it) is accompanied in the individual by violent psychic disturbances. Then follow schools of prophets, wandering bands of enthusiasts, such as Saul joined. They have their techniques, one of which is music, for casting themselves into their clairvoyant trances. They are of the shaman type, with its mixture of priestly and prophetic functions. They are in part professionals. They can be hired for special jobs, or even set up in business by an entrepreneur. The concept of the prophet is very primitive at first—it has very little to do with what I have discussed in the last chapter. Gradually it lifts itself into higher meaning.

To illustrate the beginning of the process:

We read in Judges that a rich man in Ephraim, named Micah, bought himself a set of sacred implements—gods, ephods, and teraphim, or figurines—and engaged an itinerant Levite to be his priest, permanently attached to his household, in exchange for board and lodging and annual payment of ten shekels and a suit of clothes. A band of Danites, on the prowl for new territory for the tribe, consulted the young Levite, and liked him so well that they carried him off, together with the sacred paraphernalia. When he protested, they said: "Hold thy peace, lay thine hand upon thy mouth, and go with us, and be to us a father and a priest." In this early and curious instance of forced labor the chronicler, aware of certain irregularities, mentions that in those days there was no king in Israel. But he does not imply that this prophet-priest was unreliable, or that his craftsmanship was affected by the irregularities.

The characteristics of these dawn-figures of prophetism lingered on into later generations, when the pre-prophetic was evolving into the prophetic, when the Jewish type was lifting itself clear from the general matrix of the surrounding world. Samuel, in the period following the Judges, was half priest and half prophet. But he also did little divining jobs. He was consulted, for a small fee, on the matter of some strayed and stolen asses. In a later period Elisha, when asked to prophesy in regard to a war against Moab, called for music, so that he might achieve the right condition of ecstasy. The association of prophecy with magic foresight and the performance of miracles never died out completely. At the highest stage Isaiah was intermediary for a miracle, in which the motion of the sun dial was reversed for King Hezekiah. But by that time the miracle was an altogether unimportant element in prophetism.

We do not know what the dawn-prophets taught, if they taught anything beyond the techniques of their craft. The first great ethical prophetic utterance is that of Nathan, directed at King David. But it is Elijah, that wild, tremendous folk-figure, who is the clearest compound of the primitive and classical types; *and historically he stands half-way between them*. Elijah was priest, magician, and morality prophet. He sacrificed in successful competition with the court prophet-priests. He was prodigal with miracles: he brought a dead child to life, he renewed the meal and oil of the poor widow, he burned captains and soldiers with a word, he foretold drought and rain. He becomes the morality prophet in the story of Ahab, Jezebel, and Naboth. There, like Nathan before him, he sounds the authentic note. But, again like Nathan, he falls short of the highest achievement.

Both Nathan and Elijah, by the power of their utterances, unveiled the moral insight that is beyond the retributive principle; that is, beyond prudence, calculation, and reason. But they dealt with the individual. It was not until a century after Elijah that Amos initiated that phase of Jewish prophetism which is its complete fulfillment: the identification of nationhood with moral purpose. From now on, the national destiny is placed under the sign of moral perception.

As in all historical developments, so in the development of prophetism the old persisted side by side with the new, in a diminishing ratio. Primitive manifestations of prophetism never died away completely—they merely lost importance. Nathan began the moral tradition of prophetism; but another prophet at the court of King David, Gad, Nathan's contemporary, is the embodiment of the tabu tradition. Gad brought punishment to David not for a moral misdemeanor, but for having transgressed the tabu against the taking of a census. The contrast between Nathan and Gad is startling: juxtaposed, they make one think of an illustration in a popular book on anthropology: Homo sapiens and Ape-man.

Instructive, too, is the contrast between the destinies of the two stories associated with Nathan and Gad. The story of the slaying of Uriah the Hittite, and of the annihilating rebuke it drew down on King David, is never forgotten; centuries afterwards it is quoted in the Biblical text, a blot on the memory of David. The story of Gad sinks into obscurity, and David's contravention of the tabu makes no impression on later generations.

When Amos and Isaiah and Micah and Jeremiah were fulfilling the supreme functions of prophecy, some contemporaries of theirs, mentioned in the history books of Kings, still lagged behind in earlier stages. A superficial reader of the Bible, failing to distinguish between these strata, also fails to grasp the evolutionary process that is here presented. He is also apt to be confused by the fact that many of the climactic passages in the highest prophets are—as we shall see—later additions. But that is of no importance in the establishment of the pattern. *What matters is that these additions were conceived in the original spirit of the prophets.* The mold had been created.

The prophets have been called the archetypes of the democratic tribune, the defenders of the common people against the kings, of the poor against the rich. This view, which has much truth in it, is liable to abuse. We must note that the prophets were not demagogues: they did not take up the attitude that the poor are sinless, that the oppressed are, as such, always and naturally and axiomatically in the right. They did not assume that the masses are not in want of moral admonition, being the helpless victims of "the system." Victims the masses are, to be sure, but to deprive them of moral choice is to complete the victimization. The main burden of the prophetic accusation is, of course, turned against those who are in power, for they have a larger range of choice. The princes, the men of substance, the counselors, the judges—these are in the first line of attack: "What mean ye that ye beat my people to pieces, and grind the faces of the poor? saith the Lord God of Hosts." And there is also extenuation for the sins of the weak: "O my people, they which lead thee cause thee to err, and destroy the way of thy paths." But we have just seen that when Jeremiah assembled the refugees in Egypt—and they must have been very poor to recall with such longing the "victuals" of the happy time in Judea—he threatened them with even greater calamities for their perverse and obstinate loyalty to the uncleanliness of the Astarte cult.

To defend the poor without toadying to them, without pauperizing them spiritually, was of the essence of the prophetic purpose. In oppression and poverty the masses must not be encouraged in the destructive belief that they are devoid of responsibility. That leads to mechanism, and mechanism is either all or nothing. For if one cannot talk of responsibility to the poor, one cannot talk of it to anybody; the rich, too, are "victims of the system."

The prophetic vision was not of a prosperous, well-managed nation, but of a nation permeated with the moral spirit; that is what issues from amidst the stratified confusions and occasional obscurities of the prophetic utterances. The prophets (the classical prophets, that is) were nationalists exclusively in this spirit; and though it is correct to call them the guardians of Jewish nationalism, we must always remember what purpose they ascribed to it. For them a nation that was not a moral instrument had no reason for existing, and had no "right" to exist. This is the substance of the prophetic national policy. The formula is not: "Let the nation live though all moral value perish," but: "Let the nation perish if it has no moral purpose." This is the symbolic meaning of the threats of total national destruction.

Sometimes the prophets sentimentalized about the past. Hosea, in the time of Jeroboam the Second (eighth century B.C.) thinks back to the idyll of the national birth, and prophesies a renewal of the spirit of old: "And she [the Jewish nation] shall sing there [in Jerusalem], as in the days of her youth, and as in the day when she came out of Egypt." Jeremiah, nearly two centuries later, speaks thus to the sinful people in the name of God: "I remember thee, the kindness of thy youth, the love of thine espousals, when thou wentest after me in the wilderness, in a land that was not sown."

Yet, not long before Jeremiah uttered these poignant words, another prophet, unnamed, delivered this blasting message from God to the apostate King Manasseh: "I will forsake the remnant of mine inheritance, and deliver them into the hand of their enemies . . . *because they have done evil in my sight, and have provoked me to anger since the day their fathers came forth out of Egypt, even unto this day.*" The record, which must have been known to Hosea and Jeremiah, bears out this anonymous prophet, at least in regard to the misbehavior of the Jews who left Egypt. It would be pedantic to take Hosea and Jeremiah to task for historical inaccuracy; the contradictions of great spirits add up—it is only those of small spirits that cancel out. The final effect adds up to this: the vision of the nation as a moral organism, the vision of the moral spirit as a self-subsistent reality, and the vision of the world fulfilling itself in that spirit.

The curve of the prophetic growth is associated with the curve of the history of the Jewish people from the time of the Judges to the Babylonian exile. In six or seven centuries the people passed through a tremendous series of experiences. They saw the monarchy established, and within a century after the anointing of the first King they saw the nation split into two parts. Two centuries later the larger part, Israel, the northern kingdom, where the first of the universal prophets had ministered, was wiped out by the Assyrians. The remaining part, the southern Kingdom of Judea, forefelt its doom; a century and a half later it was wiped out as completely—to all appearances—as the first. Within those centuries the prophets evolved from the medicine-man of Micah and the wandering schools of the days of Saul—those who left no message—to the uniquely individualized types of Amos, Isaiah, and Jeremiah, whose written messages were carried into the Babylonian exile.

The trajectory of prophetism is not associated with the trajectory of national power, but with the trajectory of national experience. The prophets were a projection of the people in growth. They were the people in utterance or, to borrow from psychoanalysis, the national superego struggling with the id. Their denunciation of the nation as such was a national self-denunciation; though they were often persecuted by the rulers, there never occurred a popular uprising against them. In all the long record, there is not one instance of a prophet being slain by the people (an interesting reflection on the story of the Crucifixion). The masses as a whole, they who were less guilty than the rulers, felt—without always obeying—that the prophets were the national mouthpiece, even though they often foretold universal and indiscriminate destruction.

This thesis of the national-structural character of prophetism is of such importance in the understanding of the Jewish people and its potentialities that it is impossible to ignore the criticisms which the more informed reader will bring against it, and which the less informed reader knows to exist.

There are scholars who believe that Jewish ethical monotheism developed very late in Jewish history, fighting upward against Canaanitish and surrounding polytheisms. There are others who believe that Jewish monotheism, ethical or tabu, is older than the existing records, and that the oldest codes of law which we possess derive from a common source of still greater antiquity. There is, in Biblical criticism, a great to-do about plagiarism and priority of ideas as between the Hebrews and other ancient peoples. We are told on the one hand that ethical monotheism was known to Egyptian and Babylonian priests before it was known to the Hebrews; we are warned on the other hand against seeking the origins of prophetism or of ethical monotheism in the practices and institutions of other peoples. Two features usually dominate the discussions: one is emotional interest in giving credit to the Jews or withholding it from them; the other is a journalistic addiction to phrases like "the more modern theory is . . ." and "more recent research shows . . ." (For a brilliant résumé of this material the reader is referred to Solomon Goldman's *The Book of Human Destiny*.) As for the prophets, a great distinction is made between those whose names are attached to their own books—the "literary prophets"—like Amos and Isaiah, and those who appear only in the historical accounts, like Nathan and Elijah. (The historical accounts are, for this purpose, the books of Samuel, Kings, and Chronicles.) It is noted that the "literary prophets" are not mentioned—with a few unimportant exceptions—in any of the historical records covering their periods. Various deductions are made from this circumstance, the most important being that we must not confuse the two types of prophets and their relative influence, if any, on the Jewish people.

We are told, further, that practically all of the prophetic books and nearly all of the historical books were produced very late—say in the Babylonian exile, or even in the following centuries—long after the periods with which they purport to deal. They are (some say) products of the third, fourth, and fifth centuries B.C., and are utterly unreliable as pictures of what took place in the sixth to the tenth centuries B.C.

None of these analyses and conjectures have any bearing on the crucial phenomenon—historically speaking—of Jewish prophetism: namely, its patterned deployment within the framework of Jewish history, the internal, unshakable proof of its *national* character. If this phenomenon is an illusion, we should have to accept one of two wildly improbable theories:

1. Out of a hodgepodge of plagiarisms, of tangled and intermingled texts separated by centuries, there accidentally emerges the consistent and cohesive historical picture I have presented:

2. The writers of the Biblical texts, living more than two thousand years ago, anticipated our modern and sophisticated sense of the historical. Groups of Judean Jews, writing and editing in the third, fourth, and fifth centuries B.C., collaborated—consciously or unconsciously—to throw backward into the sixth, seventh, eighth, ninth, and tenth centuries B.C. a pattern of development satisfactory to the historical sense of our twentieth century.

Since I am not a believer in miracles, I am compelled to reject both of these astounding theories. But this is not by any means equivalent to ignoring the higher criticism. We can accept a great deal of it; we can break up Isaiah, and sundry other prophets, into first, second, third, and fourth; we can fragmentate and reshuffle the historical books; and we are still left with the historical pattern of prophetism. It is so insistent that on grounds of common sense, and of every human probability, it withstands all but the most chaotic misuse of conjecture. It imposes a limitation, because it dominates logically. Even so, as we shall see, there is ample room for disagreement on the dates of specific passages. And I shall be compelled to discuss these disagreements because it is imperative to establish, for the understanding of contemporary meanings in Jewish-Christian relations, the limits of the intrinsic values of the Bible.

I have said that what was added to the prophetic books, whether in the Babylonian time or later, does not change the national-structural character of the prophetic episode. When we read the second—or second and third and fourth —Isaiah, we can see clearly, from the historical allusions, that the passages were written centuries after the first Isaiah; at any rate, centuries after the first Isaiah is purported to have lived. And there are sections here—as there are interpolated sections in the first Isaiah—which are not inferior to the highest productions of the classical prophetic age. But they are fragments—even if inspired fragments—of insight. The pattern had been established long before; the phenomenon was there, the Jewish view of nationhood and morality had been established. Prophetism as a national production—a unique thing in the world—had crystallized. The last of the self-recording prophets, following the return from Babylon, no longer had the original stature; they are epigones.

Finally, the reader may wonder at the omission of Moses from a survey of the prophets—he who is regarded by the Jewish people as the greatest of them, and of whom it is said: "There arose not a prophet since in Israel like unto Moses." But Moses stands apart in many ways. He is unquestionably a reconstruction. He is outside the trajectory of prophetism, and he is not subject to classification. There are patriarchs, kings, prophets, priests, who fall into patterns. There is only one Moses. And though he is regarded as the greatest of the prophets, he is, because of his atypicality, never called the prophet, like Elijah or Isaiah. He is called "our teacher." He presides over the birth of the Jewish national history but does not fit into it. This gigantic figure is the nearest approach in the Jewish record to a superhuman personality, a God-man. It was perhaps because they were conscious of dangerous possibilities in the Moses story that the editors of the Passover Haggadah omitted mention of him; with the astonishing consequence that when the Jews assemble annually to commemorate, with elaborate ritual, with ancient prayers and sagas, the incident of the exodus, the central human figure in its execution is "repressed."

# CHAPTER XII

## *The Dynamism of the Bible*

❊

I F THE Bible is taken as a static document or collection of documents—that is, as a flat, even recital of events and views, of equal, literal validity everywhere—it becomes, to a child of our times, quite meaningless. The prophetic messages retain their power; the vignettes and dramatic episodes still arrest the attention. But there is no Bible; there are only points of clarity in a huge confusion.

And it is no simple matter to get a view of the Bible as a whole. Sporadic reading at long intervals, "dipping into the Bible" from time to time when one has nothing better to do, and even smacking one's lips over this or that "gem" —all this is almost worse than nothing. And yet one does not have to be a "thinker" or a "scholar" in order to see the Bible as a vivid, involved, and sometimes fragmentary record of a spiritual struggle: *one has only to read until one participates in the struggle.*

I ignore the inconsistencies in dates, genealogies, and so on. They are trivial. The real initial difficulty is with the contradictions and discrepancies—as they seem to be—in the moralities that the Bible presents. Now, these contradictions and discrepancies are, actually, of the very essence of the Biblical message. The Bible would have no dynamism and unity without them. The power that makes it, in my view, the most important document in human history would be gone from it.

There are three main types of exhorters presented in the Bible. There is the ritualist or priest, who believes that the right life consists mainly in a discipline of symbolic acts directed toward God. The discipline is complicated in its details, but quite simple in execution. It is as straightforward as a book of etiquette, which in fact it closely resembles in spirit. Its gestures, or choreography, or prescriptions, are within the reach of every type of intelligence.

There is the sage, or wisdom-moralist, who believes and urges that the right life is a matter of prudence, decency, understanding, propriety, circumspection, contemplation, dignity, shrewdness, consideration, "enlightened egotism," and respectability. His discipline is a more difficult one than that of the priest, and calls for training and worldly wisdom.

There is the prophet, who opens the way to moral illumination. He rises to a level on which "discipline" no longer exists.

There is no essential opposition between the ritualist and the sage-moralist or, as I shall sometimes call him, the sage-ethicist. For the sage seeks to come to terms with the world as it is—his *sagesse* consists in that—and to do it sensibly and decently, as becomes a civilized person. In the Biblical book that best represents the sage-ethicist, Proverbs, the ritual is commended. It is also commended in the companion book, Ecclesiasticus, or the book of ben Sirach, the only one of the Apocryphal books which is of Biblical stature. (The sage-ethicist naturally appears in other places, notably in some of the Psalms.) But sages do not care at all for the ecstasies of the prophets, with their revolutionary glimpses of other-worldly understanding; so the prophets are not commended by them, as the priests sometimes are.

139

Not that there is anywhere a head-on collision between sages and prophets; they simply slide past each other. Between priests and prophets there are frequent head-on collisons—namely, when the priests have let ritualism crowd out morality. There are, however, times when priests and prophets are reconciled. More than one prophet, we may note, comes of a priestly family.

All three, priest, sage, and prophet, seem to be equally committed to a retributive or prudential evaluation of morality. All seem to believe equally in *earthly* reward and punishment at the hand of God. But I have shown, I believe, that the prophetic message liberates itself and us completely from this evaluation.

The sage or wisdom-moralist asserts that the *individual* good life is rewarded by happiness, the bad life punished by misfortune and misery. This is often contradicted, notably in Job, Ecclesiastes, and some of the Psalms; but it is the fundamental thesis of wisdom-ethicism. The priest associates the *national* welfare with obedience to the ritual. God will reward or punish the Jewish *people* according to the degree of its over-all ritualistic faithfulness, as if there were a political alliance; however, the idea of individual retribution, in which God establishes direct relations with the subjects of the allied nation, is not excluded. The sage and the ritualist are on common ground in their acceptance of established tabus which have no moral content to us. But that is not a Jewish characteristic. We find, for instance, that Plato too speaks of an abominable person who "will commit the foulest murder or eat forbidden food."

The ritualist is a guardian of cultural forms, as well as an ethicist (cf. the medieval Church). There is a profound difference between the Jewish ritual and the rituals of other peoples of the ancient near east. It denounces human sacrifice, animal-worship, and all debasing and orgiastic ceremonials. The so-called Priestly Code of the Old Testament is shot through with moral admonition, often intruding strangely on purely ritualistic instruction. But predominantly it views the relationship between man and God as an elaborate system of graded propitiatory acts and offerings. In this respect, I do not find in the Biblical ritual what cannot be found elsewhere.

Similarly, the ethics of the sage, or sensible man, as presented in the Bible, may be classed with the ethics of the Stoics, and with the wisdom moralities found among others than the Greeks and Jews. Stoicism at its highest attains an other-worldliness, a disregard of the commonplace, which is beyond the reach of the Biblical wisdom-morality. However, it should be borne in mind that Stoicism first appeared in Asia Minor.

Biblical wisdom-morality indicates two sets of rewards and punishments for the individual. The first set is external: God metes out prosperity and destitution, success and failure, according to one's ethical rating. The second set is internal: the good man feels good, the bad man feels bad. To be ethical, then, is sensible on both counts: it is a formula for success and a specific for serenity of spirit.

A rather cagey ethical system of this kind is naturally bound up with solid horse-sense generally; and the books of Proverbs and Ecclesiasticus abound in penetrating observations and amusing epigrams on matters at large. Thus: "He that sendeth a message by the hand of a fool cutteth off the feet." "Hell and destruction are never full; so the eyes of a man are never satisfied." "It is naught, it is naught, saith the buyer; but when he is gone on his way, he boasteth." "The slothful man saith, There is a lion without, I shall be slain in the streets." (Agoraphobia as one source of laziness should commend itself to psychoanalysts.)

There is plenty of sound, stuffed-shirt advice on the subjects of industriousness and indolence. "The hand of the diligent shall bear rule; but the slothful shall be under tribute." "Love not sleep, lest thou come to poverty." "Seest thou a man diligent in his business? he shall stand before kings; he shall not stand before mean men."

A little less edifying are the admonitions against signing promissory notes for others; their frequency seems to testify to a wide prevalence of this amiable and expensive weakness. "Be not thou one of them that strike hands [make a pledge], or of them that are sureties for debts. If thou hast nothing to pay, why should he take away thy bed from under thee?" "He that is surety for a stranger shall smart for it: and he that hateth suretiship is sure." "A man void of understanding striketh hands, and becometh surety in the presence of his friends." So far Proverbs; ben Sirach echoes: "There is the kind of man that out of bashfulness maketh promises to his friends; and he maketh him his enemy for nothing."

We learn that honesty is the best policy and that crime does not pay. "The light of the righteous rejoiceth, but the lamp of the wicked shall be put out." "Wickedness overtaketh the sinner." "Blessings are upon the head of the just; but violence covereth the mouth of the wicked."

The compilers of Proverbs, and ben Sirach after them, were excessively occupied with the dangers of women and of politics, but especially of women. The one famous passage in praise of a woman presents her as a formidable combination of go-getter and home-factory foreman. Otherwise she is a snare, a corruption, a torment, and a calamity generally. A wise man keeps away from women and from revolutionaries. "My son, fear thou the Lord and the king; and meddle not with them that are given to change."

The prudential motivation of morality sometimes becomes painful. "If thine enemy be hungry, give him to eat

. . . and the Lord shall reward thee." "Honour the Lord with thy substance, and with the firstfruits of all thine increase: So shall thy barns be filled with plenty." (This intrudes on the ritualists.) One should be humble and considerate for precautionary reasons. "Pride goeth before destruction, and an haughty spirit before a fall." "Rejoice not when thine enemy falleth . . . lest the Lord see it, and it displease him, and he turn away his wrath from him." This bit must have been written by an epicure of the malicious, for it amounts to: "Gloat with moderation; it will last longer."

The most offensive expression of the prudence morality is to be found not in Proverbs but in Psalms. "I have been young, and now am old; yet have I not seen the righteous forsaken, nor his seed begging bread." It is difficult to read this unctuous verse without a start of distress. It means: "If you are destitute in your old age, if your children are hungry, you—and they—are expiating your sins." I do not understand why the Reconstructionists have deleted from the Passover service the verses beginning: "Pour forth thy wrath upon the nations that know thee not," and have left in the grace after meals this piece of heartless and sanctimonious senility.

Not quite so offensive, yet basically unacceptable, is the justification of morality as sound mental and social hygiene, wherein the sage-moralists come closer to the Stoics. On this view one cannot distinguish ethical precept from medical and managerial advice. "A merry heart doeth good like a medicine: but a broken spirit drieth the bones," says Proverbs; and: "Heaviness in the heart of man maketh it stoop: but a good word maketh it glad." And ben Sirach: "Never repeat what is told thee, and thou shalt never fare the worse." Also: "Jest not with a rude man, lest thine ancestors be dishonoured." This is particularly ingenious:

a coarse person does not feel at ease with you until he can jocularly call you a son-of-a-bitch.

The same self-regard speaks in the more serious verse from Proverbs: "He that is slow to anger is better than the mighty; and he that ruleth his spirit than he that taketh a city." The appeal here is to a man's good opinion of himself, as if to say: "*You're* too big to lose your temper." It is not what happens to the other man that should guide you—according to this view—but what happens to you. Your morality is not rooted in love of man, but in the cultivation of superiority, election, and imperturbability.

The same spirit will be found in many admonitions in *The Ethics of the Fathers*, a product of the post-Biblical Pharisees. And again we are put in mind of the Stoics. Plutarch tells of Pericles: "Such was his conduct when a vile and abandoned fellow loaded him a whole day with reproaches and abuse: he bore it with patience and silence, and continued in public for the dispatch of some urgent affairs. In the evening he walked slowly home, this impudent wretch following and insulting him all the way with the most scurrilous language. And as it was dark when he came to his own door, he ordered one of his servants to take a torch and light the man home." The toploftiness and serenity of Pericles, as here portrayed by Plutarch, seem to exclude the poor lunatic—such he must have been—from human classification. He is treated with the kindness which the gentleman shows toward animals.

Counsels of prudent wickedness often read like impish parodies of the self-regarding morality. I have spoken (quoting Symonds) of the good manners, serenity, courtesy, and balanced spirits of the Italian Renaissance villains; they reaped all the psychological rewards of a perfect wisdom-morality while flouting its social admonitions. But a good parody is only a legitimate *reductio ad absurdum*.

When Machiavelli says that it does not pay to insult anyone, or to brood on revenge, he is pushing the self-regarding
morality to its logical extreme. He explains, indeed, that
insulting someone merely makes an enemy unnecessarily,
or puts one on his guard. To seek revenge is to be deflected
from the larger-minded and more comprehensive villainy.
Be gentle and ruthless, says Machiavelli; be farsighted and
well-balanced and good-humored in your pursuit of power,
winning friends and influencing people as you go along;
avoid the little emotional indulgences of spite and malice
for the sake of the greater reward of enduring victory over
your enemies—and friends. Machiavelli goes further: he
warns soft-hearted people not to undertake villainies they
have not the stomach for. They will lose their peace of
mind. It is otherwise with those whose minds are fortified
by training. Or, as Plato says, philosophy and music are
the only saviors of virtue.

It would be wrong to close on this note with regard to
the prudence morality of the sage. It never rose to clear
moral illumination, or to the concept of goodness as the
national purpose. At its best, however, it reached toward a
loving human relationship which threw a penumbra, if not
a total eclipse, on the view of morality as self-service. We
are invited to ignore retribution and reward; sin is no
longer an impropriety beneath the dignity of superior
people; we are in the realm of pure human sympathy.
Proverbs says: "Withhold not good from them to whom it
is due, when it is in the power of thine hand to do it. Say
not unto thy neighbour, Go, and come again, and tomorrow I will give, when thou hast it by thee." The verse is not
followed by a promise of reward; but this is less important
than its tone, which is one of genuine solicitude. The same
feeling warms the lines in ben Sirach: "My son, deprive not
the man of his living, and make not the needy eyes to wait

for long. . . . Reject not a suppliant in his affliction, and turn not away thy face from a poor man." On this level, too, Proverbs says, despite the eighth commandment: "Men do not despise a thief, if he steal to satisfy his soul when he is hungry."

There are evidences, too, of dissatisfaction among the wisdom-ethicists with the mercenary theory of retribution. With them too it went against the grain, now and again, to make goodness synonymous with shrewdness. The sages who lived about the time of the fixing of the Biblical canon belonged largely to the wisdom school; among them the struggle against the theory of retribution was explicit. While one of them said: "Despair not of retribution," another said, bluntly: "It is not in our power to explain the well-being of the wicked or the sorrows of the righteous." And a third: "Be not like those who serve their masters for a reward."

But these men did not attain to the perception of goodness as self-subsistent reality, *the* reality for the fulfilled man. At least, they did not achieve the transmission of it. Here the prophets alone were effective.

The dynamism of the Bible—I speak here only of the Old Testament, for reasons yet to be given—is not that of an ordinary evolutionary historical process. Such a process is, indeed, visible in the Bible, but it is secondary. The priestly and the civic codes (which are united) bear the clear traces of change and struggle on the historical level. It does not matter whether we accept the views of the Wellhausen school on the growth of the Bible, or reject them in toto with Ezekiel Kaufmann (whose *History of the Jewish Faith* still awaits translation from the Hebrew). It does not matter whether we see the historical books of the Bible as disguised propaganda for the exclusive domination of Jerusalem, with the priestly code altered to suit; or whether they only reflect the struggle with pagan rituals. In either case, there is a historical dynamism. But that is not the dynamism of the Bible as such. The dynamism of the Bible is metahistorical. It is the struggle to replace conditioned codes by the unconditional illumination that needs no code.

It is reasonable to say that after David made Jerusalem his capital, and Solomon built the Temple there, the Temple took on a political role, and the priestly code was correspondingly affected. But there is no correspondence between the curve of prophetism and the political-historical record. Why should Nathan, Elijah, Amos, and Isaiah (the first) have appeared when they did? Why should they have appeared in that order? One plausible theory is: Amos and Isaiah appeared, with their *national* morality, when the kingdom had been split, and unity was essential. It is just as plausible to suggest that they should have appeared before David, when national unity was even more essential. To protest: "But there *must* be a connection between the curve of prophetism and the historical-political curve; we simply have not enough information to establish it," is to beg the question.

The prophetic episode incorporates two dynamic processes. The first is internal; the episode is seen to be organic within itself; it is linked with the people, but by laws that we have not yet established. The second process relates the prophetic morality to the ritual and wisdom moralities; this is the total dynamism of the Bible.

The wisdom morality is static. We might show what parts of it are related to Egyptian, Babylonian, or Greek sources; we could distribute its elements in time; but there is no curve of growth. The ritual morality (priestly-civic code) is not static. We can see that its changes correspond to changes in historical conditions. *But it is static in this very fact.* It has not an independent dynamism. It is static in being a function of something else.

147

The presence in the Bible of both the ritual morality and the wisdom morality (both of them "behavior patterns") is essential to establish the dynamism of the whole, to make intelligible the drive of prophetism.

It was necessary, as a matter of exposition, to separate out the three moralities with a certain artificial clarity. Actually the prophetic illumination penetrated everywhere. Or perhaps one ought to say that the capacity of this people to produce the prophetic episode was never wholly suppressed in any part of it by the non-prophetic moralities. At no time did this people revert to the idealization of the combative code in a sporting ritual.

The Jewish community of my childhood was not steeped in prophetism—as the Chassidim were. It was nearer, in outlook, to the Jewish variety of the wisdom morality. But it instinctively rejected the pagan glorification of life as a game and of man as fighter. So, throughout the centuries, the Jewish community of ancient Palestine might turn aside from the acceptance of the prophetic morality, yet be sufficiently linked with it to escape ultimate paganism. Where fragments of the community lost this minimum connection, they ceased to be Jewish; they disappeared from the record.

Priestly codes are universal; the *noblesse-oblige* principle of ethics could evolve in Japan's Samurai and Greece's Stoics; kindness and gentleness will be found among "savage" tribes. But a consistent multimillennial aversion to paganism incorporated in a continuing people is a unique thing; it is both the source and the consequence of the dynamism of the Bible.

# CHAPTER XIII

## *Approach to the Bible*

❀

THE Bible may be studied as a history and also as a maker of history; and of the Jewish people it may be said that most of its history was made by its history book.

Unfortunately there are many not unintelligent people who have the notion that the Bible yields its affirmations only to those who approach it in a receptive trance, a reverential hush of the critical faculties; and of such "affirmations" they are properly suspicious. This view, which has a tradition of scientific caution, is without scientific foundation. Both as prophetic utterance and as history, or human documentation, the Bible is most accessible to the mind at its most vigorous and most informed. Since the Bible is central to my whole thesis, and since, therefore, I am anxious to encourage the study of it, I feel compelled to deal with some of the obstacles that have accumulated on the approaches to it.

For me, as for many others, the Bible is a vast blend of folkloristic growths and individual creations; and this two-in-one character is of its essence as record. Were the Bible only folklore, the intensely personal element would be submerged; the prophets, for instance, would be silenced. Were it only individual creation, we should not be lifted by the groundswell of its mass travail; the people would not exist. As I pick my way through the legends, histories, prayers, fables, pastorals, visions, illuminations, biographies, past the ritualistic, genealogical, and legalistic deposits of ages, I am always aware of the single voices and the huge orchestration. But I am not always sure which is which. Sometimes the voice has the multiform resonance of an orchestra; sometimes the orchestra has the piercing and personal quality of a voice. Sometimes it will seem to me that an utterance stands by itself, is universally intelligible when detached in an anthology; then on reflection it seems to me that much of its power and meaning stems from its relations to other parts of the Bible. Thus:

Putting on one side the question of the historicity of Moses, to what extent is the Bible account of him folk—that is, inextricably composite—and to what extent individual? To get the *feel* of this problem—which is all that matters!—let us examine the passage in the Book of Numbers that describes the agony of the leader locked in struggle with his recalcitrant people.

According to the story, less than a year had passed since the Jews had been led forth from the Maidaneks and Oswiecims of Egypt, where their men-children had been systematically put to death, not in gas chambers, but in the waters of the Nile; less than a year since their lives had been bitter with bondage, and their cry had come up to God. It was also less than a year since they had been the witnesses of the miracle by the Red Sea. And now the rabble, "the mixt multitude that was among them," rebelled against the monotonous desert diet of manna, and a weeping went up from the doors of the tents:

"We remember the fish, which we did eat in Egypt freely; the cucumbers, and the melons, and the leeks, and the onions, and the garlick: but now our soul is dried away: there is nothing at all, beside this manna, before our eyes. . . .

"And Moses said unto the Lord, Wherefore hast thou afflicted thy servant? and wherefore have I not found favour in thy sight, that thou layest the burden of all this people upon me? Have I conceived all this people? have I begotten them, that thou shouldst say unto me, Carry them in thy bosom, as a nursing father beareth the sucking child, unto the land which thou swarest unto their fathers? Whence should I have flesh to give unto all this people? for they weep unto me, saying, Give us flesh, that we may eat. I am not able to bear all this people alone, because it is too heavy for me. And if thou deal thus with me, kill me, I pray thee, out of hand, if I have found favour in thy sight; and let me not see my wretchedness.

"And the Lord said unto Moses, Gather unto me seventy of the elders of Israel . . . and I will take of the spirit which is upon thee, and will put it upon them; and they shall bear the burden of the people with thee. . . .

"And say thou unto the people, Sanctify yourselves against tomorrow, and ye shall eat flesh. . . . Ye shall not eat one day, nor two days, nor five days, neither ten days, nor twenty days; but even a whole month, until it come out at your nostrils, and it be loathsome unto you: because that ye have despised the Lord which is among you, and have wept before him, saying, Why came we forth out of Egypt?"

This, then, is the people of which Hosea said: "And she shall sing there, as in the days of her youth, and as in the day when she came up out of Egypt"; and of which Jeremiah said: "I remember thee, the kindness of thy youth, the love of thine espousals, when thou wentest after me in the wilderness, in a land that was not sown." It is an extraordinary passage, and the more extraordinary the more closely we examine it.

To begin with, it is obviously composite. There are at least two distinct themes, from two sources, with two distinct purposes. One is descriptive, and it is so bitter, so personal, that we want to avert our eyes. It is almost improper to intrude, even imaginatively, on such suffering. The wretchedness of Moses is the portion of every visionary turned man of action; *this* is what goes on behind the commanding façade of leadership, this protest before God against having been trapped into a killing commitment—as if a leader does not always choose to be trapped: this rage with the imperfections of his people, as if those imperfections were not the necessary condition of his leadership.

To this *cri du cœur* God's promise to pour out the spirit of Moses on seventy elders is quite irrelevant. Not that Moses would not welcome its fulfillment. When, shortly after this incident, it is reported to him that certain young men are prophesying in the camp, he cries out: "Would God that all the Lord's people were prophets, and that the Lord would put his spirit upon them!" But the promise of the seventy inspired elders is not the answer to the heart-rending cry, which is an expression at large of the agony of leadership, the agony of the responsible man struggling with his human material as—to make comparison with something less significant—the artist struggles with pigments and stone. The cry and the answer are on different levels; they miss each other.

What has obviously happened is that a second theme, historical, folkloristic, and propagandistic, has been imperfectly joined to the first. A writer has inserted, in the basic human and personal story, a popular argument for the Council of Seventy. The relevance is artificial. God, who sent the quails, could just as easily have made Moses strong enough to bear the burden alone. Indeed, by sending the quails—which he does only after a spirited economic argument with Moses—God weakens the argument for the council; it is obvious that between them he and Moses can handle the situation without a council.

It is the number seventy that puts us especially on our

guard. It intimates an established tradition, a folk institution, seeking, after the event, predated authority. Besides, the same practical theme occurs elsewhere in the
story of Moses. We read in the Book of Exodus that before
he ascended Sinai, Moses received excellent advice to the
same effect from his father-in-law, Jethro, who saw him
overworking: "The thing that thou doest is not good. Thou
wilt surely wear away, both thou, and this people that is
with thee: for this thing is too heavy for thee. . . . Provide
out of all the people able men, such as fear God, men of
truth, hating covetousness; and place such over them, to
be rulers of thousands, and rulers of hundreds, rulers of
fifties, and rulers of tens." The advice is given quite calmly;
there is no probing into the soul-struggles of Moses. But
the numbers are different. No council of seventy; only
precinct captains of thousands, hundreds, and so on. In
the first Book of the Maccabees, written much later, after the
Council of Seventy had already been established among the
Jews, there is a return to the precinct system, with the same
numbers.

And again, Moses is represented in his last days as re-
viewing the desert odyssey, and he is made to revert pen-
sively and affectionately, as befits an old man, to the difficult past: "And I spake unto you at that time, saying, I am
not able to bear you myself alone: the Lord God hath multiplied you, and, behold, ye are this day as the stars of
heaven for multitude. (The Lord God of your fathers make
you a thousand times so many as ye are, and bless you, as
he hath promised you!) How can I myself alone bear your
cumbrance, and your burden, and your strife? . . . So I
took the chief of your tribes . . . and made them heads
over you, captains over thousands, and captains over hundreds. . . ."

The folk theme of the origin and authority of the councils

is intertwined, therefore, with the theme of a personal history. But, as we reread the eleventh chapter of Numbers, we find it beyond belief that the personal passage can have wandered about changeably in the shadowy folk consciousness, can have evolved piecemeal into this perfect expression of sophisticated and embittered weariness. This is the genius of an individual writer, not of folklore. We hear a voice, anonymous, but not composite, of the folk, but not folkloristic.

Who wrote chapter eleven of the Book of Numbers? Or, since it was put together in part from folklore and in part from a specific document, who wrote that part of it which is so clearly individual? We can hardly believe that the writer was a contemporary of Moses. Was he a contemporary of Ezra, whose wrestlings with the Jewish people nearly a thousand years later earned him the name of "the second Moses"? Was he the disciple of some prophet-statesman in between? Where did he get his insight into the longings, loneliness and frustrations of the "man of destiny"?

The problem of the authorship, single or multiple, of the passage is an interesting one; but the answer has nothing to do with the value of the passage, except to this extent: in seeking the answer we exercise our intellectual faculties, and this incidentally sharpens our perception of the human and historical elements in it. Or it should. Unfortunately some people feel that the value of the passage depends on the history of its authorship, and this attitude is of the very essence of unscientific Bible criticism. I offer another illustration of this crucial point:

These memorable verses close the nineteenth chapter of Isaiah:

"In that day shall five cities in the land of Egypt speak the language of Canaan, and swear to the Lord of Hosts; one shall be called, The city of destruction. In that day shall there be an altar to the Lord in the midst of the land of Egypt. . . . And the Lord shall be known to Egypt, and the Egyptians shall know the Lord in that day, and shall do sacrifice and oblation. . . . In that day shall there be a highway out of Egypt to Assyria, and the Assyrian shall come into Egypt, and the Egyptian into Assyria, and the Egyptians shall serve with the Assyrians. In that day shall Israel be the third with Egypt and Assyria, even a blessing in the midst of the land: Whom the Lord of Hosts shall bless, saying, Blessed be Egypt my people, and Assyria the work of my hands, and Israel mine inheritance."

Like the more famous prophecy of the swords beaten into plowshares, which occurs in both Isaiah and Micah, this one exalts the ideal of universal peace as the last phase of history. But—for me at least—it has a stronger appeal because it speaks in concrete political terms. The rivalries between the empires of the Nile and the Euphrates was the central motif in the history of Asia Minor for many centuries before and after Isaiah; it continued into post-Biblical times, when the rulers of both territories were the heirs of Alexander the Great. The little buffer states, Israel, Judah, Tyre, Ammon, Moab, Syria, were the battleground and the spoils; their occasional periods of independence—which they spent mostly in wars with one another—they owed chiefly to the internal dissensions of their gigantic neighbors; and for the rest, their only active role was to outguess their fellow victims as to who would be the next conqueror, and to outwit or mollify his acquisitive rage at their expense. Against this background of intrigue, vendetta, treachery, and bloodshed, the verses that link the oppressors and the oppressed in loving unity are in the nature of a psychological miracle.

What we must note at once is that the verses are more than a prophecy; they are the description of a condition.

Egypt and Assyria are *already* the candidates for the role of God's people and the work of his hands; therefore the verses do not merely foretell; they predispose men for the fulfillment, and herein lies their power.

Now in what manner are these intrinsic features of the passage affected by a critical examination of the text?

The Book of Isaiah differs from the Moses books in the much larger element of individual authorship. That it can be the work of one man is, even to the untrained reader, wholly out of the question. Scholars were once content with two Isaiahs, the first ending with the thirty-ninth chapter, the second continuing to chapter sixty-six. Since then the second "Isaiah"—whose real name is unknown—has been precipitated out into several individuals. But within each of the several Isaiahs, not excluding the first—he who lived in the reigns of Uzziah, Jotham, Ahaz, and Hezekiah, Kings of Judah, through most of the eighth century B.C.—there are passages that do not fit in historically, and the one we are considering is among them.

It speaks of Jewish communities in Egypt; and since nothing makes a prophetic text more suspect than its fulfillment, or even partial fulfillment, we ask first: "When, within Bible times, and after Isaiah, did such communities exist?" Now, there are, as we have seen, mention of Jewish communities in Egypt during the days of Jeremiah, more than a hundred years after Isaiah. Can the passage have been inserted then? Hardly; for the Jewish communities of the time of Jeremiah were apostatizing; Jeremiah rebuked them bitterly for their continued worship of the "Queen of Heaven." It is unlikely that they had a temple and an altar to Jehovah. The predated prophecy could not, therefore, refer to them: unless we assume that Jeremiah's strictures took effect, and there was a change of heart. Or that he was exaggerating the evil, as a prophet is sometimes likely to do.

We have, however, always known, from the Greek translation of the Bible, from Joshua (or Jesus) ben Sirach, from Philo, and from other sources, that in the days of the Ptolemies there was a powerful Jewish community in Egypt with a temple to the Jewish God. The passage may have been inserted as late as the third century B.C. But by whom? The Jews of Alexandria remained for the most part Jewish by religion, but assimilated rapidly to the Greek language and culture. It is a common characteristic of assimilating Jews to disown the stigma of "peculiarness," and of God's exclusive choice of them. They do this by saying that every people is God's people, the work of his hands. An Alexandrian Jew—perhaps a learned public relations counsel, familiar with the old-style Hebrew, which was then no longer spoken anywhere, and perhaps a learned chairman of an inter-faith committee—could have inserted the passage. It may have been at a moment when a peace had been signed between the Selucid Greeks of "Assyria" and the Egyptian rulers. It would be hard to explain, though, how he managed to get this variant of the text accepted in Palestine at such a late date. More probably, then, it was a Palestinian Jew, hired for the purpose. In any case, we have here a typical instance of Jewish moralistic self-serving propaganda: liberalism as the specific against anti-Semitism.

One could really make a great to-do round this theory; for during the period preceding the Maccabean revolt the Jews of Palestine were split between those who were content to remain subjects of the Egyptian Ptolemies, and those who favored the rule of the Seleucid Greeks of Antioch. The inserted passage is, then, an attempt at conciliation. Fortunately I lack the scholarship to be tempted into a long discussion of the subject.

In recent times this second theory was shaken by the discovery of a letter that a Jewish garrison, stationed at Elephantine in middle Egypt, wrote to the Jews of Jerusalem in the days of Ezra (about two centuries earlier than the period suggested above), asking for instruction on the services in their local temple. The passage, then, may well have been inserted in the fifth century B.C., long before there was a large Jewish community in Egypt. In that case the public-relations argument, which is valid only for a large, assimilating Jewish community, falls to the ground.

There remains a fourth alternative, of course. The whole business of postdating the passage may be nonsense, because this prophecy, like many others, was never fulfilled.

So we are left without a satisfactory explanation; and the least satisfactory explanation, though it cannot be excluded entirely, is the fourth. For the passage definitely does not seem to fit in. There is something too specific and detailed about the prophecy. Like the prophecies in Daniel, it has an overtone of intramural intelligibility; but unlike these, it is without an extra-Biblical key. Meanwhile it is well for us to note that we have fallen into a trap; we are trying to equate the value of the passage with its authorship, date, and circumstance of origin. Like amateur psychoanalysts in heat, we have become too subtle to pay attention to the intrinsic content of a human statement.

When this happens to us, we are misusing the intelligence. The date and authorship of the passage are certainly matters of interest; and a legitimate curiosity may involve the scholar in years of research. Meanwhile the ordinary reader, for whom the scholar works, notes that the history of the passage does not affect its power. If we assume that the passage was written and inserted with an immediate,

158

practical political purpose in view, we can only be the more astonished at the way it has transcended its origins. For these words: "Blessed be Egypt my people, and Assyria the work of my hands, and Israel mine inheritance," have eternity in them. By comparison, all our phrases about "international goodwill" and "good-neighbor policy" ring hollow—if they can be said to ring at all. Incidentally, this illustrates my statement that "the Bible is most accessible to the mind at its most vigorous."

The major shift of interest from the intrinsic grandeur of the passage to the technical details of the authorship is not the result of a growth of knowledge, or of a widening of perspective. It is merely evidence of a decline in spiritual and moral susceptibility. However, a refusal to acknowledge the validity of criticism and research is evidence of insecurity and lack of faith. People who say they want to cling to the simple faith of their fathers debar themselves from the possibility by the very statement. They are like the romantic medievalists who seem to think that in the Middle Ages men used to greet each other with: "How are you this fine medieval morning."

The confusions, irrelevances, and futilities of most technical discussions of the Bible spring from this decline in susceptibility; and they are enhanced by a kind of question-begging. The disputants bring to the text anterior views which have nothing to do with the text itself. They are anxious to prove by it that what is scientifically impossible is historically improbable.

Most of the Bible criticism I have read—and this includes "rebuttals" of Bible criticism—is discolored by this irrelevance. The real opposition of views is a concealed one, and the trouble with concealed oppositions is that they never come to grips. We become passionately concerned with proving our intelligence rather than using it.

159

# CHAPTER XIV

## The "Lowdown"

❁

W̲E DO not have to be Biblical scholars in order to get a
sound general view of the evolution of the Bible text. Only
a few elementary facts are needed; the rest is common
sense.

We do not know, and we do not have to know, when the
old sagas, historical memories, legends, proverbs, laws, and
moral formulations of the Jewish people were first committed to parchment or papyrus. It may have been in the
days of Saul, a thousand years B.C. It may have been earlier.
That there were earlier texts than the one we now have in
the historical books is clear from the frequent references to
written sources. All this does not change the character of
our problem. What we want to reconstruct is the general
picture of the probable process.

In the days before printing, every copy of a document was
what we now call a new edition, for it was retranscribed by
hand from beginning to end. Every copyist was, or could
be, an editor. Scrolls were lost in fires, by destruction in
wars, by suppression and decay. Sometimes an edition
would be reproduced from memory. Changes crept in by
error, guileless or purposive; often they were inserted boldly
and programmatically.

The itch of an editor to improve any document that falls

into his hands is one of the oldest afflictions of literate man. The pangs of it are perhaps reflected in the ancient commandment: "Thou shalt not muzzle the ox when he treadeth out the corn." What copyist editors did to the "original" texts of Jewish codes and stories can easily be imagined. We must think of embittered men with scores to settle or reputations to clear, of grateful men with a debt to pay, of careerists in the service of princes, of cranks with obsessions, and of tribal patriots. We must also think, however, of copyist editors who had contributions of the first order to make to the national literature, and chose to make it by way of anonymous addition to an existing and accepted body of text. If the last part of chapter nineteen of Isaiah, and the section quoted from the eleventh chapter of Numbers, are interpolations, we must be grateful to the interpolators.

There were "class" interpolations, expressions of social and religious policies, good or bad, which sought the sanction of antiquity and divinity for recent dispensations. And to all the foregoing we must add error pure and simple: marginal annotations in older copies which were assimilated to the text in newer copies; words that became archaic and were misread and "corrected"; the ascription to one man of several books that had been copied on a single scroll to save parchment.

One must also bear in mind that on the old scrolls neither words nor sentences nor paragraphs nor chapters were separated by either horizontal or vertical spaces; it all ran on in one viscous stream, without punctuation, without vowels, column after column. And nothing, in fact, bears stronger testimony to the changeableness of the early text than the violence of the intellectual methods applied later (and described in the next chapter) to ensure the stability of the final redaction.

The attempt to unscramble, even approximately, the progress of the growth of that composite work is—and the orthodox Jew and Christian will take the phrase literally—a *travail du diable;* that is, if we are concerned not with the spirit, but with dead material. For an intimate and comprehensive study of the successive changes and probable changes in the Bible text, one must have a thorough knowledge of Hebrew, Latin, Greek, Syriac, Aramaic, Coptic, Slavonic, and every other ancient language—and its dialects—in which old translations of the Bible, or of fragments of it, have survived. Where one's own knowledge is deficient, one must—dangerous recourse!—rely on others. I omit history, archæology, anthropology, economics, military strategy, religious experience, ethnology, semantics, and common sense. One must have the detailed diligence of an ant, the patience of a mule, the constitution of a horse, and the self-immolating unworldliness of a saint. And when a man possessing a fair number of these qualities—which can exist side by side with many weaknesses—acquires some of the disciplines above listed, he usually turns into a maniacal specialist at loggerheads with most of the other equally maniacal specialists. The ordinary person for whom the Bible was written disappears in an atomic explosion of perpendicular erudition.

The layman who wants to do a little investigating of his own will discover that with nothing more than a moderate knowledge of Hebrew he can get into very deep water. He can watch out for the alternating uses of the names YHWH and Elohim, for God, and obtain entry into the vast literature on the Yahwist and Elohist divisions of the Bible records. He can catch the differences in style, and perceive at once that the primitive, volcanic outburst of the Song of Moses by the Red Sea, or of the Song of Deborah after the defeat of Sisera, cannot have come from the pen that produced the adjacent material. In Daniel and in Ezra he will note for himself the lapses into Aramaic; and here and there throughout the Bible he will be struck by curious incongruities in word structure and phraseology. Such a layman must exercise care and self-restraint, or else, before he knows it, he will have given away thirty or forty years to the etymological exegetes.

Even without a knowledge of Hebrew the study of the physique of the Bible can easily be overdone. The King James version imposes a rather misleading uniformity of style on the variegated text; but differences of mood and manner break through clearly. And without stylistic differences, in strong or weak translation, the story of the origins of the Jewish people declares itself, beyond cavil, a composite. If the reader bends his mind to it he will discover, with only a little expert guidance, large fragments of differently colored material, which fundamentalists see only in monochrome. There are separate codes of law struggling for supremacy; there are inconsistent traditions respecting the tribal patriarchs; the struggle for predominance between two sets of tribes is embedded in differing accounts and interpretations of the remote past. It is perfectly clear that these chunks of tribal and national memory defied editorial abrasion or decoloration.

Common sense tells us that tendentious historians and theologians must have tampered with the text as long as they could, inserting passages of their own. Their insertions, too, must have been tampered with in turn. If we follow this far enough we are confronted with a series of Chinese boxes; we come down to single sentences, single words. By this time the attempt to assort and reassign the insertions becomes an occupation for anything but common sense.

For the curious reader—the uncurious one may skip the rest of this chapter—I will offer some examples of the sort of superanalysis that scholars apply to the problem. And I have chosen two scholars of note, distinguished for their strong common sense as well as for their erudition.

Professor Pfeiffer, in his *Introduction to the Old Testament*, says, of the Book of Kings: "The author passes judgment on every king according to his obedience to Deuteronomy 12, the law centralizing worship at Jerusalem and ordering destruction of the high places (the local altars)." But in the Book of Kings occurs the following passage: "David did that which was right in the eyes of the Lord, and turned not aside from anything that he commanded him all the days of his life, save only in the matter of Uriah the Hittite."

Now, Professor Pfeiffer finds it strange, in the first place, that the ritualistic author should set up David as the ritualistic paragon. David did not, after all, build the Temple. But once David has been accepted as the ideal king, to whom the ritualistic author constantly refers as the model, it is even stranger (according to Professor Pfeiffer) to find the case of Uriah the Hittite dragged in. The killing of a man to take possession of his wife is not a ritualistic sin, and has nothing to do with centralizing the national worship at Jerusalem. The ritualistic author therefore cannot have been perturbed—at least, not in his capacity as ritualist— by this blot on David's record. So the irrelevant reminder *must* have been interpolated by someone else: by "a reader," says Professor Pfeiffer, "who, correctly and in contradiction to the author, regarded David's virtue as spotted in the matter of Uriah the Hittite."

We ask ourselves, in some astonishment: Is it likely that the tremendous story of David and Uriah and Nathan the prophet, which must have had the deepest roots in the folk, could have been coolly ignored by *any* author? And was the ritualistically minded author in question himself so utterly perverse as to think nothing of this frightful act of David's, or so indifferent to the opinion of his readers as to suppress it? Well, it is not entirely impossible. There have been villainous ritualists and cynical propagandists in many religions. But the assumption of a fundamentally amoral religiosity among the priestly authors is not borne out by the text. Though the priests did not fight the kings as the prophets did, there are several references to the *moral* misbehavior of the kings in the *ritually* oriented record. We would have to isolate all of these as non-ritualistic interpolations.

It is, however, Professor Pfeiffer himself who uncovers the contradiction. He has this to say of the religious reforms of King Josiah:

> "At the time when the nation, faced by a choice between the old religion of cult and the new one of conduct, had discarded the latter and was sinking rapidly into insignificance, a man inspired by the prophet's ideal, but simultaneously aware of the current trend and of practical possibilities, affected a compromise between the antagonistic religions, and thus became the founder of Judaism. This man was the author of the book of Moses, found in the collection box of the Temple at Jerusalem in 621 B.C., a book which now forms the kernel of Deuteronomy. The author of D, or the Deuteronomic code, was a priest in Jerusalem on whom the prophetic teaching had made a deep impression. He realized that an agreement representing the two types of religion contrasted in Micah (6:7f.) was necessary."

The passage in Micah reads: "Wherewith shall I come before the Lord . . . shall I come before him with burnt offerings . . . will the Lord be pleased with thousands of rams, or with ten thousands of rivers of oil? . . . He hath shewed thee, O man, what is good; and what doth the Lord require of thee, but to do justly, and to love mercy, and to walk humbly with thy God?"

Because this reconciliation between the two religions had been affected, says Professor Pfeiffer in another passage, the prophet Jeremiah "welcomed the book at first, and was active in his support of the reforms of Josiah." And so a "practical" or ritualistic priest can have found common ground with a prophet! Why could not such a one have written the passage about David which Professor Pfeiffer finds it necessary to divide between two authors?

Let us turn to the other instance.

There is a passage in the First Book of Kings which tells how King David, dying, instructed Solomon with his last breath to kill two old men, Joab and Shimei, the first for having assassinated Abner and Amasa years before, the second for once having cursed David. Simon Dubnow tells us, in his monumental *World History of the Jews*, that the passage was undoubtedly interpolated, to justify Solomon's killing of Joab and Shimei.

I look on this observation as a typical "scholarism." Why did the passage have to be interpolated? The author could, instead, have deleted the story of Solomon's killing of the two old men. And if he could not do that because the story was too well known, he could easily have devised another, less offensive interpolation. He could have planted a little conspiracy on Joab and Shimei, and thus exonerated the son without slandering the father. But of course it *sounds* learned to point out an interpolation; and scholars too often write with an eye cocked on other scholars instead of on plain people. The obvious fact about this passage is that we do not know what happened beyond what we are told; we must be content to say so and leave it at that.

These are two simple instances, chosen at random from hundreds I have encountered, of the self-defeating ingenuity of the learned. There are also thousands of instances dealing with comparisons of early translations of the Bible in various languages, or parallels with ancient literary and historical records of other peoples, analogies with non-

Jewish beliefs and customs and legends which are themselves matters of conjecture. And then there are, of course, tortured attempts to reconcile the irreconcilable when the text cannot be forced. By this unrealistic over-refinement scholars seem to imagine that they can establish the detailed sources and development of the Bible text—the "lowdown," that is. But there is no lowdown. There is only common sense and your attitude.

The critical examination of the Bible, the search for the lowdown, began systematically in the Age of Reason. There was as yet no new information, no archæology as we now know it. There was only a new attitude toward the old material. There was the new type of mind, the scientific. People who resisted the new type of mind also resisted its application to the Bible; and so the Bible became the testing ground of "progress" or "inertia." It was something like a modern political trial, in which the prisoner must be condemned or discharged as a demonstration, or political act, quite independently of his guilt or innocence. And the public takes sides, not on the basis of information, but on the basis of the "line."

So, in regard to the Bible, the critics assumed that what could not be proved as "true" had to be regarded as untrue. Today we have only to read Albright's *From the Stone Age to Christianity* to see how the motivated skepticism of the earlier Bible critics, including the later Wellhausen school, is being corrected by the findings of the archæologists. Which is not to say that Professor Albright and his colleagues must not be watched for signs of reaction to the other extreme. All we can say so far is that recently discovered external and independent evidence supports the view that there is a body of reliable historical material in the Bible narrative as we have it.

I have already mentioned another kind of "lowdown"

which exercises a good many minds, and that is connected with the question: Where did the Jews get it from? What are the original sources of the aphorisms, laws, dogmas, moral insights, religious formulations, and so on, which we find in the Bible? This too is an extremely interesting field of research and conjecture; and we must be grateful for every connection established, for every proof or hint of interchange of ideas. But here too we must avoid confusing two separate fields of inquiry; and here too we must not commit the common error of displaying an over-vigorous skepticism vis-à-vis the Bible and an unchallenging deference to the scientists. The hymns of the Babylonians, the death-ritual and wisdom books of the Egyptians, the legends of the Ugaritic texts, are fascinating in themselves, and more so in their parallelism with Biblical passages. But, like the partial vindication of the historical reliability of the Bible, they have nothing to do with the value of the Bible.

The notion that the Bible was, in its essentials, in its character, in its intrinsic significance, "lifted" from somewhere need not detain us for more than a moment. The man who does not see in the prophets, in the Moses narrative, in the Ruth story, in Job, in the Song of Songs, the highest type of individual genius, should apply his literary faculties exclusively to the study of crossword puzzles.

# CHAPTER XV

## *The Capture*

❀

I HAVE said that Jewish history is peculiar in that it has been made by the Jewish history book. This does not mean that a knowledge of the Bible will explain everything in post-Biblical Jewish history; it does mean that Jewish history cannot be explained without a knowledge of the Bible. It means also that for a practical consideration of the last twenty-two hundred years or so of Jewish history it is not helpful to know how the Biblical text arose. What we do need to know is the text itself and what it did to the Jews, or what the Jews did with it.

When did the Jews become the captives of the Bible? Or, since the surrender to it must, like the production of it, have taken many generations, what were the stages? We are speaking, of course, of the Bible as we have had it for over two thousand years. During the stages of the surrender, the Jews must have accepted, piecemeal and progressively, certain sections of the Bible in the form that has come down to us. Their surrender was not as complete as it became later. To some extent these two questions: "When and how was the Bible produced?" and "When did the Bible become the major factor in Jewish history?" overlap.

Some scholars find evidence of the major Biblical ideas present in the Jewish people more than a thousand years

B.C. Many take the stand that only with the discovery of the Moses Book in the time of King Josiah—seventh century B.C.—can we speak of the founding of Judaism—that is, of the first fastening of a significant section of the Bible on the Jews. Others have it that the Judaism which we know crystallized substantially in the traumatic experience of the Babylonian exile—sixth century B.C. It was then, they tell us, that the universalism of Judaism, its essential character, first took on recognizable form; it was in Babylonia that the Jews first began studying systematically the literature they had brought with them out of Judea, it was there that they added to it some of its most important sections. Still others, not denying the creative importance of the Babylonian period, place the emphasis on Ezra and Nehemiah —fifth century B.C.—who came to Judea some sixty years after the Return of the Exiles, and re-established Judaism in the midst of a declining and apostatizing community. Out of this reinvigorated community came most of the Biblical literature.

But if Ezra and Nehemiah played this important role in the rescue of the new state, they must have brought their Judaism with them from Babylonia, as the closing Old Testament records tell us. These tell us, further, that Ezra instituted the first systematic folk teaching of the earliest Bible text—the Pentateuch—among the masses in Judea. It can hardly be doubted that by the middle of the fifth century B.C. the Pentateuch text was fixed. As to the fixing of the texts of the prophetic, historical, and hagiographic books, there is much diversity of opinion. The general conclusion is that by the time of Ezra some of these were in fairly fixed form, others in a state of flux, while others were produced between the fifth and second centuries B.C.

None of these uncertainties affects the incontrovertible fact that by a certain date flux and variation and addition had come to an end; and by that date an extraordinary technique of memorization was .applied to the stabilizing of the text. The Bible text itself was written down; but that, as we have already seen, was no guarantee of stability. The technique of memorization was applied, not to the text itself, but to a process of interpretation and exegesis; and this process made further changes in the basic text practically impossible. Every word in the text was by then considered as of sacred and eternal validity, and was scrutinized and dredged for meanings, plain and esoteric. Every letter, every canonized copyist's error, every unchangeable accidental flourish of a letter, was regarded as cosmically significant. Whatever had gone, up to a certain point, into the text and caligraphy was frozen forever.

Within that rigid framework a million flexible values were implicit. For the rest of eternity the Jews were to educe these values, and to live by them. This was the purpose of their existence. They were to apply themselves to this study, and to its practical consequences, when they rose up and when they lay down, when they were at home and when they traveled. Their reward would be, after death, the continuation of the same exercises in the Heavenly Academy, where they would have at their disposal a faculty consisting of the greatest sages of the past, from Ezra back to Moses; or (later) from Akiba back to Moses, with occasional festive intervention on the part of God himself. Always it would be the Torah, now in the largest sense of all the sacred books, and not in the restricted sense of the Pentateuch. "Turn it, and turn it again, and yet again," exclaimed one sage, "for everything is in it."

By the time of Akibah (first and second century of the Christian era) the surrender to the Bible was already an ancient tradition. The doctrine of the resurrection, almost unknown in the Old Testament, had long been a part of the faith, and was educed from countless verses. Ben Bag Bag, the sage who found everything in the Torah, lived in the second century *before* the Christian era.

When Ezra began to translate (from the original Hebrew into the Aramaic vernacular), teach, and interpret the Torah—meaning here the Pentateuch—to the Jews of the infant Second Commonwealth, two or three generations after the Return, he initiated a national occupation and pre-occupation that were to become the special intellectual characteristic of the Jews. Century after century, down to our own day (and am I not, in my feeble way, continuing the tradition?), they dwelt on the words of the Old Testament, and from these constructed system after system of ideas. The adepts were few, the general practitioners more numerous; the listeners included, in one degree or another, almost the whole people. Very few adults in my childhood environment were strangers to this tradition. They had acquired it in their childhood, and whatever the years had done to water it down, they knew the technique, and they never lost a certain responsiveness to it.

It is important for the reader to know something about this technique, which goes back nearly two and half millennia. But instead of describing it, I shall attempt an imitation of it, with occasional borrowings. And instead of using the Hebrew text, which would only confuse the English reader, I shall use the King James version as if it were the sacred and untouchable original. Also, to supply a little local color, I shall call this fragment of commentary *The Garden of Spices*, or *The Hill of Leopards*; or, in imitation of the humility of the scholars—or of *their* imitation of it—*The Book of Samuel the Pygmy*; for which reason I shall henceforth be known (according to the custom) not by my own name, but as "The Leopard" or "The Spices," or (more probably), "The Pygmy."

*"In the beginning God created the heaven and the earth. . . ."*

Now why was the letter *I*, of all the twenty-six letters of the alphabet, accorded the incomparable honor of opening the Bible? Because the two great utterances of the Holy One, blessed be He, begin with that letter: *"I am that I am"* (Exodus iii, 14), and *"I am the Lord thy God, which brought thee out of the land of Egypt"* (Exodus xx, 2). And why was the honor of being the second letter accorded to *N*? Because it begins the word *Name*, by which the Holy One, blessed be He, is proclaimed. As it is written: *"Because I will publish the Name of the Lord"* (Deuteronomy xxxii, 3), and *"Then men began to call upon the Name of the Lord"* (Genesis iv, 26).

Now the Sages, their memory be a blessing unto us, note that the first use of the *Name* is not in connection with Abraham or any of his descendants, for the verse: *"Then men began to call upon the Name of the Lord"* is spoken of the time of Enos, son of Seth, son of Adam, which is seven generations before Noah. What does this teach us? That God withholds not Himself from anyone who seeks Him, be he Jew or gentile. It teaches us further that the *Name* was known and forgotten; therefore the virtue of remembering is as great as the virtue of discovering, for without remembering, what is discovering? Thence it shall be known that the merit of Israel is not to have discovered the *Name*, but to have remembered it.

But there are other Sages who say that the second letter of the Bible is *N* because it is the beginning of the word *New*. As it is written: *"I will do a New thing"* (Isaiah xliii, 19), and *"I create New heavens and a New earth"* (Isaiah lxv, 17). From this we learn two things: first, that God did a new thing in creating *our* heavens and earth. But He did not do a new thing in creating heavens and earths as such, or He would not have said: "New *heavens and a New earth*." Thence we learn, second, that heavens and earths had existed before, and had been destroyed by reason of their having forgotten the *Name*.

Now why was the word *In* chosen to open the Bible? There are some Sages who say that it could not be otherwise, if *I* was chosen as the first letter, and *N* as the second letter, seeing that they make, together, the word *In*. But this is not so, for the Bible could have begun thus: "*I* Now *create new heavens and a new earth,*" and the first two letters would have been *I* and *N*, without, however, making the word *In*. But the word *In* was chosen to remind us: "*The Lord . . . shall be exalted* In *judgment*" (Isaiah v, 16), but, also: "*I will be glad and rejoice* In *Thy mercy*" (Psalms xxxi, 7). What does this teach us? That both judgment and mercy were applied to man from the very beginning, so that he might be moved to repentance, and not think himself lost forever because he has sinned. As it is written: "*For a just man falleth seven times, and riseth up again*" (Proverbs xxiv, 16).

One can go on like this forever, which is in fact what the Jews have done. One can thus turn out a great deal of ingenious rubbish, but also a great many penetrating and illuminating perceptions, which is again what the Jews have done. Millions upon millions of pages of this kind of writing have been produced throughout the centuries; and the process still continues, with some changes in style but no symptom of abatement. There is not a sentence in the Old Testament that has not been quoted and requoted, analyzed and reanalyzed, interpreted and reinterpreted, collated with other sentences, and made the subject of dissertation. Long before the advent of printing, this process had made impossible the introduction of any further changes in the text; long before the Jewish state was destroyed, the Bible text had become indestructible.

Now, it is true that translations of the Bible have been submitted to the same fantastic treatment; what Christian theologians have done with the Bible in Greek or Latin or English bears comparison, in some respects, with the wildest flights of fancy of the Jewish commentators. But there are important differences. The very fact that there can be several English translations of the Bible weakens the cogency of a deduction from any particular English text. Again, translations lack some of the verbal exegetical possibilities of the original. The play on words that occurs so frequently in the Hebrew disappears. The name "Isaac" connects with the verb "to laugh" only in Hebrew. The syllable *Ya* as part of a name (the equivalent of our *Theo-*) has no meaning in another language than Hebrew. But there is a much more important consideration:

No people (I do not speak of groups or sects) which has received the Bible in translation has derived its history, its laws, and its religious ritual exclusively from the Biblical text, as the Jews have done; and this not simply in Biblical times. Side by side with Biblical legislation and prescription there developed among the Jews a body of laws which they did not put into writing at first, but which they always based on the written Biblical text, perhaps, at the beginning, changing the text for their purpose. But when the text became fixed and untouchable, the Jews went on developing new laws and new religious practices, which they still justified retroactively by interpretation of Biblical texts. These new laws, beliefs, and practices were declared to be as old as the Torah itself; they had, the teachers declared, been given to Moses at Sinai, together with the other laws, the written ones, and had been transmitted orally from generation to generation. The ingenuities by which the oral law was thus connected interpretatively with the changeless text of the written law is one of the intellectual curiosities of human history. Whenever the Jews needed something new, they went to look for it in the Bible; and of course they found it. The pressure under which the Biblical text yielded its consent served to strengthen its hold on the people. If the minutiæ of the milk and meat tabus were to be deduced from the single Biblical sentence: "Thou shalt not seethe a kid in his mother's milk," the sentence was not likely to be forgotten or altered.

For many centuries it was forbidden to commit to writing

the tremendous literature—far more voluminous than the Bible itself—of interpretation and exegesis. The feats of memorization that this prohibition called forth would be entirely incredible to us if we had not, among our contemporaries, Yeshivah students who have mastered *the entire Talmud* by heart.

It might be argued that if the Jews were so devastatingly ingenious at deriving meanings from the Biblical text, they could in fact do and think whatever they liked—and find Bible authority for it; and it is therefore absurd to speak of the Bible as the maker of Jewish history. Theoretically this argument is unanswerable. In practice and at long range it turned out otherwise.

There were, in fact, times when the Bible itself was less known among erudite Jews than the works deriving from it, like the Mishnah and the Talmud. But the foundations of these works compelled a periodic return to the Bible itself. Hundreds of regulations of Jewish life are only remotely and tortuously connected with the Biblical text: such are the directions for making the ritual fringes worn by every observant Jew; the form of the phylacteries for arm and head, and of *mezuzot* for doorposts; the complicated symbolism of the Passover; the instructions for the building of booths for the festival of that name; the order and the content of the prayers; the laws of the Sabbath; and, on top of all this, the code of the civic law—in so far as Jewish law could be called civic—which had to meet requirements unknown in Biblical days. If the Jews put the Biblical text to these tortuous uses, it was because they were afraid of diminishing its sanctity and its creative possibilities; and in effect the Bible reasserted itself against the dangers of the method invented for its perpetuation.

In the continuous war between pedantry and inspiration, the latter had the advantage. The contact with the Bible was maintained, and the extra-Biblical exegesis did not smother it. The ritual of the festivals was a re-creation of Biblical and Palestinian custom; the most familiar figures in Jewish folklore were everywhere the Biblical; the longing for the re-creation of the Jewish state was a Biblical, not an exegetical, fixation. There was also a type of literature, moralistic, but not legalistic or philosophical, which led back direct to the Bible: the piety of King David, the integrity of Joseph, the hospitality and obedience of Abraham, the humility of Moses, were the favorite themes of the homilists because these Biblical heroes were favorites with the masses; and, independently of homilies, the wisdom of Solomon, the strength of Samson, the wickedness of Jeroboam, the foolishness of Ahasuerus, the villainy of Haman, the beauty of Esther, the faithfulness of Ruth, were bywords in Jewish homes. Here was a folklore which, though familiar to many peoples (and often, as among the Puritans, deep-rooted and pervasive), had, among the Jews, exclusive dominance; it had not come from the outside; it did not have to compete with Nordic sagas, Greek myths, Arabian Nights, fairies, pixies, kobolds, and other local creations to anything like the same degree as among other peoples familiar with the Bible. It had not another "history" to fuse with. By being both sacred and secular it pre-empted the whole field of life.

The most impressive external evidence of the power of the Jewish history book to make Jewish history is the re-creation of the Jewish state after a lapse of two millennia. I shall defer to Book Three the discussion of the relationship between Judaism, the Biblical tradition, and the Zionist movement. Here I anticipate only to the extent of observing that, if to understand the total history of the Jewish people we must have a feeling for the role played in it by the Bible, we must deepen and refine that feeling if we wish to understand the sources as well as the significance of Zionism.

The reader who has followed me so far will perhaps suspect me of evasiveness. I seem to be saying: "The Bible is intrinsically valid; it is substantially a correct record of the spiritual evolution of the Jews. But even if this is not so, the Bible is given validity by the fact that the Jews have made it their major directive for over two thousand years." I have even said: "For a practical consideration of the last twenty-two hundred years of Jewish history, it is not helpful to know how the Biblical text arose." I do not believe that a contradiction arises here. I hold it to be impossible that an organic work like the Bible can have been "constructed" by doctrinaires or poets or prophets. I hold it to be impossible, likewise, that a pattern of behavior can have fastened itself on a people with such persistent, powerful effect as the result of a fictional reconstruction of the past. Certainly there are many instances of such fictional reconstructions; almost every people has them; almost every people fills in the unknown past as cartographers used to fill in unexplored continents, with imaginary creatures and names. But such inventions do not become the determinants of a people's history any more than the fancies of the cartographers are actually found to populate the waste places. The Bible could not have become the determinant of Jewish history if it consisted only of explanatory myths. Such myths it obviously contains, but these are not its essence. Its essence is an unmistakable folk reality, the folk transmission of a factual experience.

Yet it is proper to say that even if we never find any external, non-Biblical confirmation of the historic substance of the Bible, we shall be on firm ground if we take the record as it is and explain the subsequent history of the Jews by its effect on them. No other explanation of post-Biblical Jewish history is possible. One may of course ask:

"Why did the Jews surrender in this extraordinary fashion to their book?" Or: "Why has this people persisted so long?" I do not know of a satisfactory answer. But, for that matter, there is no satisfactory answer, as yet, to the question: Why did this or that people develop these and these characteristics? All the scientific explanations I have read are merely descriptions of the physical circumstances that attended the the emergence of the characteristics. They say, in effect: "Given its particular character, a people will respond thus or thus to a particular challenge." This is not an explanation; it is a tautology. Toynbee's "Challenge and Response" theory is not an explanation but a partial description. For always the question is moved back one stage. Where did the "particular character" of the people come from? It came, of course, from the interplay between a challenge— certain physical conditions—and an earlier "particular character." We might conceivably trace the line back to Chellean man, and be none the wiser.

Some readers may accept my thesis, but under a negative sign. They will say: "The history of the Jews has been made by their history book in the sense that it has led to their petrifaction." This view has been held by Jews as well as by non-Jews. But how can one hold this view after the creation of the State of Israel?

Others, not denying that the Jewish people has remained alive, will produce the stereotype answer to the question why the Jews developed their Bible- and Palestine-fixation: it was "the instinct of self-preservation" that invented this ingenious mechanism of national survival. Necessity did it —necessity, which is the mother of invention. This is the "Challenge and Response" theory in another form. Necessity is perhaps the mother of invention, but character is the father. For inventions are not parthenogenetic. To need is not enough: one must also be able. The very fact that individuals, nations, and species perish proves that necessity does not always find a fructifying mate. If I were to say that the Jewish people has survived, and has re-created a Jewish state, because it knew how to surrender to the Bible, I should perhaps be right; but I should not be saying how it knew how to surrender to the Bible.

Finally, I shall also be told that my thesis is nonsense for the simple reason that the Jewish people has not survived at all—not even as a fossil. I shall be told that those who call themselves Jews today, or have done so for the last few centuries—perhaps for the last twenty centuries—have nothing to do with the people that inhabited the Palestine described by the Bible, or with the people—itself not related to the people of the Bible—which called itself Jewish and had its center in Palestine after the so-called Babylonian exile. If the criterion is genetics, and nothing else, this view may be substantially correct. It would then appear that groups of various ethnic origins successively integrated themselves with a name and a tradition which have a continuous history of more than three thousand years. But I do not see that this in any way affects the thesis of the book. If, however, the criterion is cultural, the theory must rest on a total distortion of Jewish history.

# CHAPTER XVI

## *The Spiritual-Physical Parallels*

❀

About the time when the last of the Bible texts was being accepted as canon (middle of the second century B.C.), the Jewish people re-enacted with peculiar lucidity one of its typical message-dramas. This was the Maccabean-Hasmonean episode, which is not contained in the Jewish Bible, and is considered post-Biblical. It is an interesting episode in itself; but it is much more interesting as an illustration of the manner in which the Bible had fastened itself on the Jewish people. The Bible, now being fixed unalterably, went on repeating itself in their life. It was as if an obstinate experimenter, certain that he had found the right method, was applying it over and over again under changed conditions.

The following is a summary of the accounts put together by the standard historians from Josephus, the Books of the Maccabees, and various hints in the Mishnah and elsewhere:

The Maccabean war was precipitated, if not caused, by an apostatizing-Hellenizing class in Jewry, which invited foreign invasion in order to establish its rule and promote the de-Judaizing of the people. The leadership in the resistance to the invited invader was assumed by a group of five brothers known to us as the Maccabees, or the Has-

monean family. When the war had been won, the first
Hasmonean ruler of the succeeding generation—the son of
one of the Maccabee brothers—betrayed the people, and
the purpose of the resistance, by reintroducing the policy
of de-Judaization. The people again resisted—and again,
in the long run, successfully.

Now for the details:

For two or more generations before the Maccabean war,
a considerable group of Jews in Palestine—or rather Judea
—had been feeling the Hellenizing itch. They were of
course wealthy Jews. Judea was at the time (about 200 B.C.)
under the suzerainty of Egypt, which, like Asia Minor, had
been conquered by Alexander about a century and a half
earlier. In Egypt there was already a powerful, partly
Hellenized Jewish community. But in Egypt the Hellenizing
process did not have the same drive as in Asia Minor; the
ancient Egyptian spirit reasserted itself, the ancient gods
were more stubborn; and the Jews never took to Egyptian
gods. Thus Hellenization among the Egyptian Jews did not
take the form of religious apostasy. In Asia Minor, or Syria,
however, among the Seleucid Greeks, Hellenism was more
combative and more successful, and had a longer vogue.

According to the records, there was no Hellenizing or
other cultural pressure put on the Judean Jews by their
Egyptian overlords. The Hellenizing movement was spon-
taneous. We hear of a High Priest in Jerusalem, a certain
Onias the Second, who manifested pro-Syrian inclinations,
and withheld payment of taxes to the Egyptian authorities.
We do not know if this Onias was a Hellenizer; he may have
had personal or political motives. But that he should have
preferred Syrian to Egyptian rule is a suspicious circumstance, since Syria was actively and increasingly (though
not yet tyrannically) Hellenistic, while Egypt was passively
and diminishingly so.

For half a century Hellenization among the well-to-do Jews of Judea went on apace. Then Antiochus the Third of Syria took away Judea from Egypt. But he instituted a mild rule, leaving to the Jews the administration of their internal affairs, hence their religious freedom, and only exacting the usual tribute. He was followed by Seleucus the Fourth, whose reign of ten years still left the Jews their religious and cultural autonomy. It was under Antiochus the Fourth (Antiochus Epimanes, or the Madman—a name given him by others than the Jews) that the Hellenization of the Jews became the state policy of the conquerer; and whether or not this change would have occurred without the Jewish collaborationists, the fact remains that they encouraged it.

Dissatisfied with the traditional cult as practiced by the High Priest Onias the Third, these Jews applied to the court at Antioch for the supreme office, obtained it by promise of a larger tribute to be wrung from their people, and then used their power for the gradual dismantling of the Jewish cult, and the introduction of the customs and religious practices of the Asiatic Greeks. Central to these customs were, of course, the games, which symbolize the competitive interpretation of human relations, and focus the spirit of man on eternal contest. A palestra or gymnasium was erected in Jerusalem opposite the Temple itself, so that the young priests might be tempted to neglect the services. Since the contests called for complete nakedness, young Jews underwent a surgical operation to conceal the effects of circumcision; and since public sports were, in those days, at least semi-religious in character, the paganization of spirit that went with the glorification of sports was accompanied by a formal paganization in other rituals.

But at a certain point the Jewish masses revolted. Thereupon the Hellenizers invited the intervention of the Syrian authorities. Then followed the descent of Antiochus the

Fourth on Jerusalem, the desecration of the Temple with the "desolation of abominations" (an altar for the sacrifice of swine), the attempt to impose by force the worship of the Greek gods, and the emergence of the Maccabean family to the leadership of the insurgent Jews.

The revolt of the Jews was one of those wild outbursts of popular heroism and despair which from time to time set limits to the megalomania of power-masters. The character of the Maccabean revolt can best be seen in the light of the character of the people.

The Jews were not fighters. In the three centuries since the days of Ezra and Nehemiah they had lived a quiet, withdrawn life. Their name does not occur among the fiercely contending nations of that period. It was during these three centuries—which are a blank in the Jewish record, too—that the Bible fastened itself on them. There are no memories, for that period, even of the teachers, writers, and redactors under whom and through whom the process worked itself out. The only possible exception is Simon the Just, a High Priest, whose date and identity are, however, uncertain. In silence and obscurity the Jews had pursued the cultivation of their peculiar world outlook, had assumed the spiritual personality that they were to retain forever after, had submitted to the overlordship of the Bible, had become its people.

That "world outlook," that "spiritual personality," was not a simple thing. The Jews had not become models of goodness in the prophetic spirit. The historian Graetz paints an idyllic picture of Jewish social conditions in the period between Ezra and the Hellenizers. It is a ridiculous picture, as the book of ben Sirach—definitely written in that period —at once reveals. The Jews had neither surrendered completely to the prophets nor yet adopted completely the wisdom morality, nor become completely a ritualist people.

The threefold search and inner struggle continued; but it continued within that spiritual framework which denied the central affirmation of paganism: life as eternal gamesome combat, and, behind the gamesomeness, gods who were tied to eternal laws that they could not overcome, gods who were only embodiments of nature, gods who therefore could not inspire a moral law, which nature does not possess. Of course there were paganizing Jews: such were the Hellenizers; such were Jews before them, as described later in this chapter. But the paganizers always fell away. They did not stay inside; they did not infect the people. The people remained the Biblical people, the searching people, the arena (if I may so put it) of a struggle totally different from that which went on in the pagan arenas. The masses —the artisans, the small merchants, the small farmers— were interpenetrated with a feeling of destiny. That destiny was, briefly, to incorporate the co-operative as against the competitive interpretation of life.

I see that people as flesh and blood by looking at my contemporaries of yesterday, the Jews of Poland and Russia, the Jews among whom I spent my childhood: the masses of the obscure, as well as the scholars, the masses with their failings, their superstitions, their envies—but with their intellectual alertness, their overriding awareness of involvement in a unique spiritual process; above all, their organic rejection of the sportive idealization of the fighter.

Such a people rose, in an incredible access of fury and determination, against the outsiders who sought to obliterate its spirit, and the insiders who were ready to surrender it. Its leaders in the war, the Maccabee brothers, were, it seems, of that upper class which was so largely composed of traitors; but, as has often happened, members of the betraying class went over to the masses to render service in the national cause. Of the five Maccabee brothers, not one died a natural death; they fell in battle, or in ambush, or by treachery. Aided by a fortuituous turn of events—the rivalries among the heirs of Antiochus the Fourth—the Jews achieved independence, cleansed the Temple, and dreamed of peace and the free pursuit of their religious quest. The dream faded with the accession to rulership of the first son of the Maccabees, the first Hasmonean ruler.

What the pre-Hasmonean Hellenizers had failed to do with the help of the outsider, the Hasmoneans tried to do by themselves, armed with the prestige of their name and their priestly office. In short, the Hasmoneans reverted to their class. They sought to pollute the Jewish people with a patriotic-jingo passion. They engaged in wars of conquest. They repeated on their neighbors, in the name of Judaism, the crimes of Antiochus the Madman; they forced conversion on other peoples at the sword's point. But instead of outraging the forms of the Jewish religion—these they observed, ritually, though not without some significant variations—they outraged its spirit. The history of John Hyrcanos, the son of Simon the Maccabee (one of the five brothers), and of Alexander Jannai, the son of John Hyrcanos, who between them reigned over the Jews for sixty years, is the history of an internal attempt to convert the Jewish people into a standard pagan nation in everything but name.

The Hasmoneans have been blamed for the ultimate conquest by Rome because they were the first to invite Roman intervention in internal Jewish affairs (this happened with the third generation of Hasmonean princes). They have also been blamed for the calamities of the Herodian dynasty. If the Idumean (Edomite) nation had not been incorporated by force in the Jewish kingdom, Herod the Idumean would presumably never have become King of the Jews. Certainly it was an evil thing that the rival Hasmonean brothers should have carried their dispute to Pompey, the Roman proconsul; but it was so in itself, and not because it led to the Roman conquest of Judea, which was inevitable in any case. It was an evil thing to force foreign rule and Judaism on the Edomites, whatever the practical consequences. The accusations as formulated above toy with the "ifs" of history and obscure what I have just called the "peculiar lucidity" of the Maccabean-Hasmonean episode; they make it appear that if one of the Hasmonean brothers, after appealing to Pompey, had established a powerful Jewish state, or if the Romans had never destroyed Judea, or if Herod had never become King of the Jews, the actions described would not have been a betrayal of the Jewish people.

Such accusations also belong to the immemorial confidence trick of "ends and means," which withholds *moral* judgment on every act until the well-known "historical perspective" of future ages will presumably supply us with a criterion; actually it divorces judgment from morality and makes history as amoral as the struggle of the microorganisms in the primordial slime. For either morality is a present awareness and a present guide, a present living in careful rightness, or it is nothing at all. The ultimate practical consequences of an act are certainly an element in moral calculation; but our intention to be moral must be operative throughout every step. "Ends and means" are actualities in morally neutral situations; in the moral field they are an optical illusion. The Maccabean-Hasmonean episode illustrates these truths. For our purpose it also illustrates the recurrence of the physical-social form through which the Jewish struggle to remain Jewish found expression throughout the ages.

The Jewish masses were overwhelmingly pacifist before, *during*, and after the Maccabean-Hasmonean episode. In the early stages it was the Hasideans who were the representatives of the masses, their inspiration and mouthpiece; and the masses wanted only one thing: the possibility to order their lives and worship in the tradition that they regarded as Jewish. They would accept the minimum political conditions which permitted this possibility. The Maccabee brothers, on the other hand, and the Hasmonean princes, were fighters by instinct, by temperament, and by imitative regard for the surrounding peoples. For a brief period the constitutional inclination of this clan coincided with the national-spiritual need. When the period was over, the coincidence dissolved; then the struggle for the possession of the soul of the Jewish people was resumed within the Jewish people itself.

The humble and the lowly had risen in armed rebellion only in the last extremity, and for the minimum conditions of spiritual liberty. They were so terrified by the prospect of becoming the very thing they were fighting against that at first many submitted passively to massacre on the Sabbath rather than risk its desecration by self-defense. But even though they ultimately yielded this citadel of the spirit, their purpose remained uncorrupted. *They did not acquire an appetite for fighting.* When the minimum conditions they wanted had been established, they refused to fight on; and the war was continued over their protests by those elements which had been paganized before or who had been paganized by the fighting.

Of course the rulers and fighters had the usual incontrovertible arguments: "We have to make ourselves so strong that we will not be attacked again"; and "We did not fight this war in order to relapse into our former vulnerability." But behind these arguments was that which took away the worth of strength and invulnerability. There was the power lust; there was the love of combat; there was a hunger to make a stir in the world in terms that the world respected; there was, in short, the old apostatizing impulse. The Hasmoneans became stronger and stronger—and more and more Hellenistic.

From these princes and their followers (who became the Sadducees), the Hasideans (who became the Pharisees) turned as from a Jeroboam. There were no longer prophets among the Jews; there were only teachers; the truths had been uttered; they had only to be inculcated. And the Hasidean-Pharisee teachers, though not prophets, and though tainted with the wisdom morality, suffered persecution at the hands of the Hellenizing princes in the true prophetic tradition. Thus the Biblical pattern continued to weave itself after the Bible had been closed. And perhaps because it is nearer to us in time, perhaps because the records are fuller, perhaps because it stands immediately after the transitional period from the Biblical to the post-Biblical, the Maccabean-Hasmonean episode is an excellent introduction to the parallelism of the social-spiritual struggles portrayed in the Bible.

In his work *The Pharisees* Louis Finkelstein, leaning on and extending the research of other scholars, has systematized the evidences in the Bible, the Mishna, and the Talmud of that physical-spiritual parallelism. We are speaking now, the reader must remember, not of that internal search among the Jews which is the dynamism of their Book and their history, but of the struggle to stay Jewish and continue the search. Finkelstein says:

"The clash between the opposing groups of the Second Commonwealth, and of the first centuries of the Christian era [i.e., the clash between Pharisees and Sadducees], was as significant, morally and spiritually, as that between the prophets and their opponents centuries earlier. The formal issues changed; the fundamental difference remained the same. The social forces

189

which had made the patrician landowner of the eleventh century
B.C.E. desert the YHWH of his nomadic ancestors and worship
the *baalim* of the earlier Canaanite agriculturists, and had driven
his successors of the sixth century B.C.E. to imitate Assyrian and
Egyptian manners, dress and worship, produced the Hellenist of
the third century B.C.E. and the Herodian of a later generation.
Conversely, the follower of the prophet gave way to the Hasid
(Hasidean) and the latter was succeeded by the Pharisee."

We might object to certain implications in this summary
and in the book as a whole. The words "social forces" are
a description, not an explanation. We do not know why the
prophets came into existence, why the prophetic episode
developed among the Jews alone. There is nothing in the
physical and economic picture of Jewish life that we cannot
find in the lives of other peoples: the struggle of classes, the
struggle between the national priestly cult and defection
to alien cults, are universal themes. Why did the operation
of economic law "produce" the Bible among the Jews, and
nothing like it elsewhere?

The relation between the social and the moral struggle
among the Jews is organic and continuous; but if we understand morality as the prophets did—at least, according to
my interpretation of it—it is not the relation between cause
and effect. The moral struggle expresses itself through the
medium of the social struggle (and not through that alone)
as song issues through the oral mechanism; there is an interplay between the quality of the song and the quality of the
oral mechanism; but the oral mechanism does not explain
the melody. Throughout the whole of its reconstructible
history the Jewish group seems to have been haunted by an
imperious necessity to formulate and affirm a prophetic
morality; the other moralities to which it was susceptible
(the priestly, the wisdom or Stoic morality) were affected
by the prophetic morality: and when they asserted them-

selves boldly, and cast off the influence of prophetism, they supplied the material for paganization. This impulse to prophetism was incorporated chiefly in the masses, not in the ruling classes; the people regularly threw up from within itself, or occasionally drew down into itself from the upper economic levels, the protagonists of prophetism, who fought with equal obstinacy the apostatizing efforts of the ruling classes and the relapses of the masses themselves. It was the prophets versus the princes and the landed gentry; the Hasideans versus the Hellenizers and Hasmoneans; the Pharisees versus the Sadducees and Herodians and Roman-izers.

But it was also the prophets and Hasideans and Pharisees versus the people itself when the latter flagged and failed. There were times when the hand of the teachers lay heavy on the people. It was so with Isaiah and Jeremiah and other prophets, who would not exonerate the masses from the guilt of tolerating apostatizing kings; it was so with the Pharisees. There was for a period bitter hostility between the masses and the Pharisees, especially the severer among the latter, who developed into the Shammaites. Yet in the end the masses felt that the teachers belonged to *them*, were *their* better selves.

How is it that the Pharisees, with their strong admixture of the wisdom morality, were so obdurate in their Judaism? Was not their wisdom morality nearer to the Stoics than to the prophets? It seems so on the surface. If we look deeper, we see that the prophetic morality was deeper in them than their own formal statements show. For the true, ultimate test lies in the rejection of the great sporting ritual, with everything it connotes (this we find in the Stoics), and in the concept of the *nation* as a moral instrument (this we do not find in the Stoics). It must never be forgotten that the Hasideans and the Pharisees were the ones who, besides canonizing the wisdom literature, also canonized the prophetic literature. Regarding the ritualists, we have seen that they were capable of a combination with prophetism in the days of Josiah. But they have always been the weakest link.

The transition from Biblical to post-Biblical life, and the transmission of the pattern of the Jewish struggle, are, we have noted, a historical blank. But there is a fascinating coincidence of dates as between the Jewish and the Greek traditions which, though it need not be regarded as absolutely exact, gives a longer vista to our speculations.

It was in the year 444 B.C. that Ezra, coming from Babylon, assembled the small, disintegrating Jewish community of Jerusalem and read the Torah to it, instituting the system of studies which continues till this day. In that same year he began the harsh and painful annulment of those marriages with heathen women which were threatening the Jewish community with extinction. As to the Greeks, the historian tells us: "At an early period of his career Pericles enacted, or perhaps only revived, a law confining the rights of Athenian citizenship to persons both of whose parents were Athenian citizens. In the year 444 B.C., on the occasion of a scrutiny of the lists of citizens, nearly 5,000 persons claiming to be citizens were proved to be aliens, and were ruthlessly sold into slavery."

It was like a clearing of the decks for action: the obstinate, God-seeking nation, and the most alluring and spiritually powerful of the pagan nations, purging themselves simultaneously of external and debilitating elements in preparation for a decisive struggle. On the surface, Athens had the overwhelming advantage; it was a compact and powerful city state inhabited by a people which, according to Galton, had reached the highest stage of intelligence that has ever been achieved by the human race. The insignificant provincial patch in Asia Minor known as Judea—a scattering of villages about the half-ruined city of Jerusalem—was inhabited by a loosely knit, poverty-stricken, uncultured community composed of the grandchildren of returned Jewish exiles. The ecstasy of the restoration, mirrored in the dazzling verses of the second Isaiah, had been forgotten. Jewish customs, Jewish knowledge, the basic Jewish outlook, were vanishing; the Sabbath of compulsory rest—the distinctive social glory of the Jewish people—had fallen into disuse; pagan images stood in Jewish homes, brought in by Ammonite and Edomite mothers. This pitiful group Ezra and Nehemiah, backed by a powerful Babylonian Jewry, began to reintegrate with the past of prophecy; and from this community was to issue, in the three centuries that have been torn out of the pages of history, the indestructible carrier of the prophetic tradition.

The Maccabean-Hasmonean episode is one of the climaxes of Jewish history because it testifies to the permanent re-establishment of the pattern of spiritual struggle within the Jewish people. The physical garb that makes the struggle visible had been rewoven. Other interpretations, with their heathen glorification of the fighter, or their demagogic appeal to the primacy of political values, are both banalities and perversions.

# CHAPTER XVII

## The Old and the New Dispensations

❈

Is THERE between the Old and the New Testaments so fundamental a difference that they can be called the old and the new dispensations? If there is, what is its nature?

There are some who find, in the two sets of documents, two opposed concepts of human relations. Achad Haam and others hold that Judaism, as it issues from the Old Testament, exalts the principle of justice, while Christianity, as it issues from the New Testament, exalts the principle of love and mercy: that Judaism is geared to the practical administrative problem of humanity under divine direction, while Christianity preaches the impossibilist doctrine of unlimited altruism under divine inspiration: that Judaism accepts such a doctrine only as the far-off goal of the human species, while Christianity insists on its immediate application, and thereby discredits it.

In my view there is, indeed, some difference of emphasis between the Old and the New Testaments, but not enough to make anything like *two* dispensations. If it is a question of "impracticality" and "impossibilism," the most anarchic injunction in the whole Bible is: "Thou shalt love thy neighbour as thyself." In a world in which every man loved his neighbor as he loves himself, no laws could exist, for no one would appeal to the law to his neighbor's hurt. Nothing would be needed but a commentary: "Thou shalt love thyself intelligently, in order that thou mayest love thy neighbor intelligently." The commandment appears first in the Old Testament, and is quoted with approval in the New. Let us note that it does not read: "*In that day* shalt thou love thy neighbour as thyself." It applies to the present.

Again: if it is a question of "Justice versus Love," wherein is Christ's warning to the cities that rejected him less retributive than the prophets' warnings to Israel? The warnings of the prophets are more frequent and more vivid. It is a matter of emphasis. We are not dealing with two alien and disparate worlds of morality; there is too large a common area of feeling, quite apart from the common Jewish setting.

Shall we find the difference in the central personality of Jesus? If we think of him as a prophet, the enormous emphasis on miracles places him outside the trajectory of Jewish prophetism. Prophets had long since ceased performing miracles. Prophecy itself had run its course. Yet even of the miracles of Jesus we can say that if Christianity had remained a Jewish incident these would have lost their importance, and the moral content of the Christian sect would have fused again with the tradition from which it sprang. This applies also to the claim allowed Jesus as special intermediary between man and God. Jewish life, since the closing of the Old Testament, has not always been free from an excessive belief in the miraculous. The powers attributed to some *Tzaddikim* by their Chassidic followers, in the matters both of miracles and of intercessory powers, compare with anything in the Old and New Testaments. Yet Chassidism, denounced at first by the orthodox, in part for these claims, has become a great enrichment of the Jewish tradition. The extravagant legends have dissolved into fairy tales; what remains is a great efflorescence of moral insight comparable to the prophetic.

As for the personality of Jesus as it detaches itself from the various gospels in different degrees, I find it difficult to distinguish between him and the highest prophetic figures. There is about his sayings the same power of illumination that I find in Amos and Isaiah, the same annihilation of doubt as to the self-subsistence of the moral purpose in man. There is also the same falling away of the principle of reward and punishment. When I read: "Blessed are they which do hunger and thirst after righteousness: for they shall be filled," I regard the promise of reward as a typical prophetic stylization. What shall they be filled with, they "which do hunger and thirst after righteousness"? Righteousness, presumably. But they that really hunger and thirst after righteousness are already filled with it.

Does the vital divergence between the Old and the New Testaments consist in the attribution of divinity to Jesus, or the attribution to him of uniqueness of kind as ungraspable as God's? There are millions of Christians who interpret the divinity of Jesus symbolically. They regard him as human. Yet I think that we have here the key to our problem. There is a uniqueness in Jesus, and it is bound up with a structural difference between the Old and New Testaments.

The Old Testament is a history of the moral evolution of a people, in which the facts of the history and the moral message are part of one another. We are given the moral message, and we are told what the people did with it. The vicissitudes of the revelation, the acceptance and the rejection of it, the repentance and the renewal, a continuous struggle, are themselves revelation. As against this, the New Testament is a one-time final statement of a moral revelation. The historical range of the New Testament is negligible; the record of the vicissitudes of the early Christian Church—its moral failures, the appearance of schismatics and traitors—bears no proportion to the substance of the original revelation, and to the story of the founding of the Church.

The New Testament tries to overcome this structural divergence by reducing the Old Testament to a kind of prologue; the evolutionary curve of the Old Testament, its character of history-as-revelation, is flattened out into introductory testimony. It is made to appear that the Old Testament is unintelligible without the New. But the final effect is quite different. When a Christian says: "I believe in Jesus because Isaiah foretold his coming," he seems to express greater faith in Isaiah than in Jesus. The Old Testament ceases to be a prologue, the New Testament becomes an epilogue. Then when the Christian reads the Old Testament to find out about the David from whom Jesus had to be descended, and about the prophets who foretold the coming of Jesus, he finds himself plunged into a national history to which he has no relationship. The divergence is increased, not decreased.

Modern Christians who reject the Christological interpretation of certain passages in Isaiah and other books of the Old Testament seem to be more consistent, from two points of view. First, they do not torture the text—and occasional mistranslations—into arbitrary meanings. Second, they recognize that if Jesus was—even as a human being—the absolute moral phenomenon which they see in him, he did not need the testimony of the Jews or of anyone else. Yet although such Christians do not see in Jesus an absolute "identity"-phenomenon; although they do not believe in literal prophecy; although they recognize the structural function of the Old Testament; although such are their views, they still cannot stand in the same relation-

ship to the Old Testament as the Jews. For the Old Testament tells what happened to the Jews and Judaism, not
what happened to Christians and Christianity. Neither
does the New Testament, covering only two generations,
tell what happened to Christians and Christianity. The
New Testament cannot do for the Christians what the Old
Testament does for the Jews.

Am I merely saying that the Old Testament contains
history while the New Testament contains only revelation?
No; I am saying that the history in the Old Testament is of
a special kind, interacting with revelation and actually
indistinguishable from it. You cannot teach the revelation
of the Old Testament without teaching the history of the
Jewish people. Christian revelation, however, can be taught,
is taught, independently of the history of the Christian
Church, though not independently of the life of Jesus. What
the life of Jesus is in Christianity, the history of the Jewish
people is in Judaism, with this difference: that the Jewish
people is presented as wholly human. The attempt to juxta-
pose Judaism and Christianity, the Old Testament and the
New Testament, as two systems of morality, or ethics, or
eschatology, misses the point.

The difference can best be understood by noting what
the Jews have been reading, for two thousand years, as part
of their sacred literature, and noting the absence of comparable material in the sacred literature of the Christian
Churches.

Amos of Tekoa went up to Beth-el to prophesy against
Israel in the days of Jeroboam the Second. We read:

"Amaziah the priest of Beth-el sent to Jeroboam king of
Israel, saying, Amos hath conspired against thee in the midst of
the house of Israel: the land is not able to bear all his words.
For thus Amos saith, Jeroboam shall die by the sword, and Israel
shall surely be led away captive out of their own land. Also

Amaziah said unto Amos, O thou seer, go, flee thee away into the land of Judah, and there eat bread, and prophesy there: but prophesy not any more at Beth-el: for it is the king's chapel, and it is the king's court.

"Then answered Amos, and said to Amaziah, I was no prophet, neither was I a prophet's son; but I was an herdman, and a gatherer of sycomore fruit: and the Lord took me as I followed the flock, and the Lord said unto me, Go, prophesy unto my people Israel.

"Now therefore hear thou the word of the Lord: Thou sayest, Prophesy not against Israel, and drop not thy word against the house of Isaac. Therefore thus saith the Lord: Thy wife shall be an harlot in the city . . . and thy land shall be divided by line; and thou shalt die in a polluted land: and Israel shall surely go into captivity forth of his land."

Thus the prophet Amos to Amaziah, priest of Israel, in the sacred text that is both history and revelation for the Jews. And thus the prophet Isaiah, to Ahaz, King of Judah, and the pious Jews of his time:

"Hear the word of the Lord, ye rulers of Sodom; give ear unto the law of our God, ye people of Gomorrah. To what purpose is the multitude of your sacrifices unto me? saith the Lord: I am full of the burnt offerings of rams, and the fat of fed beasts; and I delight not in the blood of bullocks, or of lambs, or of he goats. When ye come to appear before me, who hath required this at your hand, to tread my courts? Bring no more vain oblations; incense is an abomination unto me; the new moons and sabbaths, the calling of assemblies, I cannot away with it; it is iniquity, even the solemn meeting. Your new moons and your appointed feasts my soul hateth: they are a trouble unto me; I am weary to bear them. And when ye spread forth your hands, I will hide mine eyes from you: yea, when ye make many prayers, I will not hear: your hands are full of blood."

Where, in a sacred book of the Christians—obligatory ritual reading, part of the supreme authority and dogma—

shall we find similar denunciations of a Christian high priest, say of a fanatical and murderous Torquemada or Pobiedonostsev, or of a hedonistic villain like Roderigo Borgia, better known as Pope Alexander the Sixth? Certainly there was Savonarola, whose words against the Borgia had something of the prophetic tinge, and whose life ended in martyrdom. But Savonarola's record is secular; he has not even been canonized. And Luther's denunciation of the Catholic Church is not in the sacred book of the Christians. St. Charles Borromeo, officially of the blessed, is called by Lord Acton (a good Catholic) "an infamous assassin"; but it is Borromeo who is canonized, not Acton, though a fitter candidate for sainthood could hardly be found.

One might argue that in an important sense the Christian Church, or at least the Catholic Church, did extend the sacred history beyond the New Testament by the institution of sainthood. But canonization is not history, and the devotional books of the Christians do not tell of the Church as something implicated in the vicissitudes of the original revelation. The villainies of Jewish priests, the abominations of the Jewish people, the failures of the Jewish church, are part of the Jewish lesson. But the villainies of Christian priests, the abominations of Christian peoples, are not in the canon. The Christians salve their conscience in church by reading about the moral failures of the Jews. In the New Testament there is, of course, denunciation of teachers and priests—but they are Jewish teachers, and Jewish priests, those that would not accept Jesus. There is no "Bible" of the Christians in which pious-seeming popes, metropolitans, presbyters, synods, and eucharistic congresses are damned for their part in the history of the Church.

Certainly the Protestants have called the Catholic Church

the Whore of Babylon, and the Catholics have denounced the Protestants as heathen—but this is not part of the Christian Bible; and in any case the mutual denunciations of rival Churches do not serve the purpose I am speaking of. What is lacking is a Catholic prayer-book of equal rank with the New Testament calling down the wrath of God on St. Peter's of Rome, or a Protestant prayer-book of that standing which performs that service for, and is accepted in the services of, St. Paul's of London and St. John's of New York.

But perhaps I have set too recent a date. Sacred books must crystallize at some point, and the canon of the New Testament had to be fixed, as the canon of the Old Testament was. Still, one cannot say that the New Testament is to the Christians what the Old Testament is to the Jews, if the former does not even contain the history of Constantine, multiple murderer and founder of Christianity in the Roman Empire. And a Church of England Bible which says nothing about the crimes of Henry the Eighth is not a Bible in the Jewish sense. The effect is a clear-cut division between nation and church; history becomes a secular process with standards of its own; the moral standards of the sacred book are not given direct and specific application to examples of the national history. God has not declared any Christian war to have been unjust, any Christian high priest to have been a sinner. The Christian peoples go to church, their history does not.

To put it popularly, then: the Old Testament was sweated out by the Jews, while the New Testament was handed to the Christians on a platter; and the latter statement applies to all religions that are produced by an individual rather than by a people. The Jews could not say of the Old Testament: "This was given to us after we had become a people, when we already had a history." Not even the orthodox could say it. They did, indeed, learn that the

201

Torah was given to the Jews at Sinai; but they also learned that the first connection with it had been established by the patriarchs. As against this there is nothing in the pre-Christian history of the western world to suggest a previous appointment with the Bible. On the contrary—and this has not been helpful to the western world—the suggestions of such promise and appointment are referred exclusively to the Jews.

When neo-pagans protest that the Bible was imposed inorganically on the western world, and must therefore be rejected, they point a sound premise to a false conclusion. What is wrong here is not the Bible, but its inorganic imposition. To live themselves into the Bible, the nations needed their own extensions of it, resulting from the application of its method to their separate histories and the makers of them. And either this will yet come about for the civilization we know (perhaps I should say: "the species we know") or the prophetic effort must be written off for the foreseeable future.

I reach with this what is perhaps the touchiest point in my entire thesis. I seem to be saying: "If the Christians could work out a relationship to the Bible such as the Jews have, all will yet be well." Or, worse still: "If the Christians could only be like the Jews!" I ask the reader for a little patience; my position is not as simple as all that.

To say that the Bible has had no moral effect on the world of Christendom would be to indulge in facile, dema-gogic cynicism. It would be equivalent to the popular communist appeal: "The capitalist world couldn't be any worse than it is." It could—and may yet be. On the other hand, to say that the Jewish people has the highest standard of moral behavior in the world would be fatuous. I wonder if the Jews have been as good as Ruth Benedict's famous Zuñis. We are concerned here with *direction* and *effort* in a humanity at such a primitive stage of morality that there is not much difference between the worst and the best, *except, precisely, in the matter of direction.*

I have not forgotten, I have not deliberately discounted, the acceptable fruits of Christianity, the Christian individuals and groups that have turned their backs on the competitive concept of man, the saints who have rejected the sporting formulation of life, and with it the entire world it represents. There is deep meaning in the St. Francises, the Thomas à Kempises, the Husses, the Shaftesburys, the Tyndalls, the Actons, the Bunyans, the Wesleys, Pascals, Boehms, Hutchesons, Roger Williamses, and others. These are the "Jews" of the western world, the Jews in western man, to whom I referred in Book One. The Quakers and Mennonites, the Waldenses and the first Anabaptists—all the associations of the humble and the pure in spirit, whose struggles with their own sins and the sins of the world were conducted on the spiritual level of Jesus and the prophets— these are evidences of the obstinate hold that Christianity has on western man.

And where Christianity thus maintains itself, the moral continuity with the prophets is easily discernible. I cannot find an underlying difference between the moral purpose of the Old Testament and the New, between Judaism and Christianity, between Bachya ibn Pakudah's *Duties of the Heart* and Boethius's *Consolation of Philosophy* or Thomas à Kempis's *Imitation of Christ*. There is, on the contrary, a deep and moving similarity of spirit between Israel Baal Shem, the founder of Chassidism, and Francis of Assisi, though the former had never heard of the latter, and had never looked into the New Testament. What is perhaps more important for my thesis, the gentleness and warmth that I have found in plain Jewish homes in Manchester, New York, Warsaw, Vilna, Johannesburg, I have found also among gentile

Lancashire weavers, and midwest American farmers, and French peasants—all deriving from the same tradition.

In some of the greatest carriers of the western pagan tradition there are flashes of the moral vision that have the prophetic, not the pagan character. The Shakespeare who dazzles us with Henry the Fifth can also write:

> *Between the acting of a dreadful thing*
> *And the first motion, all the interim is*
> *Like a phantasma, or a hideous dream. . . .*

And the Goethe whose brilliance and worldliness went hand in hand with a basic paganism could also write the famous lines:

> *Wer nie sein Brot mit Tränen ass,*
> *Wer nie die kummervollen Nächte*
> *Auf seinem Bette weinend sass,*
> *Der kennt euch nicht, ihr himmlischen Mächte.*

True, these gifts are often abominably misused, and placed at the service of pagan immorality: these passages are often inserted as sentimentalities. Yet sometimes they can rise above the purpose basely planned by the author, by the paradox of human behavior which can be better than it intends.

It would be dangerous and misleading to deny to the gentile world as direct an insight into the nature of the human problem as the Jews ever possessed. Who can read Tolstoy, or Dostoyevsky, or the Foerster who wrote *Europe and the German Question*, and not perceive Christ and the prophets at work? Were there no such evidences, the writing of this book for anyone but Jews—and it is not written for them alone—would be meaningless. The distinction lies elsewhere:

This I found in the world of Christendom which I did not

find in the Jewish world: *A universal alternative ideal which is respectable but profoundly pagan and immoral.* In Christendom, side by side with the world of the New Testament, *The Consolation of Philosophy*, the *Imitation of Christ*, and St. Francis of Assisi, there is a rival world, a rival literature, a rival pantheon, pagan, playful, and destructive, but with universal and coeval status, and of wider acceptance. On the upper intellectual levels Plato is the teacher; on the lower intellectual levels, Kipling and the *Union Jack*. One could escape from Christ to these without incurring conscious censure. The two worlds are so intermingled that the escape does not even call for a formal defection. One could attend church on Sunday morning, and hear the sermon I first heard in a church; and in the evening one could burst with pride hearing *Gunga Din* recited—by the pastor.

Within the Jewish world there was no respectable escape into a tolerated paganism. One could escape into it, of course; but one knew it to be sinful; and one had to go for it to the non-Jewish world.

There were Jewish sinners—power-seekers, snobs, exploiters, enemies of God and man. But sin could not take on pagan charm. The enmity of man for man had no uniforms, arenas, heralds, and trumpets to dazzle or deafen the moral perception. There was no intoxicating or hypnotic ritual to put the intelligence to sleep. Above all, there was no recognized philosophy of contest, and no traditions of canonized contestants.

The summation of life as a game, with the concomitant implication of life as a hideous tragedy, was completely unknown in the Jewish world; and this attitude of seriousness is the direct consequence of the interweaving of revelation and history. History was not left to take care of itself, as it were. It was shown by the sacred books to be within the framework of revelation. Fighting was not a lark, armies were not masquerades; and sporting contests, the charades of war, with their wild practice excitations, were an abomination to the Hasideans who fought Antiochus the Fourth, and a foolishness to the Jews among whom I grew up. If competitive brutality existed among them in the ordinary daily struggle—and it did—there was no philosophy to make it seem the proper order of the universe.

From all the foregoing it would seem that a Jewish state in Palestine, if it is to be Jewish in my sense, ought to be what we popularly call a theocracy. Unfortunately that word conceals a propaganda trick. A theocratic state is one in which public opinion is dominated by a consciousness of the divine and independent source of morality. Jewish history-revelation warns us specifically against confusing this with the domination of a politically organized priest-hood—the popular conception of a theocracy. In the latter sense a theocratic state is an abominable inversion of purpose. It is not only the recognizable prophetic text that utters this warning; the historic text repeatedly denounces priests—from the time of Solomon on—who abetted the idolatry of kings. The prophets were also painfully aware that the prophetic office was as subject to misrepresentation as the priestly. There were false prophets as well as careerist priests.

What is the answer, then? There is none—if by answer we mean a formula, a foolproof device; for such formulas and devices are themselves the contradictions of the ever-alert, ever-living, ever-self-renewing moral perception in the mass of the people. This perception alone constitutes a theocracy, and there is no organizational substitute for it.

A theocracy in the genuine sense might be based on the Old Testament, by the Jews alone. It could not be based by Christians on either the Old Testament or the New. The former is not their history; and the latter, too, has no extension into their experience. Popes have denounced emperors; but even where a genuine moral issue was involved —which was rarely enough—this is secular history. St. Thomas Aquinas teaches that bad kings may be deposed, but St. Thomas is not the canon. Dante has placed popes in hell, but Dante is "literature." The failure of Judaism is the failure of human beings to live up to what they have been taught and have in the main accepted; the failure of Christianity is the failure to have provided the lesson. We might even say that the Jews are therefore the more to be condemned—and the Jews have in the main accepted this view; they have interpreted their exile as a punishment. But Jewish self-condemnation, so vehement and so persistent, does not spring from proportionate guilt; it springs from the absence of a refuge in paganism—that is, in the accepted combative philosophy which is open to the Christian world.

There have been Christians, groups and individuals, who have achieved clarification, who have cleansed themselves completely of the pagan sporting spirit. But we must not confuse the rejection of the sports rituals with that clarification. It depends on the motive. The Puritans, for instance, rejected the sports rituals, but not in a denial of the combative meaning of life. They were not pacifists. They rejected the sports rituals because of the pleasures connected with them—and they rejected all pleasure as unpurposive. (There is Macaulay's famous observation that the Puritans prohibited bear-baiting not because of the pain suffered by the animal, but because of the pleasure experienced by the spectators.) Their discipline was military and militant; their asceticism, denying the value of this world, fitted them for the conquest of it. Their approximation to the spirit of the Old Testament, claimed by them and generally allowed them by others, was one-sided and astigmatic. To return to the essence of the question: they never established a history-revelation of their own to implicate them, as a nation, in the permanent canon.

How deeply and permanently the Jews were implicated in their canon I learned both from my childhood and from the classical Yiddish literature with which I became acquainted in later years. It is a warm and homey literature, untouched by worldly gallantry and adventure. The absence of the nature-theme is certainly associated with the imposed absence, in the Yiddish masses, of a broad rural base. But the continuous interweaving of the Biblical texts and their commentaries turned the privation into an affirmation. The transformation of a medieval German dialect into a wholly independent and utterly dissimilar language, in which ninety per cent of the words have undergone little formal change, cannot be accounted for without a knowledge of what the Old Testament is in Jewish life. It is not the ten per cent or so of Hebrew words that make Yiddish unintelligible to the German; it is the irradiation of Yiddish with the traditional concept of national being.

A new dispensation for the Jews will be possible only when they will break the continuous line that still makes the Old Testament the source and explanation of their specific attitude toward life.

# CHAPTER XVIII

## *A Peculiar People*

❀

N ow, what has all this to do with Judaism as that is generally understood, with the synagogue and the festivals,
with the six hundred and thirteen precepts, with the *Shul-
chan Aruch* (the authoritative Jewish code of ritual), with
the *Kaddish* (the memorial prayer for the dead), with
*Yahrzeit* (annual memorial day for the dead) and memorial
candles, with *kashrut* (dietary laws), with circumcision,
*tefilin* (phylacteries), *mezuzot* (doorpost signs), with the
*tallit* (prayer-shawl), with the ritual baths, with fasts, with
*mazzot* for Passover? What has it to do with belief in the
resurrection, with Eden and Gehennah, with penitence
and prayer, with adoration and supplication? What has it
to do with the forms, values, beliefs, and attitudes that are
presented, in such an attractive blend of eloquence, lucidity, and learning, in Milton Steinberg's *Basic Judaism?*

And suppose the Jewish reader finds himself in substantial agreement with what I have said about the Bible and
the Jewish people, how does it help him to bind himself to
his people, to become associated with the processes I have
described?

Recalling my childhood, I have told of the deep impress
left on me by the Day of Atonement and the Passover, the

*Kaddish* and the *Shivah*, the Sabbath candles, the Ninth of Ab, or Black Fast, and other symbols and rituals of Judaism. If the fragmentary traditionalism of that community has meant so much to me, how much more powerful must be the effect of a full and rounded technique of observance! What I cannot confirm from personal experience, I gather from reading and observation. In their long exile the ritual of the Jews was their homeland. It was often a homeland under siege; at no time was it wholly secure. But what the beloved woods and fields of the countryside are to a normally circumstanced people, what the intimate nooks and corners of one's native land, these the symbols and rituals of the Jews were to them. But since the symbols and rituals were the corporeal counterpart of the faith, they carried a load of associations which other peoples could distribute over larger areas. How, then, can I speak of the Jewish people, and its embodiment of a principle and a dynamic process, without giving first place to the form of the embodiment? If I assert that the Jewish people is a peculiar people, shall I not best convey that peculiarity, if it can be conveyed at all, by a careful and intimate description of its manners and mores?

I shall answer the last question first, and with an unqualified No. The rituals and religious tenets of the Jews do not make of them a peculiar people, except in the sense —not intended here—that all peoples are peculiar peoples. Just as it would be possible for a nation of Jews to inhabit Palestine and not be Jewish, so it would be possible for an exiled Jewish people to observe the ritual and believe the tenets of Judaism without being Jewish either. There is no automatic guarantee of a spiritual value, *even in formally correct beliefs, since these are intellectual matters only*. And this is true despite the fact that for all but the rarest minds—and these only of a special kind—a spiritual value suffers if it cannot find expression in plastic and choreographic form, as well as in verbal and moral.

In ancient Palestine the chief dangers were: apostasy first, petrifaction second. In the exile the order was reversed (until lately). The danger of the petrifaction or fossilization of Jewish life within its customs, symbols, and formal beliefs was so continuous and so immanent that many people have assumed, without further ado, that the Jews could not have overcome it. That is why I have been so concerned with the Jewish *people*, the masses I knew in childhood, those with whom I have since re-established contact. I am probing *their* spirit, and the history of its growth and retention. This spirit, suffusing the customs, symbols, and formal beliefs, and not the customs, symbols, and formal beliefs themselves, makes the Jews a peculiar people.

I have said: "If the Bible is taken as a static document or collection of documents, as a flat, even recital of events and views, of equal, literal validity everywhere, it becomes, to a child of our times, quite meaningless." But I shall be told that the Bible was so taken by the Jews for thousands of years, and it is so taken by many Jews today. Why has it not become meaningless to either group?

As to the first, the obvious answer is: since they had no feeling for the dynamism of history generally, they did not have to find it in the Bible. Obvious—but superficial, and here irrelevant. For we must also ask, of them as of certain Jews today: how could they accept the obvious, flatfooted contradictions in such simple matters as the prophetic promise of a peaceful death for King Josiah, and his violent death in battle in the next chapter? I do not know what enables people to swallow two straightforward, mutually exclusive statements without choking on one of them. I asked a learned friend for the comments of the orthodox exegetes on this particular textual difficulty; the information I got was entirely unhelpful. But our larger question is about something other than formal belief; it is about the spirit with which a body of beliefs is endued. What I have said regarding the spirit that accompanies the body of Jewish ritual and custom applies to the body of formal Jewish beliefs. From our point of view, a man unaware of the dynamism of history is not exempt from its effects—and a man who is aware of the dynamism of history may himself be petrified. What the Bible does to a man is not to be gathered from his answers to a technical catechism.

I have tried to avoid the impertinence of defining what an orthodox Jew "really" believes, his own statements notwithstanding. I have, it is true, defined the spiritual bond between him and the Jewishly orientated unorthodox Jew; I have the right to speak only for the latter, and that a limited right. The former may repudiate me entirely. But a certain presumption is inherent in having any views at all; and without analyzing the beliefs of the orthodox Jew, I state it as my conviction that what he has in common with the unorthodox but Jewishly feeling Jew is the essence of the Jewish being, the substance of Jewish peculiarness. I do not feel at home in the formal beliefs of orthodox Jewry; but I feel at home in its spirit, which, with its serious, ungamesome, and unpagan attitude toward life, is the same as the spirit of the ritualistically unorthodox community of my childhood.

The peculiarness I speak of, this standing apart from the rest of the world, is something over and above the differences that exist between all peoples, including the Jews. It is a peculiarness that the Christian world does not understand at all, because it has no access to the inner life of Jewry; and many Jews do not understand it either, because, like the Christians, they try to grasp the difference in the terminology of creed and custom.

A PECULIAR PEOPLE

There is another peculiarness about the Jews that has
little to do with their character—a peculiarness of position
(I do not mean geographic, social, or political position).
They are a reminder of the split in the personality of Christendom; their presence in the world today gives presentness
also to the New Testament, and draws attention to the
divergence between the potentialities and the failures of
Christ's ministry.

Anti-Semitism is not aware of what the Jews are, therefore cannot be a resentment of their qualities. Even the
dislike of Jews—like most dislikes between groups, and
even between persons—is only partly based on experience,
free perception, and significant rejection. Anti-Semitism is,
however, not dislike; the characteristics of anti-Semitic
literature, from Drumont's *La France juive* to sections of
*Mein Kampf*, are not dislike and resentment, but horror,
loathing, terror, and hallucination. There is no room here
for ordinary distastes and irritabilities, even of the sharper
kind; no room for ordinary lies and slanders, such as will
be found in pre-Christian anti-Jewish literature. It is an
overwhelming convulsion.

It should not be inferred, either, that anti-Semitism sus-
pects in the Jews today a reincarnation of the spirit of the
Bible. If the Jews had completely changed their spirit, but
were still remembered as the descendants of the creators of
the Bible, they would precipitate the same maniacal anti-
Semitic rages. I have said that Christians can escape without formal and conscious defection from Jesus to paganism.
This does not mean that Christly Christianity and paganism
have come to terms within the defecting Christian. They
do not live peacefully side by side in him on the subcon-
scious level. They torment each other, and make a whole
life impossible for each other and for him. But he does not
know whence his distress comes. He is only somehow aware

213

that it has to do with the Bible, with the Old Testament promise of Christ, with the New Testament fulfillment; and therefore the creators of the Bible—or rather their descendants—become the objects of his wildest outbursts of fury.

Jews are in error when they suppose—as some do—that they are hated because of their real or inner peculiarness, their faithfulness to the Old Testament. And their geographic, social, political peculiarness, though it irritates, is not the source of the deeper anti-Semitism. It is their positional peculiarity, as defined in the last paragraph, that is their curse. Nor are they suffering for the sins of their forefathers. Actually they are suffering for the virtues of their forefathers: at least, in respect of anti-Semitism. In respect of being disliked as a minority group, they suffer like many other peoples, for the usual reasons. It is impossible to isolate, in field-work observation, the two sets of factors. But they are there; we cannot, without assuming both of them, account for the full range of anti-Jewish phenomena.

I am perplexed and fascinated by the changes in the essential peculiarness of the Jews, by its enrichment throughout the ages, by the question of the Jewish attitude toward it. When the Jews first conceived themselves to be a peculiar people, in Biblical times, they claimed an exclusive relationship to God, and to his laws and revelations. Yet this was only a relative peculiarness; every people had an exclusive relationship to its gods, and to their laws and revelations. When the God of the Jews, and his laws and revelations, became the heritage of the western world, the Jews achieved, paradoxically enough, a higher peculiarness. They were pointed out as the precursors—and rejectors—of universal salvation: *il gran rifiuto*. They said: "That was not what we meant!" They then reached their true, or inner, peculiarness; but, challenged to say what they meant, they lost themselves in arguments and texts. This last and true peculiarness, the highest and richest, could not be the subject of a universal discourse; it was and is a peculiarness of personality, describable in its origins and effects, but not transmissible as doctrinal statement.

BOOK THREE

Jew and Israeli

# CHAPTER XIX

## *A Technique of Suicide*

❀

Today, wherever Jews discuss seriously their special problems, the central question is: Will the creation of the State of Israel help perpetuate the Jewish people, or will it facilitate its liquidation?

The startled reader will ask: "They mean, of course, will the creation of the State of Israel encourage or discourage Jewish survival *outside* of Israel. Surely the Jewish people, or *a* Jewish people, will survive in Israel." But that, exactly, is what the question is aimed at. One might rephrase it thus: Will the State of Israel help liquidate the peculiarness of the Jewish people *everywhere*, so that Jewries outside of Israel can easily assimilate, while Israel itself becomes a nation like all other nations?

Those that ask the question may not share my view of Jewish peculiarness. They may use the word "peculiar" not in the classic sense which Jews once applied to themselves: a special people, a people with a distinguished destiny. They may equate it with "queer," "irritating," "incomprehensible," "unadaptable": above all, "maladjusted," as that word is used today by amateur psychoanalysts (that is, by most of the population), applying with the same force to a man who has genius and a man who has a clubfoot: "maladjusted" without regard to content and value, without regard to whether the maladjustment is creative or destructive, whether it is the man who ought to be changed or the society.

With this last concept of Jewish peculiarness, which makes Jewishness nothing more than a sociological disease, they are sure to favor the dissolution of the Jewish identity. And even if they accept my interpretation of Jewish peculiarness, they may heartily welcome the prospect of its extinction. They may say: "We are tired of highfalutin mystical visions, tired of being the carriers of the word of God. Let us have a homeland where the Jews will live a normal life and be a normal people; a people with a government of its own, with a flag, an army, and a navy; a people with its rich and poor, its respectable classes and its quota of criminals; and yes, its sports clubs and its Test Matches or World Series. Let those of us who are persecuted, or cannot adapt ourselves elsewhere, settle in the State of Israel; let the rest of us forget we are Jews. We are fed up with 'destiny.' "

At a first reading, these hopes and wishes may strike us as rather perverse. What an elaborate technique of personality-suicide! To set up a Jewish state with so much labor, at so much cost in idealism, blood, and money, only in order that Jews may cease to be Jews! But the perversity is not willed; it is inherent in the Jewish position. The suicide-seekers, many of whom helped to create the State of Israel, may misinterpret the will of Jewry, but they have a case.

If Jews could not find a more direct and less costly and laborious way of assimilating, it was because the world would not let them. For it is not enough for a people to want to assimilate; it must find an assimilator; it is not enough to want to be eaten; one must find someone with an appetite. And the Jews were not appetizing; they were "queer."

Even when their assimilation was welcomed in principle, it could not be carried out. One-time offers to receive them wholesale into the Christian Church were perhaps sincerely meant, but they were sociologically impracticable. The sudden conversion of all or most of the Jews would merely have created a "Jewish-Christian" people—a mass as unassimilable as the overtly Jewish people. The rate of solution of the new group in Christendom would not have been high enough to overcome the internal increase; and impatience on the part of non-Jewish Christians would further have retarded the process. In modern times the assimilation of the Jews has not always been welcomed; but where it has, this difficulty of tempo has at once appeared. As a simple illustration: Americans want the Jews to assimilate, but when Jews move into a Christian neighborhood, the Christians begin to take flight. The cry is: "Let them assimilate somewhere else!"

In pursuing the assimilationist program, then, the Jews had to be changed in three ways: they had to be made more acceptable, more palatable, and more digestible. Let us take these in reverse order.

If the indigestible core of the Jewish groups could be taken out and segregated in a Jewish homeland, the residues would become more assimilable. Assimilatory Jews did not see it that way at first; and therefore they were violently opposed to Zionism. But there were many Zionists, and leaders among them, who did see it that way from the beginning. Such Zionists, who forevisioned a transformation of the entire Jewish people, from A to Z, may be called Assimilationist-Zionists. Now that there is a Jewish state, most assimilating Jews who think at all about the Jewish question agree with the Assimilationist-Zionists.

The palatability and acceptableness of the Jews are interrelated problems. Jews have faults, and are to that extent unpalatable; they have a bad reputation, and are to that extent unacceptable. (We might roughly compare the reputation to the smell, the palatability to the taste.) However, their reputation is worse than they deserve (they themselves say), first, because they are labeled with faults they do not have; second, because the faults they have are contingent, not inherent. The program therefore calls both for propaganda and for curative measures. In both of these the Jewish homeland will play its part.

Certain defects the Jews are fairly ready to admit to outsiders (the defects they admit intramurally make up a kind of confessional which outsiders always misunderstand): that they have been uncreative middlemen and traders out of proportion to their numbers; that they have been aliens to the soil and its virtues. The Jews argue that the non-Jewish world is both right and wrong in disliking them for these features; right because the features are unlikable, wrong because the outside world is itself responsible for them. The Jews did not leave the land, in early medieval Europe, of their own accord; they did not of their own accord neglect the handicrafts. They were driven from the one, excluded from the other. With the above-mentioned defects go others: urban slickness or intellectuality, urban nervousness and rootlessness. Other defects commonly laid at their door the Jews justifiably deny: for instance, physical cowardice, inability to feel patriotism.

A Jewish homeland will, according to the view I am discussing, have both a propagandist and a curative value. The admitted defects will be shown to be the result of persecution, for the Jews will point to the Jewish homeland, with its healthy distribution on the soil and in the cities, in the crafts and professions. This will also encourage Jews elsewhere to leave the city for the field, the store for the factory. As to the groundless accusations of cowardice and lack of patriotic feeling, the Jews will point to the exploits of the Jewish army.

The argument was sound in theory but rather shaky in practical application. It neglected, first, to ask whether anti-Semites would look when Jews pointed. Second, it ignored the important difference between Jews who are torn up, or tear themselves up, from their old environment and go to a new one—the Jewish homeland—and Jews who remain where they are, or who only change their place of residence while still remaining in the Diaspora. The former can more easily be redistributed in their occupations, especially since numbers of them are ideologically prepared; the latter will find it difficult to struggle out of their old setting, especially since the continuation of anti-Jewish feeling will encourage the old impulse to stay together in large groups. On the whole, however, the argument sounded reasonable, and, backed by a little wishful thinking, found wide acceptance.

There are other Jewish characteristics, real or fancied, which cannot be classified as defects, but the possession of which might be considered inexpedient. Such would certainly be the Jewish peculiarness which I have called basic and characteristic; such, also, the high level of Jewish intelligence. There is, runs the argument, an excess of Jewish talent, and even of genius, in the world; there are too many top-rank scientists, jurists, mathematicians, and philosophers credited to the Jewish people. This provokes envy and distrust. Fewer Jewish Nobel Prize winners are what the Jews need; a Jewish Peace Prize winner makes life less peaceful for the Jews. A Jewish homeland would bring the Jews down to earth—literally; and everywhere in the world there would be fewer Jews in the colleges and professions; there would be more room for non-Jewish talent. A decrease in the Jewish role on the higher levels of civilizational activity would benefit the Jews everywhere.

223

I must caution the reader that the last paragraph is written soberly, not satirically. It represents the considered, or at least the frequently repeated, opinion of a large number of Jews. As against this, other Jews—of both the assimilationist and the anti-assimilationist schools—feel that they suffer from the "repression" of Jewish achievement. In their opinion not enough gentiles know that Einstein is a Jew, and out of a hundred who do, only one also knows that Ehrlich, Wilstätter, and Haber were also Jews. Freud is an Austrian and Bergson a Frenchman. We are robbed even of the half-Jew in Proust. Elaboration on this point is impossible here, also perhaps unnecessary. As men of genius Jews are automatically credited to the land of their birth rather than the people of their origin—we need only look them up in a standard encyclopedia to see the justice of the complaint. Thus, by an error of bookkeeping, or by deliberate falsification, the most creative people in the world is made to appear parasitic. In this argument one value of the Jewish state will be the undeniable stamp of locality, the non-removable trademark, which it will place on a large proportion of Jewish talent: "Made in Israel." For these Jews at least there will be no more stealing of credits.

Somehow this view is reconciled with the desire to demonstrate that the Jews are a "normal" people; which means, among other things, not insufferably over-gifted. It is further reconciled with a program of assimilation. Pride therefore struggles with expediency, as it might in a man who is suing a cardsharp, but is ashamed of looking too much of a fool.

What the Jewish assimilationists who opposed the creation of the Jewish state could not take into the reckoning was the effect that would be produced in *their* emotions both by the actual creation and by the manner of it. The return to life of a nation destroyed two thousand years ago is a kind of portent in history; it is something that the world has not seen before and is not likely to see again. One must be dull of soul indeed not to be moved by it. And again, the manner of the rebirth testified to such qualities of ability, imagination, and physical courage in Israel that the temptation to associate oneself with it was too much even for assimilationists.

Other factors had been subtly at work on assimilationist Jews. They had been shaken and sickened by the slaughter of Jews in Europe; many had contributed and still contribute generously to the rescue work and to the rehabilitation of the survivors. Rescue work and rehabilitation alike had been, and still are, focused on the Jewish homeland. Whatever their long-range views on Jewish survival, the assimilationist Jews had been warmed and impressed by their association with the Jewish state, in the making or made.

Let us grant that they did not look deeply; that they were carried away by the spectacular; that they did not see something far more impressive and significant in the long process of laying the foundations of the Jewish homeland than in the last, brilliant phase of the achievement of independence. During that long process the assimilationist anti-Zionists either stood aside (except toward the very end) or interposed obstacles, to the bewilderment of the Assimilationist-Zionists. For the latter believed they were entitled to expect help from all assimilationist Jews (and for that matter from anti-Semites, too!). It would be so much easier for the assimilating Jews to lose their Jewishness if numbers of their fellow Jews—the most Jewish, at that—went to Palestine; in other words, if there were fewer Jews around. But the Assimilationist-Zionists often contradicted themselves; they also said that the creation of a Jewish state would enhance the self-respect of *all* Jews, wherever they lived: their self-respect as Jews, be it noted. This, however, was the last thing that the assimilationist anti-Zionists wanted.

Even those Jews who, while worrying about the Jewish problem, still refuse to have anything to do with Israel—they are a small minority—are trapped in a paradox. They find themselves being identified with a Jewish majority that cannot suppress or disguise its pride in the Jewish state. They insistently proclaim that to them the Jewish state is just another foreign state, and that their attitude toward it is the same as that of all other Americans—or Englishmen, or Frenchmen. But that they should have to make these protestations when other Americans do not already sets them apart. Perhaps they want to say: "Israel is to us like any other foreign state, only more so." They might, from their own point of view, do better to keep quiet. True, they would still be identified as Jews by their fellow townsmen, for they still have their own temples, they are still segregated socially, they still take a suspiciously enthusiastic part in the combating of anti-Semitism; but at least the whole country would not always be hearing about them, and wondering.

Besides, to them Israel is not a foreign state like any other; it happens to be the one state the birth of which they fought tooth and nail, and over the existence of which they are inconsolable. Into the mouth of such a Jew an Israeli has put this brief lament: "For two thousand years the Jews have prayed for a homeland, and it had to happen to me!"

From this unhappy minority we may now turn back to the large number of assimilationist Jews who have come to terms with the Jewish state; and the most important thing to note is that *the old assimilationist anti-Zionists and the Assimilationist-Zionists have become identical*. They always were identical, in fact, as regards the ultimate objective, which was to dismantle the distinctive Jewish character everywhere; they only differed as to the method. One group believed that total assimilation could best be achieved through a Jewish homeland; the other group thought the suggestion self-defeating and was terrified by it. Now that there is a Jewish state, the argument as to the method is over; the unifying objective has come into its own.

But the position is still far from clear.

When assimilating Jews say: "We want to be like everyone else," they either assume that the world is uniform or else that they want to be like the majority of the rest of the world. But if they accept a special relationship of pride toward the Jewish state, they want to be like a *minority* of the rest of the world: in fact, they want to be one of the respected and respectable minorities, loyal citizens of foreign origin or ancestry with a kindly sentimental attachment to the old home country.

So, just as Irishmen and Poles and Frenchmen, wherever they live, are permitted to think affectionately of the land of their origin, so Jews shall be permitted to indulge a special regard for Israel. As Americans of Irish, Polish, and French descent are permitted to observe St. Patrick's Day and Kosciusko Day and Bastille Day, and are none the less ordinary Americans—or as nearly so as matters—so American Jews can observe Israeli or Jewish Independence Day and also be considered ordinary Americans.

There are, of course, conditions and limitations attached to the permission. If a war should range America on one side and Ireland, or Poland, or France on the other, the secondary affection is overridden; or it is so interpreted as to call for the defeat of "the old country" for its own good. So it will be with American Jews and Israel. Becoming thus one of the many standard and respectable minorities, they will know where they stand, and so will the world. They will be cleansed at last (they assume) not only of the defects already discussed, but of that stigma of indefinableness, ghostliness, historical homelessness which, they believe, has also contributed to their maladjustment.

This happy theme is based, alas, on an optical illusion. The American Jews (or the English, or the French) did not come from the State of Israel. Their association with it is grounded partly in a tradition of immense age, reaching into that monstrous past which is such an intolerable burden to the Jewish identity, and partly in very recent events and decisions. In respect of these recent events and decisions, the relation of the Jews to Israel is quite unlike that of the emigrant French to France, or of the emigrant Irishman to Ireland. Israel did not create the Jews, as France created the French, Ireland the Irish. On the contrary, it was the Jews of America, England, France, South Africa, South America, and so on, who created Israel. It is as though these Jews were saying to their neighbors: "You don't want to have in your midst a people of mysterious attributes and baffling identity? You want us to fall into the familiar pattern of immigrant minorities? You want us to have a country of recent origin to which we have a permissible attachment? Right: we've just created it."

It won't do. For the Israeli observances that American Jews may permit themselves, and in virtue of which they are now happily "like everyone else," are of a peculiar kind. They do not end with financial and political help to Israel, with the showing of the Israeli flag on festive occasions, with cheering the Israeli President or the Israeli representative on the U.N., and with observing Israeli Independence Day. To point the problem, we may well ask with regard to the last item: "Which is Israeli Independence Day? May 14 or the Passover? The most recent festival of national liberation or the oldest in our civilization?" Then one might go on: Are the universal Jewish festivals of Pentecost and of Booths

—and we might even include New Year and Atonement—purely religious in content? Is it to be regarded as a hangover of history, without repercussions in the present, that all Jews everywhere, in and out of Israel, observe these festivals simultaneously, without a single non-Jew participating anywhere?

Do what he will, the devotional Jew is tied to Israel and to the total past of the Jewish people with a bond quite different from that of the Irish-American with Ireland, or the Franco-American with France. This bond he can alter, loosen to the desired weakness, only by abandoning his religion, or by changing it into something unrecognizable, which comes to the same thing. If Israel and American Jewry both remain Jewish, and if Jewishness is what I have described it as being, a spirit transcending religious form, it is certainly idle to classify Jewish-American with Irish-American and Franco-American. Jews and Israelis then constitute a single people which has evolved a single destiny. That unity and that destiny must be denied by American Jewry if it wants to acquire the regulation, easily understood minority pattern. And even if Jewishness is only a form of worship, a set of rituals and prescriptions, *the exclusive cultivation of it by Jews, and, I must repeat, by Jews only, gives a special meaning to the word Jewish-American, separating it from Irish-American, Franco-American, and the like.*

Still, the obstacles may not be insuperable. Destiny or ritual, Jewishness may fade, in America, in Israel, and everywhere else. The identity called Jewish-American, meaning Israeli-American, may not be as transmissible through the generations as the identity called Jew. In time it will really fall into the class of Irish-American. The rest will be easy. For one of the reasons that create acceptability for immigrant minorities is the knowledge that they rarely last, as groups, more than two or three or four generations.

After that the very recollection of a non-American origin is lost, except among very distinguished families; and even if it is retained, embedded in a name or a family record, it is without force.

We may now review the hopes and beliefs of the Jewish assimilationists, Zionist or anti-Zionist. The State of Israel will have a wholesome effect on the world's attitude toward the Jews. It has, in fact, already done so. It has shown that Jews can fight like everyone else, till the soil like everyone else, administer a country, negotiate treaties, issue eulogies of democracy, send teams of athletes abroad—do all the things that normal folk do everywhere. Jews everywhere should *feel* normal. As time goes on, these external and internal effects will react on each other. As the world realizes that its bad opinion of Jews was based on error, anti-Semitism will diminish, and Jews, in turn, will feel it safe to scatter. They will also scatter out from their occupational concentrations, partly influenced by the example of Israel, partly influenced by their own progressive geographical diffusion. The *Wechselwirkung*, the cycle of effect and countereffect, will continue steadily, to the gratification of all parties concerned. Diffused geographically and occupationally, the Jews will stop crowding the colleges, professions, and Halls of Fame; the same effect will be produced in Israel, where the diffusion will be only occupational. Relieved from this pressure, the non-Jewish world will open its arms wider still. Stage by stage, in counterpoint, the ancient evil of anti-Semitism will shrink, the ancient identity of the Jew will fade. The Jewish connection with Israel will become feebler and feebler. In time the very name Jew will disappear, except as a remote historic echo, like Ammonite, Moabite, and Girgashite. There will be Israelis in Israel and, outside of Israel, a few families will display, with mild vainglory, genealogical tables linking them with the common ancestors of the Israelis. There will be no Jews; and, strangely enough, there will be no anti-Semitism.

The Zionist movement will have solved the Jewish problem, as was promised by the founder of the Zionist Organization, Theodor Herzl.

# CHAPTER XX

## *Amputation*

❀

A LESS radical forecast of the total Jewish future, by other Zionists, makes a sharp distinction between world Jewry and Israel, between the Diaspora (the dispersion, or scattered Jewish communities) and the homeland. In this view the Diaspora Jewries will cease to be Jewish, but Israel will not. In what sense Israel will remain Jewish is a matter for discussion; some think in ritualistic terms, some in social, some in intellectual. All have the feeling that it is impossible for so gifted a people to develop a homeland that will be nothing more than another Levantine state, another Lebanon or Iraq, and for that matter another "ordinary" country. Something of the ancient ardor will awaken again, and the new Israel will perhaps rival the old Judea in the importance of its contribution to civilization. Nevertheless, this high hope often goes hand in hand with an emphasis on "ordinary" forms, on the normal and respectable attributes of statehood, on protocol and parade—all the ego-tickling, blood-stirring, heart-warming gewgaws that Jews, as Jews, have so long been deprived of.

The Diaspora, however, is done for. As many Jews as possible must be drawn into the State of Israel; the gates must be open both for the persecuted and for those who, though they could manage in the Diaspora, are so strongly

Jewish that they want to live in a Jewish state. The remainder must be written off. They will continue to call themselves Jews for quite a long time, but with diminishing justification and in diminishing numbers. There are already Israelis who regard outside Jews as distant and somewhat degenerate relatives, useful financially and politically, but morally and culturally negligible. These Jews have a limited usefulness for Israel, and they should not be relied on too heavily. They have the *galut* or exile mentality or they would come to settle in Israel; and the exile mentality is the one thing that Israel cannot stand for. It was for the purpose of destroying the exile mentality in the Jewish people that Israel was created.

What Israel would do if several million American Jews evinced a strong desire to immigrate is seldom considered; but this is beside the point. They do not, and that is the end of the matter.

The above-described attitude toward Diaspora Jewry is not a new thing; it is familiar in Zionist discussion under the Hebrew name of *Sh'lilat ha-Galut*, the Negation of the Exile, or Diaspora. It has, however, wider implications than those so far mentioned.

"The Negation of the Diaspora" extends its concept backward through nearly two thousand years, and classifies the entire period of Jewish history—if it can be called that—since Hadrian's suppression of Bar Kochba's rebellion, or even since Titus's destruction of the Temple, as a negative phenomenon: something to be remembered, if at all, with horror and shame, but best forgotten. The persecutions, displacements, humiliations, and insults, the defenselessness, the psychological stigmata that defenselessness produces, the shifts and devices to which the defenseless were reduced, the overcompensations of impotence, the mendicancy for the simple right to live, the toadying to the powerful, the successive acquisitions of different languages, generation after generation, the adaptations to a landless and craftless economy, the apologies and petitions, the martyrdoms—all of it, all of it, must be erased from the memory. It is a disgrace to have to reflect on such things, a crime to force them on the attention of the young. Let the gap between the fall of Judea and the proclamation of the State of Israel be closed. Let the nightmare disappear from the national memory.

And in order that it may disappear the sooner and the more completely, let the Jews of the Diaspora, the unrebellious heirs of the ignominious tradition, the memorializers and perpetuators of it, the slavish and unredeemable victims of it, make their peace with the non-Jewish world as fast as they can, and be swallowed up. A new and glorious chapter is opening for the Jewish nation in the land of its first triumphs; let no shadow be cast upon it by the dragged-out existence of Jewries of the exile, with their endless pleas for tolerance, their interminable explanations of what is Jewish and what is not Jewish, their dreary and revolting protestations of good citizenship and loyalty, their Anti-Defamation Leagues, their Better-Understanding Committees, and their Jewish-Christian Goodwill Conferences and prizes.

This furious rejection of two out of the three or four millennia of Jewish existence occurred in Zionist propaganda from the beginning; it has increased in intensity with the proclamation of the Jewish state. But it was not the Zionists alone who dwelt on the wretchedness and squalor of Jewish life in the Diaspora, and particularly in eastern Europe—the greatest of recent Jewish centers. There was a general literature of Jewish self-disgust in the nineteenth century, and the Zionists drew heavily on it, pointing the moral in the direction of a Jewish homeland. Other writers dwelt on the hope of general human improvement, in which the Jew would get his chance to develop normally.

The more one studies Jewish exile history, the more difficult becomes this total and contemptuous rejection. The episode of Babylonian Jewry, for example: the Babylonian Talmud, which overshadows in importance the Jerusalem Talmud, and has been a treasury of folklore, history, law, and ethics to world Jewry, cannot have been produced by the crushed and repulsive kind of life which the excited Negator of the Diaspora draws for himself; or the episode of Spanish Jewry under the Arabs, or of north African and east Arabian Jewries: Maimonides and Yehudah ha-Levi and ibn Gabirol, the Jewish viziers and physicians, as well as the philosophers and poets. There is something to be remembered with more than pity and horror in the Jewish life of medieval northern Europe, which produced such massive figures as Rashi and Rabbenu Gershom and Meir of Rothenburg. It is fantastic to speak of the most recent phase of Jewish exile history, the Yiddish-speaking episode in Jewish civilization, as a negative thing. Chassidism was one of the greatest religious episodes in world history; Yiddish is a lovely and lovable language; the associations with the Talmudic academy towns of Mir and Zhitomir and Volozhin are exalted and tender, as well as unhappy. And is my childhood environment something to be remembered with distaste?

Besides, half the miracle of the rebirth of Israel disappears if the two-thousand-year interval is closed up. If a national reawakening after two thousand years is a miracle, is not a two-thousand-year vigil of faithfulness also a miracle— and perhaps the greater one? And it was not merely an immobile vigil: Jewish history, or Jewish life, was not suspended. The productivity of the Jewish people in the fields of moral, legal, and religious literature (to take only the bookish side) during the vigil is downright incredible. One would have thought that the exertion of sheer physical survival would leave nothing over for spiritual adventure, and that under these circumstances a people could survive only if all its faculties were devoted to the practicalities of day-to-day existence. But the life of the Jewish people in exile makes one think of some fabulous wandering scholar, who turns up in a dozen countries, spends a few years here, a few months there, now finds a patron, now starves obscurely, now is beaten up and expelled by the police, or languishes in prison and, when he dies, leaves behind him an enormous body of important work; so that we ask, in bewilderment: "How and when could he have done it? Without peace of mind, without a decent period of stability, without acknowledgment and encouragement—how, when, and, above all, *why*?"

I am less than a tyro in the literature of the Jewish people. I have been a constant reader of the Bible, but I have only dipped into the Mishnah and into the Talmud—the latter by way of a digest of its non-legalistic sections. I have read in some of the medievalists, in Bachya ibn Pakudah, in Solomon ibn Gabirol, and in Yehudah ha-Levi; but far from exhaustively. I have taken a few samplings from the master-thinkers and commentators, from Maimonides and Rashi. I have looked into the Hebrew modernizers, know something about the Hebrew literature that was the swan-song of European Jewry, and somewhat more of the Yiddish aspect (a cosmos in itself) of our history. I have tasted of the Chassidic writings and maintain sporadic contacts with the latest Hebrew literature. But it is nothing. One has only to go through Zinberg's *History of Jewish Literature*, in Yiddish (in seven volumes, and awaiting translation), and Gershom Scholem's *Major Trends in Jewish Mysticism* (this is available in English, and is a great book), to get a glimpse of the vast libraries that the Jews in exile have produced in their un-ending search, started off by the Bible, for the true way of life. How, then, can an informed and thinking Jew desire to forget the exile? Where, in known human history, will he find a comparable experience and achievement?

But of course an Israeli who wants to see his country and his people "normalized"— that is, regularized and stand-ardized into a nation like all other nations—though a very brilliant example—will also want to forget anything in Jewish history which is so extraordinary as to border on the freakish. He will also want to forget the Jewish spiritual output of the exile because it excludes, as pagan, the concept of the standardized nation, and ignores completely the gal-lant, sporting, and combative view of life. He should, finally, and most importantly, forget the Bible. This he cannot do, because of its prestige. But he can make it a purely Sabbath-day salutation; *and in this, above all, he will have become part of a standardized nation.*

As a more limited concept, Negation of the Diaspora ap-plies only to the future. It denies that the miracle of survival in an alien environment can continue for world Jewry; and it offers several reasons. To begin with, the most powerful mundane drive in the Jewish ritual, its practical motif, had as its purpose the rebuilding of the Jewish homeland. This purpose fulfilled, the remaining motifs, outside of Israel, are not compelling enough to sustain a people in the face of all the discouragements of dispersion. Again, the cultural pressures and demands of modern states have become so powerful that we can no longer draw conclusions from the past; modern universal education, the penetration of the home by books, the press, and, latterly, the radio, has cut down to nothing the survival chances of cultural minorities without a territory and local cultural autonomy. Third, the stubbornly Jewish Jews will sooner or later migrate to Israel; with every such withdrawal the Diaspora communities will lose a little of their remaining vitality.

A reason of a different character, of frightful and shameful origin, has been added by some Negators of the Diaspora in the last decade or so: the possibility, and for some even the likelihood, that what happened to six million Jews of Europe will happen to Jewish communities elsewhere—America not excluded.

A whole world of argument opens up here, and I will not enter into it beyond saying that this world of argument is insane through and through. For if that should happen in America which happened in Germany, the world would be in dissolution. This is not Negation of the Diaspora; it is negation of the human species and belongs to another order of discussion. Still, we may observe in this connection that it is easier for the world to be optimistic on behalf of the Jews than it is for the survivors of the great massacre; and it is a little inhuman to be impatient with Jews for not recovering so quickly and so completely from the Hitler episode.

A stronger point is made by the Negators of the Diaspora in regard to Russia. There the soul of the Jewish people is being systematically strangled. Zionism has always been, and still is, illegal in Russia. The suppression of Zionism was accompanied by fraudulent offers of Jewish national centers (at that, for Russian Jews only) in the Crimea and Birobidjan; their real purpose was not to create Jewish cultural-national centers, but to provide Jewish communists outside of Russia with propaganda based on "Jewish interests," and to weaken the Zionist movement. In 1947 the Russians, after having crippled the Zionist movement for three decades by cutting off Russian Jewry from Palestine and world Jewry, supported, in the United Nations, the motion for the creation (more properly, as we shall see, the *recognition*) of a Jewish state. Subsequently Russian policy again became negative. In any case, there was never a question of legalizing Zionism in Russia, or of permitting the departure of such Jews—there are tens of thousands of them—as are still attracted by the idea of a Jewish homeland.

There was a time when Russian Jewry was the great reservoir of Zionist strength. The foundations of Israel were laid largely by Russian Jews; and but for the Bolshevik revolution, the Jewish state would have been created in half the time. Russian Jewry is no longer a factor on the world Jewish scene. Weakened and discouraged in its Jewishness by a mixture of isolation, propaganda, and cultural repression, it has been bribed and thrust into assimilation. That which has happened in Russia, say the Negators of the Diaspora, can happen elsewhere, under different economic and political conditions.

It can, of course. One of the purposes of the Zionist movement, as I shall argue in the next chapter, was in fact to provide a new technique for Jewish survival in the Diaspora, answering to the new circumstances. For the Negators of the Diaspora have always been a minority in Zionism, though not a negligible one. Now they also have a new generation in Israel, young people who have never known the exile, and who are not yet linked with Diaspora Jewry by a common Jewish outlook. Such have said to me, more than once: "*Mah lanu ha-Galut*—what is Diaspora Jewry to us?" They meant: "If Diaspora Jews are like us, they will come here; if they are not, what have we to do with them?"

That which we foresee, we often tend to bring about, either by resignation or by a desire to adapt ourselves in advance to the "inevitable." The danger of the split in the Jewish world—Diaspora and Israel—is a real and urgent

one; therefore the philosophy of the Negation of the Diaspora must be examined and understood. It is not the less
real for being falsely formulated; for actually it is only another aspect of a total Assimilationist-Zionist program. For
a *Jewish* Israel, in the sense I have given Judaism, cannot
have a negative or indifferent attitude toward the existence
of Jewish thought and feeling anywhere; only an Israel that
misuses the word "Jewish" can retreat from the concept of
the Jews as a world people.

As in many other areas of Jewish thought and feeling, we
have here also an echo of a general, world-wide change of
heart: in this instance, toward the question of national
minorities. Because they have been misused, especially in
the twentieth century, for the purpose of extending nationalist claims, minorities are generally regarded as dangerous
abnormalities. Wherever possible, they should be liquidated
by absorption into the mother country (this is the "liberal"
solution); in this fashion the frictions, frequently of a border
character, between nation and nation will be diminished.
In particular, the failure of the Versailles minority-rights
treaties has helped discredit the theory of permanent minority groups.

But the forced withdrawal or removal of minority groups
into the mother country is a concession to the totalitarian
concept of the state. *Minority groups are positive phenomena by
nature.* They are the transitional areas of common understanding between nations. Often bilingual, they can be
interpreters, in the narrow and wider senses. The misuse of
them for international intrigue, which tempts us to ask for
their liquidation, blinds us to their normal function in a
non-totalitarian world. The belief that the elimination of
minority groups, and the more rigid compartmentalizing of
the world which would result from it, will make for more
peaceful relations is a tragic error. Behind their more per-

fected barriers the nations will only accumulate more rapidly, to the explosion point, their charges of egotism, provincialism, and suspicion. A world that cannot make affirmative use of its minorities cannot live in peace.

# CHAPTER XXI

# Jewish Zionism

❈

THE longing for the "Return" which existed in the Jewish masses was a complex thing. Superficially one would have said that its substance was threefold: first, the longing for the security of a permanent home; second, the longing for political self-determination, partly in connection with the first element, security, and partly in connection with: third, the longing for the self-respect that springs from the exercise of the standard national functions. Outside of these three "real" elements, everything was presumably sentimental and inessential.

Thus Herzl, when he first conceived the idea of the Jewish state, did not even think of Palestine; that was a sentimentality. But thus it also came about that when, in 1903, England offered Uganda to the Zionists, it was the Russian Jews, then the most persecuted and humiliated group, who predominantly rejected it. *But they were the most Jewish of the Jews.* It was the western Jews, the least persecuted Jews, who predominantly favored it. *But they were the least Jewish of the Jews.*

Actually the real substance of the longing for the Return was the desire to remain Jewish! *Political self-determination, assumption of the standard national functions, were secondary and instrumental.* To the extent that they were sought for themselves, *they* were the sentimentalities. Even security, if divorced from Jewishness, did not attract the masses. Had it done, they would have accepted Uganda. More properly, had it done, they would not have been in existence to need Uganda.

Contrary to Herzl's theory, the *Judennot*, the Jewish need, did not provide the motive power of Zionism. It was the *Judenwille*, the Jewish will, or, better, the will to be Jewish.

Yet fifty years ago, and even twenty-five years ago, the Jewish masses were not Zionistically activated, except in Russia. Only a minority—to be sure, the effective minority —had plunged whole-heartedly into the movement. My childhood environment, Jewish through and through, stood off. The longing for the Return was real; it colored every aspect and corner of the Jewish consciousness; but it lacked faith in its realizability; it was paralyzed by the inertia of centuries; it was possessed of an ancient fear—a very reasonable one, as it happens—of "trying to force the hand of God," *lidchok et ha-ketz*. And if we look back through the centuries of the exile, we shall see that all previous attempts at a Return had in fact been premature. This not because they failed, but because an objective estimate of conditions shows that they were doomed to failure.

Herzl's incomparable service to the Zionist movement was his contribution to the breaking of the paralysis. Like all significant historical figures, he had to appear at the right time, and the time was right. Like most significant historical figures, he helped set in motion forces he did not understand, and died before he could see the effect of his contribution. His reward is the Herzl cult, a falsification of his meaning in Jewish history. Seldom has a great man been more unfortunate in his personal life and in his immortality.

The rightness of the time for Herzl's self-immolation and the activation of the Jewish masses must be seen under two

aspects. First, the conditions for the re-creation of the Jewish state were emerging with the decay of the Turkish Empire and the creation of a partial vacuum in the near east.
Others than Jews and Zionists could see that, too. Second,
the modern conditions of Jewish Diaspora life had become
such that it needed a new technique of survival. It was no
longer possible to resist the pressures of the western world
(I speak of the time when Russia was included) without a
Jewish homeland in Palestine as the center of Jewish self-
expression.

I am not referring now to the physical pressures of nine-
teenth-century anti-Semitism, and not even to its hideous
fruition in the twentieth century. I am referring to aspects
of Jewish life already mentioned, those aspects which have
been seized upon by the Negators of the Diaspora. They
may be summed up under one heading: the impending
dissolution of the Jewish *folk* life in the communities through
the world.

There was a time when it was fashionable to sneer at
Jews who wanted to reconstitute a ghetto; and the fashion
has not wholly disappeared today. When we remember that
it was German Jews who set the fashion, and that German
civilization was the model held up before the ghetto Jews,
we cannot help wondering at the bitter ingenuity of history.
Not that the sardonic lesson—still unlearned by a considerable number of idiots—depends entirely on this contrast.
The world at large has not quite justified itself; it was not
in the ghetto that the atomic bomb and bacteriological warfare were born. But comparative merits have nothing to do
with the case; the ghetto is dead, and cannot be revived;
the time of Jewish *folk*-communities throughout the world
is gone, never to return.

Compact bodies of Jews living a life apart, speaking predominantly a language of their own, subject only to periph-

eral contacts with the outside world, no longer exist and cannot be re-created. Such bodies were formerly the carriers of the Jewish spirit in the Diaspora. They rose successively in Babylonia, in Spain, in northern Europe, in eastern Europe, and, already in weakened form, in America; and from each national Diaspora center, life streamed to the others. They were so massive, or so cohesive, that they could assimilate external cultural material into themselves, through the periphery, turning it to their own use. They could eat as well as be eaten. But long before the most recent phases of mass attack on the body and spirit of the Jewish people, such centers were beginning to dissolve. A threat never faced before had risen for world Jewry; and in this respect the diagnosis of the Negators of the Diaspora was wholly correct.

But their prognosis was wholly incorrect. Zionism arose, and became activated, partly because the Jewish people took alarm at the new situation. The purpose of the Jewish homeland was not directed simply at the ingathering of the homeless and the persecuted; it was never intended, either, to withdraw the Jewish people in its entirety from the Diaspora; still less was it proposed to abandon the Diaspora communities to their spiritual fate; *the Jewish homeland was projected by world Jewry for the maintenance of world Judaism.*

This last sentence is an extreme formulation, but it must be made thus, even if it must later be modified, in order to arrest the attention. The objection immediately arises: "But it is obvious that the great drive for the Jewish homeland began only with the Hitler time. There were less than two hundred thousand Jews in Palestine in 1930, and fifty years had already elapsed since the coming of the first modern pioneers. In 1949 there were a million Jews in Palestine, or Israel, of whom a third had entered in the last year and a half. The Jewish state was made possible by sheer Jewish need, then, not by an idealistic longing for the preservation of Judaism. The outpouring of financial and political support by world Jewry, and particularly by American Jewry, the five- to ten-fold increase in Zionist membership, were consequences of a direct physical threat to one part of Jewry and a humanitarian response by another part; a prophetic spiritual program had nothing to do with it. The bulk of that support, and of that new membership, was not drawn from specifically Jewish masses, such as you describe; you have just stated that large numbers of assimilationist Jews co-operated latterly in the creation of the Jewish state. Before them, according to your account, there were Assimilationist-Zionists in the movement. Herzl himself, the most important individual figure in Zionism, was not Jewishly Jewish. How can it possibly be said that the Jewish homeland was created by world Jewry for the maintenance of world Judaism?"

The answer lies in the perspective. The Jewishly Jewish masses were mostly inert fifty years ago, and Herzl did more than any other single person to set them in motion. But it was the Jewishly Jewish masses that were set in motion, not the assimilated and semi-assimilated Jews. Herzl's appeal to the latter was ineffectual. Nor must we underrate the Zionist activism that already existed before the coming of Herzl. Distilling out of the inertly Jewish masses of eastern Europe, it was a concentrate of Jewish purpose, of Jewishly Jewish purpose. It made grateful use of Herzl, but did not surrender to him. As the Assimilationist-Zionist element, largely but not wholly of western origin, increased, the Jewish-Zionist element reacted strongly, and remained in control. The spirit that pervaded the crystallizing Jewish homeland was Jewishly Jewish; the combative-nationalist concepts played no significant part in it; the symbolism of the pagan life and of pagan statism, the love of parades, flags, contests, and mob demonstrations, the fierce competitive thrill, individual or sublimated into the national group—all these one had to seek in a minority. And this minority was not creative; to put it quite bluntly, it did not do any real work.

It did not want to do any real work. Its political philosophy was opposed to practical construction in Palestine before "the right political conditions" had been created. It was forever seeking effective world recognition of a Jewish state *as a principle* before it would begin contributing to a Jewish state *as a substance*. Such was the rationalization. But the rationalization was interpenetrated with the emotional frivolity of statism as a principle instead of an instrument, so that the energies of the Assimilationist-Zionists were exhausted in demonstration and psychic indulgence, leaving nothing over for craftsmanship. So they did not build the colonies and the co-operatives; they did not create the *Histadrut* (the labor union of Palestine); they did not lay the foundations of the Jewish state-in-the-making; they did not put their stamp on the *Yishuv* (the pre-state Jewish community of Palestine). Even their support of the world-Jewish funds for the building of Palestine was weak and irregular; and at one point they set up a rival World Zionist Organization, which confused world Jewry without adding anything to the tangible or spiritual assets of Palestine.

The work was done by the representative elements of the Jewishly Jewish masses, by the activated section of that Jewry which wanted a Jewish state for, among other things, the maintenance of world Judaism. Theirs was the stamp that was placed on the entire organism. The question today is not in regard to this historical fact; it is whether, in the cataclysm of the last ten years, forces have not been released which will obliterate this stamp. This, again, is a reformulation of the question: Will the creation of the State of Israel

help to perpetuate the Jewish people, or facilitate its liquidation?

It is not at all easy to get a composite picture of what
world Jewry projected for itself and for the Jewish state as
its spiritual mainstay in the new age. If a Jewish folk life
had become impossible in the Diaspora, was it possible to
construct one in Palestine? Can a folk life be *constructed*? Is
not the essence and virtue of a folk life its anonymous and
undirected growth? Programmatic folkism sounds as silly
as sophisticated medievalism. There was, indeed, one Jewish writer who said that the national ideal will have been
realized in Palestine when its Jewish population will contain its proper proportion of Hebrew-speaking illiterates.
This is intellectual affectation with a vengeance. One can
almost imagine the appointment of a Committee for the
Creation and Maintenance of the Natively Shrewd and
Unschooled Classes.

The writer just quoted was, however, not in the main
stream of thought. Whatever the confused longings of the
Jewish masses with regard to the Jewish state-to-be, a
hankering after creative illiteracy was not among them.
They wanted a farmer class, but not peasants; a working
class, but neither economic nor intellectual slums. And the
practical work in Palestine reflected this choice clearly. The
core of the pioneer movement, from the 1880's on, consisted
of intellectualized persons; the hunger for a return to the
soil did not undermine the insistence on high educational
standards; and there were times when the budget for schools
exceeded the budget for colonization—to the bewilderment
of neutral observers and the disgust of Assimilationist-
Zionists. "Is this," the latter asked, "the way to build a
state? Is it from these spiritual *shlimihls* that you expect the
political salvation of the Jewish people?"

For that matter, the folkism of the spiritually self-subsistent Jewish communities of the Diaspora was of a peculiar kind. Its base was not the soil, but an idea, or set of ideas; Yiddish, for instance, is extremely poor in nature terminology, extremely rich in emotional and intellectual idioms. The true technical illiteracy of earth-bound masses was practically unknown among the Jews; even the relative illiteracy was "spoiled" by a widespread hankering for book-learning. Yet it could be called folkism in the sense that its substance was transmitted anonymously and informally in the masses by oral tradition more than by books, being interwoven inextricably with the ordinary business of living. This folkism, with its rejection of the competitive ideal of man, its self-conscious fixation on ideas, its Palestino-centric memories, projected the rebuilding of the Jewish state (doing very little about it at first) as the reply to the threat of new conditions. What it projected could not, in fact, be grounded in the kind of folkism which was alien to it: that is, of a peasantry without a taste for books; of masses untouched by the intellectual activities of the élite; of a broad base of instinctual living which feeds and renews a sophisticated group at the top without being fed and renewed by it in turn.

What, then, did this Zionism mean, what did it make for? With or without formulation, it "had in mind" a world-Jewish people which lacked the usual folk element either in the Jewish state-to-be or outside of it. With formulation in the case of Achad Ha-am and his school; without formulation in those who were not bookish enough to read him. The world was becoming such that Jewish folk groups could not continue on their own momentum; and the Jewish state that was dreamed of could not artificially give itself a folk basis. The survival of Judaism therefore depended on a change of plane: Jewish values could henceforth be carried only in forms, symbols, and ideas that were systematically and consciously cultivated. And even this concept, which sounds so artificial and improbable, was already inherent in the kind of unearthly folkism which characterized Diaspora Jewries.

A people of philosophers! This description of the Jews has been attributed to Aristotle. We need not cringe before the description; and if we find the word too portentous, let us say: a thinking people. Even this notion strikes terror into the hearts of those who keep their eyes fixed on other nations, and whose program is—to borrow a recently coined political phrase—"me-too-ism." But it is no longer possible to think of being Jewish without a solid Jewish education, without a deliberate and alert yea-saying to Jewish moral and intellectual creation.

All the inverted snobbery of upper-class worship of the folk will rise up at the foregoing picture. "Give us our folksy masses or we perish!" "What a monstrosity of a people!" Inherent in this reaction is the feeling that the enjoyment of intellectual values is the privilege of the few, for whose benefit obscure and lovable masses must, in blind subjection to forces greater than they know, produce patterns that only the refined can truly relish. And not far from it is the spirit of the Nazi who said: "Whenever I hear the word 'culture' I reach for my revolver." Opposed to it is the tremendous utterance: "Ye shall be unto me a kingdom of priests."

One might, however, ask reasonably: "Having gone so far, why not go a little farther? Why not achieve complete liberation from the earth-bound and learn to perpetuate Judaism without a Jewish state?" The question was, in fact, asked challengingly by Jews who called themselves Diaspora nationalists, of whom the most consistent spokesman was the historian Simon Dubnow. They believed that the Jews had demonstrated a unique principle: they were teaching the world how a people incorporating a culture could survive without the accounterments of territory, government, army, navy, or internal legal compulsions. They believed that the demonstration could continue indefinitely, despite the increased pressure and penetration of the modern world.

They underestimated, even forty or fifty years ago, the solvent properties of the new organization of education; they certainly did not foresee the implacability of the new nationalism. They put their trust in treaties for the safeguarding of minority cultural autonomy; and even if these treaties had been faithfully observed—as faithfully, that is, as they could be technically—which they were not, the propaganda for national-cultural conformity, directed continuously at what radio executives call "a captive audience," was developing into something mankind has not known before. But the Diaspora Nationalists, too, were "folkists" of a special kind. They too were—for the most part—Jewishly Jewish; and though they gave Yiddish the preference over Hebrew, they did not think of Jewish peasant classes to be created in a primitive mold, and of a Jewish proletariat without intellectual aspirations.

Now that Zionless Diaspora Nationalism is no longer a real force in Jewish life, we must ask: What exactly did the Jewishly Zionistic masses feel that a Jewish state would do for them—for those of them who did not go to live there? What help would it give them in the struggle to remain Jewishly Jewish?

Let us observe first that merely to participate in the creation of a Jewish state, a Jewishly Jewish state, was already a unique response to the new pressures. Zangwill once criticized the Zionist movement because it had presumably been intended to end the exile and had actually given Jewish survival in the exile a new lease of life. Zangwill struggled from 1904 to 1917 to shift Jewish public opinion to Territorialism—that is, the acceptance of another center than Palestine for the new Jewish homeland. What was paradoxical to Zangwill was straightforward, programmatic cause and effect to Jewishly orientated Zionists. The effort to incorporate the Jewish philosophy of life in a Jewish community refreshed by contact with the center of Jewish origins already slowed up the dissolution of the Jewish communities elsewhere. That central Jewish community, Hebrew-speaking, deeply influenced in its emergent structure by the non-competitive spirit, offered some assurance to Jews of the Diaspora that their adherence to the Jewish spirit was not just talk; it was translating itself into form; it was becoming objectively visible—that is, outsiders too could see it. The Jewish spirit, then, was not a hallucination; it had its own craftsmanship of life.

The hope for the later time was: a continuous interchange between the Diaspora and the Jewish state, a continuous consultation of each other on practical matters, on the most effective way of perpetuating Judaism with the help of new instrumentalities of form. The song that pioneers sang in Palestine: "We have come here to build and to be built," could have been sung by those who entered the Zionist movement in the Jewish spirit. It was not to be a folk relationship between the Diaspora and Palestine, but a partnership on another level. It was not conceived that the Jewish state would ever regard itself as completed, a thing-in-itself; for the effect of the Jewish state on the Diaspora Jewries was one of its attributes. Such was the reconstruction of Jewish life which, it was hoped, would replace the folkist instrument of the past.

This philosophy was caricatured by some Zionists who seemed to think that the Jewish state would take over their obligation to be Jewish. They consigned Jews to live a Jewish life in Palestine "for our account." In Palestine Jews would do the praying and Hebraizing, and practice the social justice, which the Jews in the Diaspora had not the time or inclination for. They would point to the Jewish state and say to the world: "Do not judge us by what you see here. Look over there to see us as we really are." Palestine as the better self of world Jewry, as its Sabbath-day exhibition, was not Zionism. It was only a Jewish version of an endowment fund for the singing of Masses.

Now it is easier to understand why the Zionist movement insisted so obstinately on Hebrew as the necessary language of the new Jewish state, even though most of the Hebrew-speaking leaders (and even writers!), themselves a minority, were more at home in Yiddish. The last national language of the Jews in Palestine was not Hebrew; it was Aramaic! And we must reflect with wonder that if the Jews had never been driven out of Palestine, the Hebrew language would perhaps never have been revived for the masses. On the other hand, fifty years ago the prospect of a revived Hebrew language, current outside scholarly circles, looked even more improbable than it had done two thousand years ago in the Second Jewish Commonwealth. The Zionists achieved the climax in absurdity and impracticality when, having piled on the Ossa of occupational self-retraining the Pelion of refructifying desert Palestine, they completed the dizzy structure by proposing the revival of the Hebrew language. They proposed, in short—and to change the figure—to pull themselves up by their own bootstraps without having either boots or straps. What inspired them to this Munchausen extravaganza, and how did they make good on it?

It is here that I must return to the thesis that it is utterly impossible to make sense of the Zionist movement if one leaves out of account the Bible and its textural identification with Jewish life. Jewish Zionism cannot be accounted for—as so many Jews think it can—as an intelligible, rationalist, socio-political phenomenon, a mass manifestation of the simple instinct of physical self-preservation. Were it that, the Jews would not have chosen desolate Palestine for colonization; having committed that folly, they would not have added to their other burdens their self-re-education into Hebrew. Yiddish, a highly attractive and adequate language, was spoken by the vast majority of the *Chalutzim* (pioneers). When we are told that Hebrew was chosen by the Zionists because it offered a neutral base for unification of Yiddish-speaking and non-Yiddish-speaking pioneers, we are asked to accept a secondary advantage as the explanation of a major achievement. Besides, it is no explanation at all. One does not "choose" a language for a people. The return to Hebrew, a difficult, not to say tormenting, as well as laborious self-transformation, was part of the organic wholeness of Jewish Zionism. The Biblical fixation which made for the non-combative vision of life, which molded the Jews generally, demanded Palestine—and Hebrew. To ignore one demand was to invalidate the other.

There have been millions of Jews without the Biblical fixation, without the non-combative vision; they have always disappeared from Jewish life. Others of their kind have replaced them: *they* have disappeared. But there have also been millions of Jews who have been Jewishly Jewish without being able to speak Hebrew; though in all such masses—including those of the Second Commonwealth— there was a living contact with the language. Hebrew was always the language of prayer; a rich admixture of Hebrew words crept into Yiddish and the other Diaspora languages of the Jews; Hebrew and Aramaic are nearer to each other than French and Italian. I have insisted that my Yiddish-speaking childhood environment was Jewishly Jewish; the *Chalutzim*, Yiddish-speaking at first, were certainly so. But the longing for the Return, and for its activation as the great countermove to the threat of modern conditions, was a longing for the first sources—Palestine, the Bible, Hebrew —as the maximum safeguards. Quite possibly, if the Jews had never known exile, but had remained Jewishly Jewish in Palestine till this day, they could have done well with Aramaic. The maximum threat of the Diaspora called forth the maximum organic response. Yiddish was a beloved language among both pioneers and Zionist leaders; but a living-together of the Jewish state and the Diaspora called for Hebrew. There were millions of Jews who would not learn Yiddish, because it had no status outside its own circle; many of them would, however, learn Hebrew.

Not that Hebrew would ever become, in the Diaspora, what Yiddish was once; but it would have the double advantage of Biblical ritual and modern applicability. That it must always be, in the Diaspora, an additional and not a primary language, a language learned specially, a deliberate, disciplined acquisition, a sign of culture, is clear. This, however, is increasingly true of Yiddish, which has not the double advantage of Hebrew. Yiddish is becoming more and more a pidgin language among the masses, or else the possession of cultured classes. The "YIVO" (Yiddish Cultural Institute) is actually a learned society, and its attention is focused on the past. Its excellent publications will no doubt prolong the life of Yiddish, and they should be encouraged for that reason; if Yiddish must pass away, let the end be delayed as affectionately as possible, and the necessary preference for Hebrew must not be interpreted as a rejection of Yiddish. But there is simply no comparison between their future roles in the preservation of Judaism. The submission to the painful and artificial revival of Hebrew shows how profound the demand for it was. And the increasing study of Hebrew throughout the Jewish world shows two things: the demand was rooted in a still deeper demand for the preservation of world Judaism; and it did not err as to results.

The re-creation of a Jewish state as an instrument for the preservation of world Judaism is not a new thing in Jewish history. (Hardly anything is.) Despite the poignant prophecies in Isaiah and elsewhere of the complete ingathering of the Jewish people after the first destruction, more Jews remained out of Palestine than returned to it. A remarkable feature in the creation of the Second Commonwealth is the role in it of Babylonian Jewry. When, as I have described in Book Two, the Palestinian colony founded by Zerubbabel (leader of the Return) was falling into decay, Babylonian Jewish leaders, Ezra and Nehemiah, came to its rescue. Judaism was far stronger in Babylon, in Ezra's day, than it was in Palestine. Similarly, it was far stronger in Russia in Herzl's day than it was in Palestine, fifty-odd years ago. What made Ezra and Nehemiah feel so deeply that a Jewish National Home had to be re-created in Palestine after two generations had made such a failure of it? Why could not their own powerful Jewish community become the guarantor of Judaism?

The standard Jewish historians unite in telling us that Judaism became a "universal" non-nationalist concept in Babylonia. There, detached from the parochialism of a native land, the Jews first realized their spiritual destiny. It may be so. But it was Babylonian Jewry that sent the first contingent of forty thousand, under Zerubbabel, to rebuild the Jewish state; and some sixty years later sent the second, and more successful, contingent to retrieve the failure of the first.

From the work of the second contingent issued the Second Jewish Commonwealth; and this second contingent, removed from the first by the space of two generations, differed greatly from it in spiritual composition, motive, and outlook. Of the first contingent, Zerubbabel's, it is written that it contained numbers who had lived in Palestine before the expulsion by Nebuchadnezzar; old men who saw the walls of the second Temple rising, wept, remembering the first. Of that original forty thousand, we may say that they were drawn to Palestine by sheer homesickness; and, significantly enough, they lacked the character to found a Jewish state by themselves. But Ezra's and Nehemiah's companions were, like themselves, already grandchildren or great-grandchildren of Babylon, and they were drawn to Palestine by a more powerful impulse. It was not homesickness; neither was it philanthropy and humanitarianism; it had nothing to do with refugees; it did not patronize "our unfortunate brethren"; it came to place upon them an immense burden, and to co-operate with them in the setting up of an instrument for the preservation of Judaism; or, more correctly, *the* instrument.

But the Diaspora was not liquidated; and we must note that from the time of the Babylonian exile, and throughout the Second Jewish Commonwealth, there were more Jews in the Diaspora than in Palestine. But though living in Palestine was always considered meritorious, there was no propaganda for a total return as long as the state existed, and there was certainly no intimation that remaining outside of Palestine was a forfeiture or even a diminution of one's Jewishness. The Jewish state was not a self-justifying thing; it had a higher purpose than itself.

Six centuries after Ezra and Nehemiah, the Second Jewish Commonwealth was completely destroyed, and Babylonian Jewry, which in the interim had drawn sustenance from Palestine, emerged once more, to be a sustenance for succeeding generations to world Judaism. Could Babylonian Jewry have thus survived, and thus played a great role a second time, if there had not been a Jewish state in Palestine in between, if there had been no Hasideans, no Pharisees, no Mishnah (still uncodified, to be sure)? No one can answer this "if" of history, but the mere possibility that the answer might be No should be enough to give us our perspective.

In the thirty-five to forty centuries of known and surmisable Jewish history, it is an idea or an attitude toward life that has been the concern of the Jewish people; no arbitrary idea, no mere variant on current and popular ways of life, but a grimly realistic recasting of the foundations of human relations—without which both foundations and superstructure will be reduced to atomic dust. A people so burdened with responsibility, and so long acquiescent in it, cannot take its directives from the day's events alone, or from changes in philosophic fashions; nor can it entrust the formulation of its philosophy to public-relations counsels. If it has indeed reached the end of the road, cannot carry the burden further, let that be made apparent. But it is an outrage on so sober and responsible a past to transfer the old name to a new and irresponsible enterprise. The demand for the world-wide relinquishment of Judaism is a clear and manageable proposal; but the proposal to divide the Jewish people into Israelis and American Jews, Israelis and English Jews, to assign a future to Israel and consign the others to paganism, is quite as negative but much less honestly so; and its intention of parading a paganized Levantine state as the inheritor of the unique Jewish experience must be repudiated in a last gesture of Jewish piety.

# CHAPTER XXII

## *"Dual Allegiance"*

❄

THIS is a subject that must be treated separately, if briefly. It exercises the minds of a great many Jews who have recently acquired an affirmative relationship to the State of Israel, and even of Jews whose Zionism goes back a generation or two. In another fashion it is also a matter for deep concern among the minority which claims it has no relationship (we have seen that it really has a negative one) to the Jewish state, and which issues periodic statements propounding its own patriotism and impugning the patriotism of the other Jews.

The last group cannot be taken seriously; one cannot have an intelligent discussion with a man who proclaims his superior virtue in the newspapers and wants to make a public issue of it. Most of the Jewish pro-Israelis who are bothered by the problem of dual allegiance have solved it along the lines indicated in a previous chapter; they are loyal Americans in the same way as Americans of Irish, Polish, or French origin who have an affirmative attitude toward "the old country." These pro-Israeli Jews are fundamentally of the assimilationist or Assimilationist-Zionist groups. The Jewishly orientated Zionist is not bothered by the problem.

Why, then, should it be treated at all?

The answer is that among the old-time Assimilationist-Zionists, those who look forward to the final dissolution of Diaspora Jewry, with Israel remaining as the sole repository of Jewishness, there are dissatisfied spirits who realize that there is something wrong with this idea: they suspect that it amounts to the same thing as total assimilation—that is, the dissolution of the Jewish identity and spirit throughout the world, Israel included. Yet they feel they owe it to America to consider themselves one of the "normal" immigrant groups, and Israel one of the "normal" foreign countries with which such groups are permitted, within limits, to identify themselves emotionally.

Before the creation of the State of Israel these Zionists did not suffer from any perplexities. The Jews of Palestine, and the Jews of the Diaspora who were being helped to settle in Palestine, did not constitute a state. The Zionists were not compromising themselves by co-operating with a foreign government; they were doing a humanitarian work, and even if this work had political overtones, if it aimed at the creation of a state, if it involved the organizing of propaganda pressure in America against the misdeeds of England in Palestine, there was no foreign state as such, no foreign government capable of contracting alliances and making war, which was the beneficiary. But now Israel *is* a state; it has a government; it can contract alliances and declare war. Is it possible for an American Jew to be as whole-heartedly with the Jews of Palestine as he was before? Must not a new code of relations be drawn up, to anticipate and prevent an unconscious lapse into defective Americanism?

It is questionable whether the above arguments are the real ones. For it is quite misleading to say that the Jewish state came into existence on May 14, 1948. It was certainly proclaimed then; but a state does not come into existence in a day, or a year, or even a decade. There was a Jewish state in Palestine—even if only a state within a state—before the British withdrew; that was, in fact, the chief reason for Britain's withdrawal. That state within a state had its agricultural, educational, and foreign-affairs departments. It had its representatives abroad. It was even able to conduct war of a kind, and did so. The world's acknowledgment of the existence of this state, which was made on May 14, 1948—or really in the U.N. on November 29, 1947—was an important phase in its development; but it was not the act of creation.

From this it appears that either the fear of "dual allegiance" is a purely formalist problem, or else it had existed before, and was repressed by a sophistry. In the latter case, the anti-Zionists, with their much earlier raising of the problem, were right; in the former case, we are concerned here with a verbal-legalistic question.

But if we examine the *facts*, we are completely baffled because we have nothing to work on. No one has ever suggested that, among the Jews, Zionists ever showed themselves remiss, in peace or war, in their duty as Americans. No one has ever suggested that Louis D. Brandeis was less American than Louis Marshall—or, to take a better contrast, Julius Rosenwald—because the one was a Zionist, the other a non-Zionist or anti-Zionist. If anti-Semites denounced the Jews as unpatriotic, they made no distinction between Zionists and non-Zionists. That wild fantasy *The Protocols of the Elders of Zion*, the seriously accepted myth-center of modern anti-Semitism, did not report a Zionist congress; it reported a conspiratorial meeting of omnipotent assassins dedicated to the destruction of western civilization, and not to the creation of a Jewish state.

What is it, then, that bothers these old-time Zionists?

I believe it is their inability to reconcile with their Americanism a concept of Judaism which flickers somewhere in their minds, and which would make of the Jews a peculiar people, and of Israel a peculiar state. They have surrendered so much of themselves to the commonplace that they dare not entertain openly the notion of a people and a state altogether different in their purpose and relationship from all other peoples and states. They have not surrendered completely; if they had, they would be at ease, seeing themselves in the regulation pattern of the loyal minorities. They dare not clearly remember, they cannot wholly forget, that they belong to a people that cherishes this tradition: "Let the Jewish state perish if it abandons the moral idea," in contradistinction to all other states, whose motto is: "Let the state live, at any cost to any idea."

This, as I have said in various forms, is the essence of Jewish Zionism; and I repeat: "*The determinant element in the longing for the Return was the desire to remain Jewish; political self-determination, assumption of the standard national functions, were instrumentalities; and where seen as more, were sentimentalities.*"

Certainly there was sheer physical longing for a home, weariness with displacement, weariness with humiliation and maltreatment. But with these alone the people would long ago have perished; with these alone it could not have created a state. The longing for Palestine had an obstinately *ideal* character. That the Jewish spirit was not evolving in its own place tormented the Jew as a disaster in itself, apart from his personal insecurity. "The Divine Glory is in exile," was a folk saying. And while he studied the sacred books or, if he was a simple man, repeated the prayers, practiced at least part of the ritual, and wept on the day of the Black Fast, he brooded over the alienated and desecrated sanctuary which was Palestine. He conceived the land as hankering for sanctification, and for those who had sanctified it. The land was frustrated, even as he was; and, like himself, it suffered less from the physical usurpation visited upon it, or the cruel neglect of its physical welfare, than from the spiritual frustration.

The Jewishly orientated Zionist, who is in this relationship, who does not get it by description, looks blankly at those who want to "reconcile" it with his Americanism. Only a thoroughgoing atheist (disguised or self-deceived) and amoralist places God and patriotism in that sort of juxtaposition. A man's business is to make his patriotism fit into God, not God into his patriotism.

Perhaps the misunderstanding that prompts the problem of "dual allegiance" is grounded in the formulation of the official Zionist Program, the Basle Platform adopted in 1897: "Zionism strives to create in Palestine a legally secured, publicly recognized homeland for the Jewish people." Those who imagine that this is the full definition of Zionism must also imagine that the Zionist movement is dead; it has triumphed into extinction, and Zionists must now find another name and field of activity. But the Basle Platform neither described nor defined Zionism; it only defined its most easily definable project. The literature of Zionism—for those who want enlightenment on the subject—is coterminous with all Jewishly Jewish literature, beginning with the Bible; and the objectives of Zionism are coterminous with the objectives of the Jewish people.

To this Zionism it is misleading to apply the terminology of familiar political phenomena, and to saddle it with a problem of "dual allegiance." There is, I have pointed out, a kind of Zionism which does invite that treatment; but it is not the Zionism of the historic Jewish people. It is the Zionism of Jews who want Jewishness to disappear from the earth; and the problem of "dual allegiance" as it exists for them is solved easily and uninstructively.

# CHAPTER XXIII

# *The* Chalutzim

❀

Jewish folk life, as we have seen, was already dissolving before communism came with its program of compulsory assimilation, and Nazism with its program of physical annihilation. Perhaps folk life is dissolving throughout the world, and the folk of every people has only two alternatives: to transpose itself into cultured humanity or to become the mob. But this dissolution in the Jewish people was accompanied by geologic splits, so that larger areas were exposed to wastage. The following is a rough classification of the sections that were in existence fifty or sixty years ago, when Zionism was becoming activated:

1. Assimilating Jews: of at least two kinds; those who, with their obsessive self-obstructing desire to stop being Jews, made a philosophy and self-perpetuating movement of it, and those who chose to drop off quietly.

2. Semi-assimilating Jews, who, with a partly-Jewish social idealism, were primarily concerned with local and world social transformations, revolutionary or evolutionary. They too were also of at least two kinds: those who wanted the perpetuation of the Jewish identity, and those who did not care. Some, of course, thought that a hankering for Jewish identity was counter-revolutionary or illiberal; but it is difficult to decide whether these belong in this para-

graph or the preceding one. Cutting across the two divisions here noted, were further divisions: Jews in search of a non-Palestinian territory for the Jewish people (Territorialists, organized in 1905); Diaspora Nationalists (not exclusive of the Territorialists), who should perhaps not be called semi-assimilating Jews, because they did not want assimilation at all (for example, Yal Peretz). But I let the description stand, because in effect non-Zionist Diaspora Nationalism, in a world no longer capable of tolerating a Jewish folk life, meant ultimate assimilation.

3. Jewishly orientated Jews, folk and cultured and the blend of both. Among these were extreme pietists who opposed Zionism because its leader was Herzl, instead of the Messiah. But perhaps these, too, should be classified among the semi-assimilating Jews. Their piety was often petrifaction, the Diaspora equivalent for pre-exilic apostasy; and they too refused to understand that without a folk life in the Diaspora, and without a reconstituted Jewish state or homeland, assimilation was inevitable.

Personal assimilation was not confined to any group. It was at work everywhere, with a different tempo in each group. The body within which was lodged the essential spirit of Judaism was growing steadily smaller. Dozens of communities like the one I have described in the Manchester of nearly half a century ago have lost their folk character and, where they have not renewed themselves by Zionist work, have lost nearly all Jewish content.

But, as I have shown, Zionist work has not necessarily meant Jewish self-renewal; or, to put it more exactly, working for Palestine and a Jewish state has not always been Zionistic. Those who, while speaking loudly of "social justice" and "democracy," projected in Palestine a state like all other states, even of the liberal western world, belonged in various degrees to the Assimilationist-Zionist groups: and they were the more assimilationist precisely because they used such words dishonestly, thereby acquiring one of the characteristics of western nationalism. If Jewish nationalism was Jewish at all, it was so in the continuity of the prophetic interpretation of it; a pervasive moral will working on the national home from the very beginning, and creating its own forms before the character of the state was pre-empted by pagan nationalism. This prophetic interpretation was incorporated in the *Chalutzim*, who have so far been the highest embodiment of Zionism.

By a rough analogy we may thus relate the three principal divisions in Zionism to the Biblical classifications I have made in Book Two: the Mizrachi, or religious Zionists, correspond to the priestly philosophy; the General Zionists to the wisdom philosophy; the Labor Zionists to the prophetic philosophy. There is some overlapping, as there was in ancient times. Mizrachi Labor Zionists have, in the prophetic spirit, developed non-competitive forms of life side by side with the "non-religious" labor groups; large sections of the General Zionists have always sympathized strongly with Labor Zionism. On the other hand, Labor Zionism itself has been tinctured with a philosophic materialism that contradicts its true character: of this more below.

Let us pause first on the curious phenomenon, already mentioned, of the revival of Hebrew, and on the part played in it by the *Chalutzim*. The large majority of them, I have noted, were originally Yiddish-speaking, and, unlike the smaller Mizrachi group of *Chalutzim*, they did not usually come from a formally religious environment. Many of them even belonged originally to the semi-assimilating Jewish social idealists. The self-transformation of these pioneers into a Hebrew-speaking people must forever remain a cardinal point in the understanding of the nature of

Zionism; and when we shall have learned to take for granted the fact that the Jews of Israel speak Hebrew, we shall have lost the clue to that understanding.

The language of Palestine before the coming of the Zionists was Arabic; the pre-Zionist Jews in Palestine spoke Arabic or Yiddish. The language of the *Chalutzim*, we note again, was Yiddish. Arabic or Yiddish, or a mixture of the two, should "inevitably" have been the language of the Jewish masses of Palestine. That immigrants into a new country should have used neither their own language nor that of the overwhelming majority of the population, but should have imposed upon themselves the crushing discipline of a language that only a few specialists had mastered, cannot be accounted for by the usual materialistic formulas. It was in many ways a really brutal business: an apparently superfluous submission to the hair shirt of a linguistic transformation on top of other agonizing self-transformations: from city dwellers to dwellers in the wilderness; from inhabitants of the temperate zone to inhabitants of a subtropical zone; from white-collar work (more often the lack of it) to the habit of manual labor (and what labor!) without the assistance of environmental masses. Those who have watched the transformation must remember it as long as they live; they must ponder it the more closely because the *Chalutzim* were not refugees; that is, not in the technical sense of the word.

They could have chosen easier countries. Visas were hard to get, but for a sensible person it was better to wait five or six years and reach America or the Argentine or South Africa than be buried alive in Palestine. Because they chose Palestine they were regarded by rich Jews as doctrinaires; and their obstinacy, reprehensible enough in any applicant for public funds, was the more so because it was fixed in total Jewishness. So the Zionist funds languished, and the

*Chalutzim* starved. The solicitude that is properly expended on refugees was withheld from them. They did not show the refugee's preoccupation with sensible objectives. They were a rebuke to the successful. They could dispense with the solicitude, but they could have used the money; and not the least of the burdens they took upon themselves was the knowledge of the *stupidity* of wealthy Jews.

Even without these reflections it was almost shocking, in those days, to see groups of workers, back from draining swamps, or breaking stones for roads, or bringing in the harvest, denying themselves in their public places the relaxation of discussion in their mother tongue—Yiddish. A feeling of intolerable disharmony, something more than mere bad taste, or incongruity, thrust their Yiddish into the background; they were under an imperious necessity to make Hebrew the language of *Chalutziut*; and had they felt otherwise, the great preparatory work of Eliezer ben Yehudah, who is regarded as the reviver of Hebrew as a spoken language of the people, would never have taken hold of the masses.

The compulsion had at least two aspects, which played into each other. The language of Palestine was fixed not only in the Old Testament, in the book, but in the place-names that designated the surroundings of the *Chalutzim*. The place-names could not be changed without disrupting the record. If the *Chalutzim* had done what all builders of a country in new territory do, they would have brought with them familiar names to displace the local ones, driving into oblivion the memory of the experiences associated with the latter, or leaving them here and there as museum pieces of a vanished life. This we have done in America with the Indian names: we have brought New England and New York, St. Louis and San Francisco, Charleston and New Orleans, from the places of our origin; we have left Omaha and Tallahassee and Chickamauga as curiosities, mastodon bones, witnesses of an unintelligible past. Suppose, then, the *Chalutzim* and the newcomers generally had renamed Mount Carmel Mount Grodno, and the Jordan the New Dnieper, and to their settlements had given preponderantly new names (as they have done to a few): instead of Ain Charod, New Berdichev; for Arava, K'far Odessa; for Tel Aviv, New Warsaw. It would have been, to begin with, a confession that they were really newcomers, not returners. And then, how queer it would have been for their children to learn—if they learned at all—that Elijah had had his famous contest with the false prophets on Mount Grodno, formerly Mount Carmel, that Gideon had gathered his band at New Berdichev, formerly Ain Charod, that Joshua had crossed the New Dnieper, formerly the Jordan.

Even where the etymology of place-names is lost, historic association gives them content. But it often happens that place-names retain recognizably their original purpose. The name Jordan, in addition to its countless associations in all languages, has a descriptive force in Hebrew. It comes from the verb *yarod*, "to descend," and the Jordan is in fact the most descending river in the world, falling as it does into the Dead Sea, the lowest exposed point on the surface of the planet. *Yardein* (the Hebrew for Jordan) is the Descender; but in Hebrew, not in Yiddish. And the area known as the *Shefelah*, to both Biblical and modern Jews, is the low-lying stretch along the seashore, above and below Tel Aviv. It is the Hebrew equivalent for *Netherland*, but it has no meaning in Yiddish. The Valley of Jezreel is still one of the most fruitful places in Israel, and its name, from of old, meant "God will sow." Something would have been wrong if to Jews in Palestine, speaking Yiddish, these words, *Yardein*, *Shefelah*, *Yizreel*, and many others, would have become merely syllables, like Kalamazoo and Rappahannock to Americans. The land would not have recognized its returning children; the tradition would have had to speak through a veil.

The second aspect of the compulsion toward Hebrew relates to world Jewry and the preservation of world Judaism; and to this I have already referred. We need only add here the reflection that the retention of the old names, which *might* have taken place without a return to Hebrew, has additional significance for a Diaspora Jewry which is itself returning to the study of Hebrew.

And now, bearing in mind that there were no rational compulsions of any kind on the *Chalutzim* to torture themselves into Hebrew, let us return to the observation made above: "Labor Zionism itself has been tinctured with a philosophic materialism that contradicts its true character."

The technical language of Labor Zionism has always been Marxistic in varying degrees; its inspiration has been Biblical and prophetic. Its non-combative, non-competitive view of life is in the everlasting Jewish tradition, and equally in the tradition is its relationship to world Judaism. The collectives and co-operatives of Israel, the great achievement of Labor Zionism, talk Marxism and act Judaism. They are regarded with contempt by Marxists throughout the world, and they are forever trying to make themselves intellectually acceptable to the Marxists. Men who have found it necessary, for their spiritual health, to read and reread Isaiah and the other prophets until they know large sections by heart, plead for admission into the community of the orthodox materialists to whom the Bible is the desolation of abomination. Nothing points up the absurdity of this complex more aptly than the inexplicability, in Marxist terms, of the wilful, the implacable, one might almost say perverse—and now successfully normalized—revitalization of Hebrew. The handful of communists in Israel, who had proved by the book that the revival of Hebrew was impossible, since it contradicted historical materialism, are now preaching historical materialism in Hebrew—rather good Hebrew, too. Not all the inherited or transmitted Talmudic ingenuity of the Jews can derive a Marxist thesis from the linguistic admonitions of a landscape. But the revival of Hebrew is only one illustration, if the aptest. The whole of Jewish history is a continuous contradiction of the sufficiency of the materialist interpretation.

Of late the Jewish liberals, progressives and semi-Marxists of the world have turned a tolerant and sometimes very friendly eye on Israel. They do not claim to have changed their general views; they cannot claim, either, that Labor Zionism has changed. Finally, they cannot deny that they have been receiving the literature of the movement for the last twenty years. It would be ungentlemanly to suggest bandwagonism. Perhaps the two riddles propounded here have a common solution: the liberals may, without realizing it, have lost the old feeling that a Jewish fixation on the Bible is necessarily reactionary; the Labor Zionists may have been drawn to Marxism only for its valuable negative element, its Biblical and prophetic denunciation of social injustice.

Another factor may be relevant. Before Marxist materialism had a real chance to show its implications in action, its apparent intentions were extremely persuasive. I find it hard to sympathize with those writers who erred on Marxism for twenty years, recanted in six hundred pages, and made the same hullabaloo over their recantation as they did over their original error. A silence of ten or fifteen years would have been more becoming, as well as more convincing. But it is true that until ten or fifteen years ago one could ignore the Marxist line for the sake of necessary co-operation; the more so as the vast majority of "spiritual" leaders were either brutally indifferent to the problems of war and poverty, or criminally implicated in the conspiracy against peace and social justice. We have now learned that communist materialism is actually the replica of capitalist materialism (both of them atheistic and amoral); but the disadvantage of communist materialism is its newness, which imparts to it a ferocity of morale now absent from capitalist materialism. For when capitalist materialism unveils itself—as Nazism or Fascism—a large part of the capitalist world is shocked. The communist is shockproof.

In their re-creation of themselves and Israel, the *Chalutzim* were aware of two things: they were being carried by the Jewish past, and they were answering the Jewish problem of the present—the problem, that is, of world survival under new circumstances. They never thought of themselves as a segment of the Jewish people which was evolving into a new and separate nation. They were not Negators of the Diaspora; they were a function of the adaptation to the new danger. They *were* Diaspora Jewry, the product of its activation, the articulate part, or, rather, the articulateness itself. They believed that hundreds of thousands of Jews would follow them from the Diaspora; but not all the Jews; and those that would remain behind would still be Jews. If they felt the impulse toward Palestine sooner and more strongly than the hundreds of thousands, it was not because they were separate; on the contrary, they were the focus of the historic and national impulse. The Jewish people was *one*, throughout the world. Its purpose was one: the continuation of the struggle toward the serious understanding of life, the continued rejection of the dominant combative paganism and frivolity of the western world.

I must take up this refrain once more: *political self-determination, assumption of the standard national functions, were secondary and instrumental; beyond that they were sentimentalities.* The *Cha-*

*lutzim* wanted a Jewish life; they wanted a maximum of co-operativeness in their living; they wanted it in Palestine and in Hebrew. Whatever would give them this was good enough: as a colony, a British dominion, a province—it did not matter. The moral substance of life was their sole concern; and the pagan passion for statism that seized on some Jews, the mad, un-Jewish hankering for the thrill of status, was not only alien to the *Chalutzim*; it was the very essence of that danger of Jewish dissolution which Zionism was countering, and which the *Chalutzim* most articulately rejected. Within the Zionist movement the hostility between the pagan, state-orientated Assimilationist-Zionists and the *Chalutzim* was sharp and continuous.

It was not only the economic collectivism of the *Chalutzim* that the Assimilationist-Zionists hated; it was, even more, the indifference to the sacred frenzies of statism, the refusal to identify Jewish nationalism with standard nationalism, and to draw from that identification all its consequences of eternal combat. It may properly be said that the Assimilationist-Zionists were in the Hasmonean tradition, the *Chalutzim* in the Hasidean tradition. I shall return to this parallel.

The *Chalutzim* were in their way as singular an episode in human history as the prophets were in theirs. There has been no lack of fellowships in ideal social enterprises in the ancient, medieval, and modern world; and it is not on the plane of personal morality that the singularity of the *Chalutz* as type must be sought. It is in the peculiarly Jewish motif of *the redemption of the idea of the nation.* To derive a social-moral impulse from a national need and tradition, to devote the impulse, in turn, to the nation as a whole, to make morality and nationhood a unity, is Jewish as theme and experience; the highest Christian fellowships have denied nationhood instead of redeeming it; they have therefore denied

273

the organizing need of mankind, and placed their trust in a vast and unmanageable abstraction. The *Chalutz* man recognized, as the prophets did, the inescapable necessity of the organizing of the world into groups called nations; like the prophets, he did not turn his back on that necessity, leaving nationhood to paganism; he accepted it, affirmed it, sanctified it, and gave his all-human interpretation of it.

*Chalutziut* must not be confused, as it often is, with pioneering as such; and the present-day demand for Jewish pioneers for Israel is not necessarily a renaissance of the *Chalutz* spirit. In the present transitional phase of Zionism and of the development of Israel, many surface imitations of authentic forces appear; many enterprises of limited usefulness, and sometimes of wholly harmful quality, take the labels of old, approved, and now perhaps suspended forces. The events of the last decade have left a terrible impress on the Jewish people and on Zionism, and unless we take this into the careful over-all reckoning, we shall not understand the nature of the struggle through which Israel and Jewry are both passing.

# CHAPTER XXIV

## *The Unrealizable Calamity*

❀

IT WILL be a long time before the Jews will be able to realize the extent of the calamity visited on them by the Hitler episode. They will first have to forget or subdue the wild horror of the incident itself, which overwhelms them when they recall the last ten years; they will have to learn —and this is among the abominations of the situation—to assess with a quiet, clinical measure the effects of an action that cannot, so to speak, be tasted by a quiet, clinical measure. In a sense, then, they will never realize the full extent of the calamity; at best, standing outside of themselves, they will talk in artificial, objective phrases of something that only an inarticulate madness can begin to grasp.

Let no one confound the Jewish calamity in this period with the general calamity; and let no one complain that I am asking for preferential pity for the Jews. Much more than pity is at stake here, and much more than physical torture and mass murder.

Our time has witnessed two opposite climaxes in Jewish history, one negative, the other positive: the Hitler episode and the re-establishment of the Jewish state. I call them negative and positive, but while the first is overwhelmingly and irredeemably negative, the second is only provisionally positive. I believe that a Jewish state in Palestine is indispensable to a good Jewish life everywhere in the world; but—as I have tried to show—the notion that a Jewish state, whatever its character, automatically improves Jewish life anywhere is immoral and un-Jewish. Like life itself, then, the Jewish state is only provisionally positive; but the Hitler episode was negative through and through.

I have heard it argued that inasmuch as the Nazi onslaught on the Jews called forth acts of generosity and heroism among Jews and non-Jews, *and also helped in the creation of the Jewish state*, it cannot be described as a wholly negative phenomenon. I would observe at once that the moral significance of a human act cannot be judged by its accidental or unintended results for the good; the guilt of a murderer is not mitigated by the kindnesses that strangers show the widow of his victim. But even on this level of consequences the argument is fallacious when applied to the case in hand. The flood of evil feelings—affirmation and intensification of the anti-Semitic creed, brutal indifference to Jewish suffering—which the Nazis released in the world, left the surviving Jews worse off in their general relationships than they were before the coming of Nazism. As to the "help" that the Jews derived from their six million dead in the creation of the State of Israel, I shall show shortly that this too is an illusion, that the "benefit" is obliterated by the mischief.

The virtual extermination of Polish and central-European Jewry by the Nazis is generally classed as an act of genocide, or race slaughter. This is a misleading description. It was as much an attempt to destroy or discredit an idea as to wipe out a people. Behind blood lust as such, behind hatred of Jews as persons, behind calculated (or miscalculated) advantages of various kinds, there glowered in the Nazi mind a maniacal loathing of something spiritual, something with which the Jews and Judaism are historically associated. I refer the reader again to the last pages of the chapter "The Old and New Dispensations." The Nazis did not direct their fury only against Jews in their own and conquered territories; they did not kill Jews as they killed Poles and gypsies. They wanted to make the whole earth uninhabitable for Jews. It was of the deepest moment to them that Jews should be loathed everywhere; not strategically and temporarily, as part of a passing political combination, but intrinsically and permanently, or at least as long as there were any Jews to speak of, or even any recollection of them. With Poles and Ukrainians in reduced numbers the Nazis could come to terms, after acquiring their territories and reducing them to slavery. For people of Polish or Ukrainian descent in America they had no special hatred. But the existence of Jews anywhere, in any numbers at all, was intolerable to them.

The reasons for this extraordinary and pathological hostility, with its attendant hallucinations and seizures, I have examined in my book *The Great Hatred*. I am concerned here with the consequences of the onslaught, unforeseeable in 1941, and even today beyond assessment.

When the Nazis accompanied their farsighted direct campaign against the Jews—first repression, then mass extermination—by a world-wide indirect campaign, an appeal to universal anti-Semitism, they sincerely saw and represented themselves as the proponents of a great liberating idea—the cleansing of western civilization from all Jewish influence, past and present. It is a frightful mistake to look on this as a maneuver or stratagem. It was an act of deepest faith. They were not, with their anti-Semitism, seeking primarily to split the democracies, as is generally assumed. They were seeking universal admiration as the first unashamed and consistent protagonists of a Jew-free world. Whatever smacked of the Jewish influence in the secular or religious aspects of western civilization was to be destroyed; the preliminary to this action, the spiritual and symbolic accompaniment of it, was the destruction of the Jews themselves. It did not matter that many Jews were un-Jewish; it did not concern the Nazis that the internal life of the Jews might be a contradiction of the spirit which the Nazis hated; the Jewish episode in human evolution had to be repudiated, and the most spectacular way of beginning it was with the extermination of the Jews.

This was not genocide as such, and it was not systematic bestiality, whatever play it gave to both of these. It was a call to arms against the restraints of the moral law; it was an offer to lead western man out of the labyrinth of the moral problematic, and back into the lost paradise of the primitive, pre-Christian world. Therein lay its appeal; therein still lies its appeal to millions of men and women who do not understand, have never quite understood, its explicit purpose, but have felt and feel its attractiveness none the less.

We might even have said that Nazism was in the last accounting a positive phenomenon if it had left behind it a full realization of its hideous nature, if the revulsion from it had illumined for former adherents—and even for opponents—the dark places of the western mind, the unexplored implications of the combative and competitive principle of life. Nothing like that has happened. The anti-Semitic aspect of Nazism is still regarded as "incidental," "subordinate," or "strategic"; the sources of anti-Semitism are still confused with the banalities of racist illusions; and the majority of Jews, looking for a simplified definition of their position in the postwar world, are still incapable of confronting the basic difficulties.

The Jews were bewildered, at the time of the Nazi onslaught, by its utter implacability. "What," they asked in horrified astonishment, "have we done to deserve this?" They were bewildered, too, by the echo of approval that the onslaught awakened in some places, and by the disapproval that it failed to awaken in others. They were immeasurably grateful for a word of protest or a friendly gesture; but they never understood what it was all about, and therefore they could not ask that others understand. Their historical, cultural, folkloristic position and role in the immense division of the western mind, between Christianity and paganism, remained completely hidden from them. In this respect too the whole ghastly episode was a negative phenomenon.

The history of the Jewish reaction, in democratic countries, to the Nazi campaign of anti-Semitism is one of confusion, cross-purposes and panic, not untouched with treachery. There were in the 1930's prominent Jews—and among them some, still living, are still accepted in certain Jewish quarters as Jewish spokesmen!—who decried the anti-Nazi propaganda, the boycott against Germany, which other Jews launched in self-defense. They asserted that protest only made matters worse. They also felt that their position in America, or England, was being jeopardized by this Jewish emphasis on the Jewish danger in other countries. Among them were members of American and English political groups which were by no means antipathetic to the spread of Nazi and Fascist principles. They called this putting the interests of their country first—that is, before their Jewish interests. In reality they were actuated by class interest; and they had their own theory of Jewish interests, too. They persuaded themselves that if Nazism and Fascism, or something like them, were to win out in America—a prospect to which they were not averse—it would be well for the Jews to have established at least a partial record of pro-Nazism and pro-Fascism, though without their anti-

Semitic "incidentals," of course. They erred viciously on two counts: first, Fascism and Nazism are not anti-Semitic "incidentally"; and their cunning policy of having a friend at court *auf alle Fälle* would have done them and any other Jews as little good as it had done in Germany. On this point the reader may consult the history of Jewish pro-Nazism in Germany. Second, they strengthened the isolationist elements that almost succeeded in bringing about the ruin of the democracies.

During this period the warnings of the Jews that the Jewish persecutions in Germany were the preliminary to a general assault on all human liberty (Weizmann said to Lord Halifax: "They are burning the synagogues now, tomorrow they will be burning the British cathedrals") were often classed as "war-mongering"—particularly by the organizations referred to in the last paragraph; and some Jewish members of such organizations or groups were often willing to suppress their inmost agreement with the Jewish warnings in order that their public reputations might remain unspotted. It was more important to them to *appear* to be good Americans than to *be* good Americans. All this is set down not as a reminder (though that is necessary too), but to establish the background of the Jewish position.

There are divisions of interests and purposes in all peoples and nations; accusations and counter-accusations of defective patriotism are also universal commonplaces. The first demoralizing effects of the Hitler episode in the Jewries of the free countries was to precipitate out, with horrifying clarity, the quite unique significance of Jewish collaborationists. Whereas a French or British collaborationist was willing to sell out his people for his class or personal advantage, but always with the tacit understanding that his people had some sort of claim to existence, the Jewish collaborationist started out with the basic philosophy that the

Jewish people had no right to exist! He certainly did not want to see the Jewish people slaughtered; but as an assimilationist he regarded its obstinate persistence on the historical scene as—at least—an irritating indiscretion. He never got rid of the idea that the Jews themselves were to blame, for not having disappeared long ago—as a normal, decent people would have done under such discouraging circumstances. Thus the divisiveness in Jewry, accentuated by the Hitler episode, had no parallel elsewhere.

During the first phase of the Nazi assault—preceding the gas chambers—the Jews watched the pacifist democracies retreating from position to position (we are apt to forget that time of the world's humiliation) until it seemed that nothing worth fighting for was going to be left: nothing, that is, except life itself, which as a bleak, unadorned concept is worth very little indeed. That which happened with the democratic world at large—the stripping down of the value of life to mere life itself—began to happen with the Jews. Particularly during the days when boatloads of Jews were being shunted from port to port, shaken off by humanity like a pest, during the days when even the partial succor of Palestine was denied them—during those days there spread among the Jews a sense of desperation which pushed into the background the affirmations of Jewish life. More especially, Zionism began to lose its original character as a projected new device for the safeguarding of world Judaism. The simple saving of lives, divorced from ideologies, historic missions, world purposes, and the rest of it, became, understandably, the dominant purpose of the movement.

In the second phase of the assault, one third of the Jewish people was exterminated—the overwhelming majority of the Jews of Europe. Now the democracies were fighting for their lives—*and* their principles. But that third of the Jewish people which was being destroyed was the last great cohesive center of folk-Judaism—Polish Jewry and east-European Jewry generally—the main repository of implemented Jewish principle. Coming on top of the loss, to Russia, of a still greater and more powerful Jewish folk-community, this dealt a shattering blow to the content of Zionism: how much Judaism was there going to be left in the world to transmit into the emerging Jewish homeland—which, for that matter, itself seemed to be on the verge of dissolution? And how much world Judaism was there going to be left for the homeland to safeguard?

During this second phase a change came over American Jewry. There were two elements in the new response, often overlapping. One was compassion, the other, rage. Between them they did much to produce an appearance of unity, especially at the later time when Israel was struggling for independence against the British policy of repression. How insane that policy was we can best realize now when we try to imagine those six hundred thousand Jews subordinated to the Arab leadership which led the mass flight from the country; but before 1948 it was not the insanity of the British policy that infuriated the Jews; it was its savage heartlessness. Yet I speak of "an appearance of unity" among the Jews because the temporary coincidence of purpose masked a profound divergence of ultimate effects.

In the panic of pity—in itself no ignoble phenomenon—it became almost a sign of callousness to be concerned with the principles of Judaism, which had been more than three millennia in evolving and which the Jewish homeland had been intended to perpetuate. Even short-range practical questions as to the feasibility of this or that proposal sounded obstructionist. There was one cry: "Get the British out of Palestine! Get the Jews in!" In so far as this cry issued from sheer compassion, in so far as it expressed the frustrated longing to remove the survivors of the Hitler slaughter from the revolting environment of Europe to the friendliness of Palestine, it was an affirmation. Even so it could be self-defeating if it could not pause to consider the structural possibilities of the Jewish homeland; and very obviously it had no relationship to all the long-range historical and spiritual needs of Israel and world Jewry.

The other emotion, rage, was not an affirmation. Whatever excuses we try to find for it—that it was natural, that the Jews had been goaded beyond endurance—it must be condemned on every conceivable ground. To begin with, the hatred that the Nazis had awakened in the Jews, which the defeat of Germany had not slaked, spilled over into the relationship with England. The folly and brutality of British policy in Palestine after the war gave specious reason to this transference; but the psychological realities were concealed.

There is a difference between anger and hatred, between resistance and the desire to kill. This difference existed as between the mass revolt in Israel, before 1948, against British repression, and the anti-British Terror of the same period. The masses were angry, the Terrorists were filled with hatred. The difference remains clear in spite of the compulsions that sometimes brought the two together—that is, Haganah and the Irgun [1]—or the errors of moral judgment on the part of Haganah leaders.

The psychological realities that expressed themselves in the rage of the Terror were manifold. There was a long-repressed hunger to "get one's own back" on someone. There was a longing to know and show that Jews could kill as well as be killed (and this was referred to as Jewish "honor"). When the popular resistance began cautiously, unwilling to shed blood, the Terror denounced it for its

[1] The Sternist group, more extreme than the Irgun, but also much smaller, did not have the same reactionary social implications as Irgunism. It merits special study as a pathological phenomenon, but this is not the place for it.

squeamishness and mawkishness; and when the first assassinations were carried out by the Terrorists, a frightful satisfaction, a sense of equalization, welled up in thousands of hearts: "We have proved that in this field we Jews are as good as anyone else." In the propaganda of the Terrorists, in and out of Israel, a genuine gloating was mingled with justification of "policy." It was as though Jews were killing and being killed in Palestine so that Terrorist supporters in Hollywood might, after ignoring Judaism and Zionism for three decades, work off their hatred of anti-Semitism.

In Israel the emblem of the Terrorists was an uplifted arm flourishing a rifle, and the legend: "Only thus!" Outside of Israel the supporters of the Terrorists glorified the gun as the "universal language," the Esperanto of mankind, and sang the praises of the new Jew as gunman. Because the popular resistance, which was made up of the working mass, of those who had actually built the country, used no such language, held its fire, and probed all possibilities before resorting to war, it was represented as cowardly, footling, blundering, and ineffective, by groups in and out of Israel who had *not* built the country, had *not* founded the colonies and co-operatives, had *not* nursed the Jewish homeland from its babyhood at the beginning of the century to its manhood in the fifth decade. And it need scarcely be pointed out that the Terrorists drew their personnel and their support mainly from those who had never shown any sympathy with the social achievements of the *Yishuv*.

In America the predominant sentiment of the old school of Zionists was anti-Terror. But a radical transformation was coming over the movement. Hundreds of thousands were joining the Zionist Organizations, which before had counted their memberships in tens of thousands. Their "Zionism" was not grounded in Jewishness. The Jewish cultural-religious content of the majority of American Jews is much lower than that of east-European Jewry was; though it is now rising again, it is lower than that of the preceding generation of American Jews. The violent re-awakening of Jewish self-consciousness, set off by the Nazi assault, sharpened by participation in the rescue work via Palestine, and brought to a climax by the emergent Jewish state, had nothing but itself and the bare fact of the Jewish state to focus on. It was, so to speak, a great awareness with little to be aware of. In this setting "Zionism" had no meaning. From something that no one had wanted to hear about, Zionism became something that no one thought it necessary to learn about. For a large mass of unthinking people the impossible had become the self-understood, without any change in their mental habits, or any addition to their stock of information. Those who had said, if they bothered to speak of the matter at all: "Of course a Jewish state in Palestine is nothing but a crazy dream," were now saying: "Of course a Jewish state in Palestine is a perfectly natural thing." But they could not tell you why they had changed their view, if, indeed, they remembered ever having changed it; and they were not at all interested in finding out why what had looked like a crazy dream (and it really had!) should have turned out to be a solid and sensible reality.

Zionism had, in short, become a success; and the most dangerous feature of success is that one is applauded for the wrong reason, and one begins to like it; or, rather, that one is applauded at all, instead of being understood. One begins to seek the applause instead of the understanding. It is so with an individual, and even more so with a movement. In both cases it is the success, and not the content, that sud-denly attracts wide attention: the wide attention becomes wider—nothing succeeds like success. But a movement is more vulnerable than an individual. For whereas to corrupt an individual you must get his consent, you do not need the consent of a movement. You have only to join it in large enough numbers and take over.

At this point in a movement a struggle begins for the possession of its soul. A division appears in the leadership and in the intelligent rank and file. One group is alarmed by the spiritual inundation, or rather by the inundation of unspirituality, and tries to halt it; the other group rides the inundation and rejoices in the unwonted sensation, with the pretense or under the delusion that no principles are at stake.

Such a point was reached in American Zionism when Palestine became big front-page news, and the membership in the organizations leapt into the hundreds of thousands. The Jewish content and purpose of Zionism receded, none the less so (perhaps all the more so) as the priesthood (that is, the Rabbinate) had a large share in the official leadership. Much of the support given the Terrorists, financially and morally, was concealed with naïvely spectacular cunning. Respectability demanded that one should repudiate the Terrorists; *Realpolitik* demanded that they be supported. And so, all of a sudden, there broke out in Zionism a perfect pestilence of miniscule Machiavellis, who disassociated themselves publicly from the Terrorists, by carefully worded statements, and, behind the scenes, applauded and encouraged them. To have run counter to this tendency in American Zionism would have meant to lose the political leadership; and to lose the political leadership just at this point, when it was *really* worth having in terms of national and international publicity, would have been heartbreaking.

It was pleaded then, it has been pleaded since, that this perversion of the Zionist spirit was inevitable; moreover, that without it the practical results—the "driving" of the

British out of Palestine, the establishment of independence, the opening of the gates to immigration—could not have been achieved. This is a profoundly and dangerously false point of view, as will be demonstrated in the next chapter. But it is even worse to plead, as some do, that this perversion is the real Zionism, that Zionism has come of age because it has become "realistic," that we have at last cast off the mystical futilities of the primitive or spiritual Zionists and have emerged into intelligent modernity. It will take decades, perhaps generations, to undo the harm that the movement has suffered; and if it must be said in justice to the American Zionist leaders that they did not create the situation, it must also be remembered that they took advantage of it and confirmed it, instead of opposing and repudiating it.

A tentative list of the wounds inflicted on the Jewish people and on Zionism by the Hitler episode reveals its overwhelmingly and irretrievably negative character. It destroyed the last of the great Jewish folk-communities, which should have provided the richest and most Jewish material for the re-creation of the Jewish state, and should have continued to feed American Judaism. It accentuated the divisions in the rest of world Jewry, even while providing a temporary and deceptive unification. It left the Jews a new legacy of horror, a new trauma, and both Jews and Christians a new example of evil. It was not successful in its plan to exterminate world Jewry, falling short by somewhat less than two thirds; but it dealt a double blow at Judaism. For apart from accentuating the divisions in Jewry, it gave encouragement among Jews to the un-Jewish faith that force, and force alone, is the intelligent directing principle in human relations; and in pushing the growth of the Jewish homeland beyond a natural pace, it obscured the purposes of the Zionist movement, and deflected it—temporarily, it is to be hoped—from its historic, religious, moral, and cultural identity with eternal Judaism.

That deflecting forces already existed in the Zionist movement before the Hitler episode—a fifth column emanating from those very tendencies which Zionism was meant to overcome—has already been pointed out; but the fierce life-and-death needs which the Hitler episode created gave the deflecting forces a scope and drive they had not possessed before. A simple measure of the change is the following observation: more than forty years ago the Zionist movement dared to turn down the offer of another territory than Palestine, though the Russian pogroms had already set in; the Zionist movement could not and would not have turned down the offer of another territory than Palestine if that had been made seriously in the last ten years. And in accepting such a territory Zionism would, under irresistible pressure, have been converted entirely into an assimilationist movement.

These are some of the consequences of the Hitler episode in Jewish history—so far visible. They will probably be overcome, but they have been a setback to Judaism and Zionism, and there is not in them a single compensatory feature.

# CHAPTER XXV

## *"We" and "They"*

❧

$D$EEP-REACHING problems of a practical kind confront the Jews everywhere, and they cannot be answered in a hurry. After a period of such violent changes it is impossible to know which manifestations in an organism are backed by long-range forces and which are fleeting reactions. But it is also impossible to ignore the problems or—which is the same thing—to say: "They will answer themselves." Consciousness of purpose is itself an important force, and it must be cultivated even while the relative momentum of other forces is still in doubt. I do not pretend to "answer" the problems I pose below; but it is my deepest conviction that without a Jewish framework of reference no Jewish problem will ever be answered.

A Jewish framework of reference is a sense of Jewish unity in time, space, and destiny. It is quite possible to argue that this sense no longer exists, or that it is confined to such small groups that it has no practical significance. But this is one of the arguments that are not resolved statistically and discursively; it must play itself out; the protagonists have no "proofs," they have only their individual charges of vitality. That a sufficiently widespread sense of Jewish unity in time, space, and destiny exists is my basic assumption, as it was my assumption, more than thirty years ago, that Zionism could be activated. My conception of this destiny I have already defined, or, rather, hinted at. It is my argument, further, that Jewish problems are formulable, or meaningful, and eventually resolvable, only in terms of Jewish unity; and by "resolvable" I mean susceptible of being turned to creative account for the Jewish people and for humanity.

Let me give one instance of a creative answer, or resolution—in the field of "Jewish-Christian" relations. The Jewish problem cannot be answered by a widely organized effort to ignore it out of existence; it cannot be answered, either, by assuming that it is a socio-economic complex without meaning outside socio-economic terms. The Jewish problem must remain with us for the foreseeable future; we must try to convert it from a destructive social conflict into a creative spiritual tension. The Jewish problem can, in fact, be converted from a curse into a blessing; but only if Jews and Christians alike see Judaism and Christianity as realities, and not as the illusory byplays of realities.

But Judaism is not a reality if the unity I have spoken of is not a reality; and this unity is denied, or, rather, destroyed, when Jews of Israel and Jews of America think of themselves and each other as "We" and "They." This de-unifying tendency has always existed, because the Zionist movement, like the Jewish people as a whole, has always had in it assimilating, de-Judaizing elements. Today this tendency is once more dangerously strong. It expresses itself in mutual suspicions and warnings. Israelis say to American Jews: "Do you think that because you have provided or are providing money and political influence for our liberation and growth, you have the right to tell us what the State of Israel should be like? If you have views on that subject, become Israelis; otherwise keep your views to yourselves." American Jews say: "Do you realize that what you do affects our position in America? If you are religious or irreligious, if you are leftists or rightists, you involve us, you give us a coloration, whether we like it or not. We cannot disassociate ourselves from you even if we wanted to."

Or the argument takes another form. "The most pressing need in Jewish life today," say Israelis—and many American Jews with them—"is the rapid building of the State of Israel. Jewish needs elsewhere must be subordinated to it." Other American Jews answer: "We have too long neglected, under the pressure of crisis, our own needs, our schools, temples, cultural and social institutions—in short, our Judaism. You must slow up the rate of your growth, because we cannot continue to support it as we have done in the recent past."

These latter disputes represent genuine practical problems, which cannot be answered by formulas. They cannot be answered, either—they can only continue with mounting irritation and futility—if their basis is not the unity of Judaism in time, place, and destiny. And either the destiny is of the moral character I have described, or again such unity as still exists is only superficial, emotional, and unstable.

Nor will it do for the two groups to approach the problem in an "intelligent" bargaining spirit, as between decent strangers, each regardful of the other's difficulties and prepare to adjust claim and concession. It is not enough for Israelis to think: "Well, of course, we really must consider their position; in any case it won't do to kill the goose that lays the golden eggs. We must not embarrass them by our behavior, and we must not make fun of their so-called Jewish schools, their synagogues, centers, temples, and so on, which are quite incapable of stemming the tide of their assimilation. We must humor them and pretend they have a future." Or for the American Jews to think: "Perhaps it *is* too soon for us to slacken our efforts in behalf of Israel.

After all, they're doing a marvelous job, their task is far from completed, their security is not yet assured. We will wait a little longer before cutting loose. Meanwhile, let's be patient and hope that they will not disgrace us in the eyes of our fellow Americans."

Even this apparently adult approach, with its "We"-and-"They" implications, can only lead to dissolution. A common concern for the total spiritual significance of the Jewish people, with maximum suppression of localisms, must guide all practical discussions. This, as we shall soon see, is beset with difficulties enough, but they are not negative difficulties.

## The Equilibrium of World Jewry

It is necessary to assume that the Nazi attempt to make this planet uninhabitable for Jews has failed, and that Jewish communities will continue to exist for a long time in many places. It would be foolish, however, to assume that anti-Semitic pressures will not, here and there, compel Jewish emigration. The Jewish state must be capable of absorbing a large share of this emigration. To demand that the Jewish state shall be capable of absorbing all world Jewry in case of a universal rise of Hitler anti-Semitism is meaningless. It is like the demand, in any country, for complete military preparation against every variety and any volume of attack—a practical absurdity. Even America cannot set herself such an objective, not though she converted herself into an exclusively military organization; and if she did so convert herself she would cease to be America. Similarly, the effort of Israel to make herself capable of absorbing all the Jews of the world at need would turn Israel into something completely un-Jewish.

What, then, is the proper equilibrium of Jews inside and

outside the Jewish state? The question is unanswerable on this "security" level. Nor is it easy to answer on the other level—namely: "At what point shall we say that the Jewish state is fulfilling its Zionist function, interacting with the rest of Jewry for the perpetuation of Judaism?" This is not merely a quantitative question. Nor can we ever speak of "fulfillment" in the sense of completion. The effectiveness of the Jewish state in this regard depends on the total Jewishness of world Jewry. And for that matter it is not unthinkable that in some respects Israel will learn Judaism from world Jewry. We must, from year to year, decade to decade, generation to generation, make our estimates of the world situation, and our spiritual self-training must be based on the perpetual assumption of world unity of purpose. Sometimes the picture will be fairly clear; at other times confused.

At present the picture is clear. The State of Israel is not yet definitely established, in either the physical or the spiritual sense. Physically it is staggering under a load of immigration that only a large increase in funds can enable it to carry; spiritually it is inundated by an immense tide of unprepared and often de-Judaized Jews, which increases enormously the danger to its Jewish character. It is not only Jewish enemies of Judaism who have foretold that within a decade Israel will no longer be Jewish; the grim prophecy has been made by adherents of Judaism, too. What are the reasons for this posture of affairs, and what is to be the response of Jewishly orientated Zionists?

Some of the reasons have already been mentioned in connection with the Hitler episode: the forcing of the Zionist pace, the damage done to the Zionist spirit. We might also ask: Should the gates of the new state have been thrown wide open and an unrestricted invitation issued to all Jews to enter? Should not all efforts be concentrated now on assimilating the already dangerously large body of "foreign" material, economically and spiritually?

The factors in the postwar stampede toward Israel are so many that it is practically impossible to draw the line between the effects of policy and the effects of irresistible forces. One thing is certain: had the Israeli government sought to restrict immigration, Jews would have paid no attention. Boatloads of "illegals" would have converged on Israel in far greater numbers than in the days of British rule. The thought of turning back such boats, of meeting them at the shore with repelling parties, would never have occurred to a sane person. As against this, the willingness of the Jews of Israel to risk the total wrecking of their economy by encouraging the flood is a great moral asset. It was of course not unmixed with other considerations. Security against Arab attack called for a maximum increase of population in a minimum period. But against this, again, the decline in the quality of the immigrants indicated the rapid approach of the point at which numbers would be a liability, not an asset, if only militarily speaking. Has this point been reached? Shall an attempt be made at restriction?

There are countries from which Jews can still migrate, but which tomorrow may lower the curtain. There are countries in which the Jewish position is very precarious. Has Israel reached the stage at which it must say: "More immigrants today makes the total position worse; neither Israel nor the immigrants will be better off." And *dare* it ever say: "We might be able to accommodate refugees on the subsistence level, but the country is getting out of hand; its Jewishness is threatened. We must wait till we have caught up, at whatever cost to Jewish lives elsewhere."

These are crushing decisions to be compelled to make, and no one is justified in being dogmatic. To the extent that the decisions depend on the contributions and investments

294

of American Jews, they may lend themselves to exhortation. But in so far as they have to do with the basic concept of the Jewish state, they are not subjects for oratory or high-pressure publicity. They are matters for deep self-searching and spiritual co-operation.

## INTERVENTION

But what, at this point, do we find ourselves doing? We find ourselves directing the policy of a foreign state! And we find ourselves being invited to it, even while we are told to keep our hands off. For it will be noticed that the "Hands off!" cry always has a party bias. The laborites in Israel do not tell the Labor Zionists in America to stop interfering; and the religious Zionists in Israel do not resent the activities of the American Mizrachi. But religious Jews in Israel denounce the leftist "irreligious" Labor Zionists in America, and the Israeli laborites denounce the "interference" of the "clericalist" reactionary Mizrachi. To some extent the cry of "interference" is therefore a fake; yet it is serious enough because it accepts the principle of "We" and "They." And to the extent that it is not serious it confronts us with the curious and disturbing fact just referred to: we American Jews are directing, or helping direct, on invitation, the policy of a foreign state; we control the volume of its immigration by our contributions; we affect its legislation, its social structure, and its foreign policy by our response to its various financial appeals.

There is no escape from it. Either we stop helping Israel or we recognize that help implies at least a tacit partnership in policy. Even if we withheld all opinion and advice, the need of financial help would turn the thoughts of Israeli Jews to the question: "Are our policies likely to alienate American donors?"

The fact that we cannot help being implicated in the policy of Israel makes it imperative for us to recognize the reality. But that is not enough. *We must fortify and extend the reality.* We must declare openly: "We, the Jews of America" (or of England, the Argentine, and so forth) "are one with the Jews of Israel; and the forms which that state takes, the life it develops, is our deepest concern. We do not vote in Israeli elections, we do not participate in the parliamentary debates; but we are a constant factor in the elections, debates, and decisions, and we intend to remain so, and to become increasingly so."

There is one practical issue, handled hitherto in very gingerly fashion by American Zionism, which best summarizes all the intellectual difficulties of an ideal unity between American and Israeli Jewry: this is Israel's call for young American Jewish *Chalutzim*.

It may seem strange that when Israel cannot accommodate the masses who *must* come, it should be appealing for those who need not come. But there are several resolutions of this contradiction. The young American Jews whom Israel seeks will increase, not use up, the absorptive capacity of Israel. They will bring American freshness, know-how, good humor, physical and mental health into the stream of immigration; above all, they will bring the very fact of their voluntary self-dedication to the building of Israel. Now, this appeal for American *Chalutzim* is perhaps the very focus of the problem of relationship with Israel. Here are American Jews not only involved in the direction of the affairs of a foreign state, but proposing to migrate thither, and proposing to persuade others to migrate. How is this consonant with Americanism?

I do not propose to examine this question in the terms usually employed: to wit, by referring to the right of Americans to migrate as part of their tradition of freedom; or by talking of a new, struggling state in the near east, a state dedicated to democracy, which appeals to the generosity of all-powerful America to spare some of its manpower, as it has spared so much of its wealth, for the establishment of its principles in other parts of the world. I shall not cite the instances of Americans, Englishmen, Frenchmen going out to offer their lives for the liberation of other countries and not being thought the less American, English, or French. These arguments have their validity, but they do not bear on the essence of the Zionist case. For either Israel is not a state like other states, or else its creation is a dreary addition —the drearier because of its pretentiousness—to the long list of self-centered, competitive countries without a vision of a new nationalism dedicated to the redemption of mankind. Presumably on that level, too, it has the same title to life as anyone else. But what, on that level, is there to attract American Jewish youth, or to awaken special American sympathy? I shall be told: "Exactly what there was in the appeal of Italian freedom in the days of Garibaldi, Greek freedom in the days of Bozzaris." And this, precisely, is the answer that begs the question. For an Israel that is no longer moved by the Jewish Zionist ideal, an Israel that talks straight nationalism, and is not linked with the world-redemptive character of Judaism, is a retreat, not an advance, a subtraction from the world's liberating forces, not an addition to them.

The *Chalutziut* which went out of Europe to Palestine in the past—before the Hitler catastrophe dealt such a blow to the spirit of Judaism—was a spiritual phenomenon *sui generis*. Because, like Zionism everywhere, American Zionism has become heavily tinged with straightforward nationalism, it does not think of that kind of *Chalutziut;* hence its hesitancy and embarrassment; hence also its uneasiness at finding itself involved, or seeing itself accused of involvement, in the affairs of another state. That Israel needs and should get an ever-increasing stream of *Chalutzim* from America is obvious to every Zionist who retains the original principles of the movement; and an intelligent Americanism which is convinced that the original Zionist principle is at stake would not withhold his approval. But a *Chalutziut* movement that consists of nationalist propaganda, even when properly flavored with democratic talk, cannot hope to draw on American Jewry or American sympathy to any significant extent. And an organic link between American Jews and a purely nationalist State of Israel will perhaps be tolerated by liberal Americans, but the inspiration of a higher purpose and unique form will not be there.

Nor, finally, is there any sense at all in the quiet hints that Israeli pioneer-seekers in this country throw out: "Better come over to us, you never know what might happen to you in America." For better or for worse, American Jews love and trust America. In the unlikely if not inconceivable event of a Hitlerizing of America, the saving of a few tens of thousands of Jews into Israel (will Israel still exist in that down-going of the world?) is not an inspiring program. American and Israeli Jews must understand once for all that an American *Chalutziut* into Israel, so badly needed, so justifiable—and so possible—can only be urged in a moral setting that would be helpful to all Americans of goodwill. And the interweaving of American with Israeli Jewish life must have the same setting if it is to have meaning and fulfill a purpose.

## The Form of the Relationship

I am positing for world Jewry (including the Jews of Israel) a relationship to Israel which no other people has to any land; for the Jewish people, to remain Jewish, must still remain peculiar. The suggestion that Israel will be a sort of Vatican for world Jewry is wide of the mark, for reasons already implied. The Catholic Church is a supra-national body; the Jewish people is a national organism devoted to the creation of a non-competitive nationalism. It is that to the extent that it is Jewish. When it abandons the prophetic view that only the prophetic notion of nationalism is permissible, it becomes a standardized nation, neither Jewish nor Christian.

This looks like a demand that the Jewish people be given a special position in the world—and it is; except that the word "given" is inappropriate. The Jewish people has always had a special position in the world, and will continue to have it for a long time. But hitherto this special position has been based on misunderstanding. The world will not, cannot, and should not forget that the foundations of moral perception in the western world were laid by the Jewish people: *it can and should realize that the peculiar human enterprise which Judaism represents was not rendered superfluous by the advent of Christianity.* And let it never be thrown up to the Jews that they are asking for "privileges." God knows that in the worldly sense it is no privilege to occupy this peculiar position. Under the best circumstances it will be a difficult and onerous one.

A Jew who contemplates a standard type of nationalism for Israel, with consequent assimilation of world Jewry, is, whether he realizes it or not, proposing an unparalleled piece of historical cynicism. To have endured so long, so obstinately, in the possession of a vision, only for the purpose of achieving a magnificent climax of banality, is to turn a millennial agony of the spirit into a farce. There is nothing vicious about Jews who drift away from the Jewish spirit because they will not submit to its discipline; but those who exalt the escape into a principle and go about looking for company in their flight, deriding (sometimes in gloating and anonymous magazine articles) those who remain behind, are spiritual destroyers. And those who represent as a moral fulfillment the sublimation of Judaism into a standard nationalism seek to disinherit not only the living, but a hundred generations of the dead.

It is useless to look for legalistic definitions of the proper, creative relationship between the Jews of the Diaspora and the Jews of Israel. If Judaism means anything resembling my outline of it, we are dealing with a unique value in civilization; and if Zionism and the Jewish state are aspects of Judaism, we wrong both Americanism and Judaism by applying to them formalized definitions transferred from other, irrelevant fields of experience. It is obviously necessary to say, at the present stage of world affairs, that a man cannot be simultaneously a citizen of Israel and a citizen of America; he cannot carry two passports, he cannot vote in two countries. But this is not the essence of the problem, which can perhaps be best approached by a personal formulation: "I, Maurice Samuel, an American citizen, and a lover of this country, feel that the best I can offer it springs from my identification with the development of Judaism. In the deep moral struggles of America (as of the rest of the western world) the issue lies between the co-operative and the competitive interpretations of life, between essential Christianity and its matrix and ally, Judaism, on the one hand, and paganism, open or concealed, on the other. If I identify myself with a Judaism that is such in name only, hence with an Israel that is a purely nationalist state, I serve neither Judaism nor America, whatever approvals I can obtain for the deception. If, under the slogan of an exclusive Americanism, I disassociate myself from creative Judaism and a creative Israel, I am practicing another deception: I am depriving America of my best potentialities, and calling it good Americanism. For this deception it is particularly easy to obtain approval; but though there is a popular—and singularly immoral—advertising cliché: 'Such popularity must be deserved,' I must look for guidance to more serious considerations."

If this attitude is morally sound, what are the legalistic formulations that must accompany it? Is there a legalistic setting for it? It is probably not a business for jurists, however deeply imbued with the moral spirit; and it is certainly not a business for political careerists and patrioteers. But apart from a general understanding of such a relationship, there are details of application which individuals must work out for themselves, and for which no general formulas can be framed. Thus: in what proportions shall one divide one's attention between American and Jewish tasks? I have known men and women who have divided themselves effectively between American and Zionist affairs, giving to each a higher proportion of their energies than most of their fellow citizens gave to either. I have known some who hardly participated—directly—in American tasks, yet whose lives were exceptional contributions to the moral spirit of America. Such a one was Henrietta Szold (to quote an admittedly outstanding instance), who made Judaism and Zionism almost exclusive preoccupations, but who nevertheless radiated into American life as such, through her Jewish activity, an impulse of the highest significance.

It is the spirit that matters, and searches based on anything else lead nowhere.

## The Two-way Process

There is another approach to the "We"-and-"They" division, the Israel and Diaspora division, which is associated with the famous verse from Isaiah: "For out of Zion shall

go forth the law, and the word of the Lord from Jerusalem."
This is interpreted as meaning that the Jewish homeland
will formulate the moral law for the world; more particularly, in the Jewish field, the reborn Jewish state will teach
Judaism to Jews everywhere, while the Diaspora has nothing to teach the Jewish state.

When the verse was first applied to an exile Jewry, in the
time of the Second Commonwealth, the pagan world had
not yet been leavened by Christianity. The law had not yet
gone forth out of Zion. But the notion that today only
Israeli Jewry can create, that neither the Jews of the Diaspora nor the Christians of the world can help work out the
moral law, is nonsense. Christianity has already created
much; the Jewish prophetic moral type has appeared in the
Christian world. Confining the issue to Jews alone, it must
be understood that Diaspora Jewry cannot be the passive
recipient of Israel's spiritual creations; we cannot accept the
view that whatever Israel says and does is to be the Jewish
norm all over the world. That is a "We"-and-"They" situation again. For that matter, the record is very clear that
even in ancient times the Jewish state lapsed frequently
from Judaism. We have seen that the Jewish "state"
founded by Zerubbabel after the Babylonian exile had to
be rescued from moral decay by the Jews of Babylonia.
Putting historical parallels to one side and arguing only
from immediate realities, we must repudiate the conception
of a world Jewish unity created solely by moral radiation
from Israel (there can of course be no talk of "dictation").
A world Jewry that has not Jewish values enough of its own
to react on Israel has not values enough to accept a moral
radiation. Very specifically, the tradition of the exile, its
affirmative side, must flow from the Diaspora to Israel
(Israelis will need such tuition), while the counter-tradition
of purely Jewish living flows back from Israel.

But here too we must not fall into a "We"-and-"They" attitude, a pointing out of each other's faults and short-comings. All faults and shortcomings must be seen as general; those of the Israelis are ours, ours will in time be equally chargeable to the Israelis. The effort to remove such faults must be that of the Jewish people as a whole. The growth and development of Judaism must be a two-way process between Israel and the Diaspora—and even this phrase must imply only a geographic division.

I will illustrate the common responsibility by a recent example:

When I was last in Israel, the government arranged to bring home from Vienna, for reburial, the body of Theodor Herzl. The more I heard, on the spot, of the ceremonies that were being prepared, the military displays and guards, the catafalques and torch illuminations and processions—all the paraphernalia, mummery, and technically ingenious manipulation of mob emotion—the more deeply I was depressed. New evils were combined with ancient ones in this manifestation of the "national" spirit: an open application of that propaganda machinery which is the "non-violent" suppression of quiet thinking, plus a hidden appeal to the heathen worship of relics. The incident had about it most of the features of the home-bringing of a patron saint to a backward community; only the technical preparations were the latest thing. It was all falsely conceived from the beginning: the elevation of Herzl to this incommensurate position in the history of Zionism and of Israel distorts the meaning of all three; his heroic services deserve something better than the canonization, in an un-Jewish spirit, of what was least Jewish about him. Being falsely conceived, the program could not be creatively executed. I asked myself in amazement at the time: "What have you serious people, you Ben Gurions, Shprintzaks, Goldie Meyersons, you the representatives of a meaningful Zionism—what have you to do with this tomfoolery?"

I would not attend the ceremonies, and I could not direct the question at the Israelis alone. For the thousands of American Jews who were in Israel at the time were caught up equally in the incident; and I ascertained on my return to America that American Jewry had participated as effectively as it could *in absentia*. There is not the slightest doubt in my mind that if world Jewry—meaning here chiefly American Jewry—had not shown itself as susceptible as it did to the preparations, and the ideas that accompanied them, these would have undergone some change. The "bringing home" of the body of Herzl was a good symbolic gesture; at any rate, a permissible one. But the only content which could be read into it without falsifying history and Herzl's errors was that the Jewish people had purified him. His early death has been attributed, probably with reason, to the rebuke he received when he tried to substitute Uganda for Palestine; that is, when he tried to impose his Assimilationist-Zionism on the movement. He had accepted the rebuke. Now he was taken back lovingly to his people, his error "forgotten." But his error was not forgotten if he was being received in that very spirit which the Jews had rebuked: the spirit of a non-Jewish nationalism. The ceremonies were a frenzied glorification of Herzl as *the* Zionist. Herzl was not *the* Zionist. There is no such personality in Zionism, and no such personality must be created. To do so is pagan.

The downward drag on Zionism is world-wide because of the response that its success has evoked on the lowest levels. All the more reason, then, for vigilance on the highest levels. Zionism has now become the vogue in the cabarets and in whatever remains of the Jewish theater; Haganah is being celebrated on Second Avenue in New

York and on the rue des Rosiers in Paris in the Yiddish equivalents of the "Good-bye, Mama, I'm off to Yokohama," songs that burst forth in America after Pearl Harbor. The people who write such songs of Haganah and those who sing them with the feeling that "this is the real Jewish thing, boys," have votes for Zionist conferences and money for Zionist funds. But it is falsely assumed that their money can best be obtained by joining them in the singing, and that they will use their votes only if they are approached on their level of Zionist thought. Support thus obtained is not enduring; the exploitation of a mob mood in Jewry is, even from the practical point of view, a feckless economy. It is one more illustration of the truth that he who seeks achievement at the expense of character forfeits both. The retreat from this dangerous course must, however, be world-wide in Jewry. The responsibility rests as much with the American communities as with Israel.

## PARALYSIS

Many of our difficulties can be put under one heading: the Paralysis of Achievement. Somewhere along the line of effort, that which is only a phase of development so arrests the attention that it produces an impression of finality, of "the end in itself."

Years ago it was proper, and helpful, to rejoice in the discovery that the long exile, the long repression of certain normal activities, had not atrophied in the Jews the faculties needed for the physical creation of a self-sustaining society. Whether Michurinism or neo-Darwinism is right, we learned that the acquired negative characteristics of the Jewish exile communities were not transmissible. But how long are we going to linger over this happy discovery? When a man has been sick and has lost the use of his limbs and the control of his speech, we may cheer him on with every unsupported step and every clearly uttered phrase. But even before he walks quite freely and speaks quite clearly we must shift our attention to the purpose of his recovery. To go on applauding his return to the normal condition is actually to make a permanent invalid of him.

The analogy is admittedly faulty, for Jewish Zionism never lost sight of its purpose even while the painful physical healing was in progress: witness the extraordinary fact, already mentioned, that the *Chalutzim*, while casting off the physical habits and overcoming the physical handicaps of the exile, were already pursuing the creative spiritual meaning of a Jewish homeland. But the very faultiness of the analogy makes it the more instructive. It is forgotten that the physical struggles of the *Chalutzim* in Palestine twenty-five, thirty, forty years ago were far more difficult than those of the most unhappy immigrants in the reception camps of Israel today. If we grant, as we must, that the *Chalutzim* brought with them a superior spiritual equipment, it becomes the more evident that our excessive celebration of the physical normalizing of Jewish life lowers the tone of Zionism and delays the normalizing itself.

In our propaganda for Israel we seem to be standing in a condition of eternal stupefaction before the discovery that Jews can build houses, plow fields, milk cows, deliver the mails, elect a government, and fight back when attacked. We are forever pointing out with almost inarticulate glee that the Israeli walks and talks like a real human being. I suppose that, the technique of money-raising being what it is, and regular propagandists being what they are, some of this is unavoidable. But when the permissible emphasis on the rehabilitation of homeless refugees has been allowed for, when a reasonable area has been staked out for chairmanship oratory and high-pressure campaigners, there is still room for education in Judaism and Zionism. That room is almost unoccupied.

Many Zionists who should know better have been intimidated into accepting this situation as "inevitable": we must, they say, run the risk of spiritual pauperization for the sake of practical results. So we are being panicked into a surrender of everything that gave Zionism meaning and power. But the situation is *not* inevitable, and the risk—at least in this form—is *not* necessary. We are being bulldozed (there is no other word for it) into a total misconception of what the practicalities really are. And we shall realize this most clearly by returning to the subject of the Terrorists and the Haganah, and to the days when some of us were bulldozed into the belief that the Terrorists were the *Realpolitiker*. I do not apologize for reviving this unhappy chapter of the past; it is full of instruction for the future.

Among all the items listed above as evidence that the Jew was again a "normal" human being, the most popular was—and still is—his ability to fight. That popularity, very natural in a world at war, was an *emotional* response, but it rationalized itself into political terminology. To the fighting Jew, and above all to the obviously and spectacularly fighting Jew—that is, to the Terrorist—was given the credit for the liberation of Israel from British rule. And though the military exploits of Haganah have since eclipsed those of the Terrorists, there are still large numbers who believe that the Terrorists are entitled to much, or most, of the credit for having "driven out" the British.

The question of credits is of immense importance, not for the sake of the laurels, but for the sake of the lesson. We are concerned here with identifying the real historical forces at play in Israel and in world Jewry, so that we may stand before them in an intelligent relationship of co-operation or opposition.

When we ponder the question: "Why was England compelled to withdraw from Palestine?" the answer obviously is: "Because her position there had become untenable." But why? Because by the end of the Second World War a Jewish state was—as previously pointed out—*already* in existence. It was the only dynamic force in the whole area of the near east. The refusal to recognize this fact stemmed from a type of intellectual paralysis that is one of the occupational hazards of foreign-policy-makers. England had alienated the Jews by trying to break her promise to them when it was too late to break it; she had alienated the Arabs by making them a promise when it was too late to keep it. Faced with two evils she had reacted like Zangwill's famous pessimist, and chosen both. All the political formulas that the British designed to bridge this contradiction were verbalisms, not policies. With or without the Terrorists, Britain would have been compelled to seek from the United Nations a renewal of her "authority"; and if she had got it, it would not have done her the slightest bit of good. At the present time the United Nations can only register situations, not create them. When it fails to register them accurately, it must retreat.

The existence of the Jewish state in Palestine *before 1948* is the decisive factor in this problem. To assume that the Jews were able to put a state together only when the British withdrew, were able to organize departments, invite mass immigration, fight a war—all as it were overnight—is to think, not in terms of miracles, but of fairy tales. This Jewish state was the product of half a century of growth; its solidity and adaptability were the result of long and intelligent sacrifice; its morale was founded in the Zionist ideal; and its clearest characteristic was the dominance of pacifist and co-operative tendencies in the prophetic spirit.

In the resistance to the British policy of repression, the

significant role was played by the population as such (which was overwhelmingly anti-Terrorist), with the Haganah as its military arm. The Terrorists—largely identifiable with the Revisionist movement—had contributed nothing in the past to the solidifying of the structure that was now standing up to the supreme test. And they, who had not accepted the principle of slow and steady creation, were ready to make the supreme gamble and risk everything on a throw of the dice. They were ready to goad England, and alienate world opinion, to the decisive point at which the destruction of the Jewish state would have become a condonable act. Then half an hour of British military action, with bombers and heavy tanks, would have been sufficient. But the Terrorists, who were loudest in denouncing England —and certainly the denunciations of British government policy were well founded—have only the decency of British public opinion to thank for their failure to bring ruin in Palestine. And let it be recorded and remembered that, under extreme provocation, the *people* of England reacted with a minimum of blind anger; even the anti-Jewish demonstrations in England, in those days, were confined to the riff-raff and discountenanced by the masses.

When the British authorities withdrew from Palestine, churlishly, obstructively, obviously hoping that what they had not dared to do would be done for them by the Arabs, there was re-enacted in Palestine something like the Maccabean episode of twenty-one centuries ago. A people that was essentially pacifist turned on the Arab invaders in a fury and desperation that astonished the whole world. From the co-operative colonies which had been grounded in Labor Zionism's pacifist principles came young people altogether alien to the spirit of militarism—that spirit which had been the glory of the Terrorists—to throw themselves recklessly into a struggle that seemed all but hopeless.

These, the chief element in the *Palmach*, were the most Jewish of the Israeli Jews. The world saw a return of the Hasideans, whose only demand had been for the minimum political conditions which made Jewish life possible. Haganah was a cross-section of the *Yishuv*, but *Palmach* was its core. The fighting capacities of Israel were a function of the serious constructive and spiritual achievements of Israel. It was not a question of physical courage, which the Terrorists possessed in the same measure as the others. It was a question of character. Nor can we shrug off the response of the Haganah with the formula: "They had no alternative"; for danger as such does not necessarily call up courage and resistance. It was the final response of a people that, possessed of courage and skill, had been reluctant to descend into the arena; now, convinced at last that it must either fight or perish, it entered the struggle with a fury proportionate to its strength of character.

The preservation of this character, Jewish, pacifist, anti-competitive, is a practical matter; it is the only assurance we have of the viability of Israel. As it alone was productive in the past, it alone is reliable for the future. We are dealing with realities when we speak of the equivalence of viability and character; and as usual, it is the illiterate realists, the shortsighted worldings, who are the romantics. Of course the assurance of the viability of Israel, as of every other country, and of the whole human species, is relative; we can speak only of the maximum guarantee, not of an absolute; and when we tamper with the spirit that brought Israel so far, we are tampering with the primal source of the Jewish meaning and the Jewish sources of strength.

By "we" I mean all Jewry, world Jewry. We tamper with the Jewish spirit in our glorification of the Israeli as fighter. With the most shocking irresponsibility we begin to apply to the Israeli army all those self-serving flatteries which conceal the corruptive nature of war, and end up with the apotheosis of the fighter. We arrive at the pagan ideal of the gentleman-warrior. We close our eyes to the most ancient, most obvious, and deepest danger: namely, *even in fighting a defensive war, men are exposed to almost irresistible forces of corruption.* No army comes out of a war, even such a war, as clean as it went in; the killing of human beings under *any* circumstances is a dreadful trial of the spirit, and long exposure to it is almost always fatal. It is the proper thing to deny that American, British, French soldiers committed barbarities in the war with Nazism; the denial is a betrayal of the soldier, a surrendering of him to the worst effects of war. A good part of world Jewry was shocked by the massacre that the Irgunists perpetrated on the Arab village of Deir Yassin; but with quiet distress, with naïve disappointment, leaders of the Haganah in Israel will tell you of reprisal killings and of looting by the regular army, by those youngsters of the idealist colonies. The world is willing to forget. But the world is also willing to forget the gas chambers of Maidanek. It is the business of Jews to remember and, in remembering, to refrain from making of Israel's army the chief expression of "reborn Jewishness."

Circumstances work against us. The encouragement of a second Arab attack on the Jews goes on unabated. The Israeli army must be kept mobilized, the little local rat-race in armaments is fed from the outside. And still we have to bear in mind that war is foul, that if the foul work must be done, it must be done efficiently, expeditiously, courageously, and without illusions as to the nobility of the fighter in us.

Is this itch for glory among the fleeting reactions, or among the long-range forces? We cannot tell yet. Nor can we tell whether the intoxication of world Jewry with Israel's paraphernalia of independent government is a passing indulgence or a symptom of chronic political alcoholism. It is really pathetic to follow the Jewish press—Yiddish, English, Hebrew, French—and to mark how it lingers over the reports of the Israeli parliament, not so much for the content as for the sheer sensation of touching, smelling, and feeling a real Jewish government. For instance, in connection with the political disposition of Jerusalem, an Israeli publication reports, in excellent English, and in the classic English tradition of political writing, the following:

"The disappointment at the unexpected majority for internationalization [of Jerusalem] in the UNO Council precipitated some sharp criticism of our foreign policy. The House was not permitted to have a full-dress debate on the subject, partly because Mr. Sharett was still in New York, but in the statement of the party representatives on Mr. Ben Gurion's motion, dissatisfaction was expressed by more than one speaker. It was realized, however, that the unusual combination of U.S.S.R. with the Catholics and the Arabs had presented us with a formidable hostile front. There was much speculation on the possible reaction of Mapam and the Communists. On this issue they were not together. Mapam fully backed the Coalition, taking occasion only to demand the whole of Jerusalem, including the Old City, which Abdullah holds, within Jewish jurisdiction. It is clear that Russia does not want the Arab king installed even in a part of Jerusalem because she regards him as a tool of Britain. But that was no reason for opposing Israel's legitimate right to control the city it had salvaged and was administering. Mapam's stand was evidence of the solidarity of Israel concerning Jerusalem. The Communists were obviously embarrassed but were entitled to their view that Russia was not acting out of unfriendliness to Israel but in opposition to the British-American influence. . . ."

This is the real thing! Take out the Jewish names and you would imagine you were in the House of Commons or

the *Chambre des Députés*. There is, of course, nothing wrong
with the substance of the report. But in the spirit of it
quivers an unctuous satisfaction with the ballet in which
Jews are now free to participate. "We have arrived! We
sound just like everybody else! We did not suffer two thousand years of exile and martyrdom in vain!" For millions
of Jews throughout the world the mere fact that Jews are
governing themselves in Israel, are going through the
standardized motions of political self-determination, is the
fulfillment of Jewish history; and the passage quoted is
typical in spirit of a thousand reports in Jewish periodicals
of New York, Buenos Aires, Paris, and Johannesburg.

This is not what the Jewish people, or Judaism, survived
for; this is not what the Zionist movement intended; and
this is not what Israel and Judaism should mean to themselves or to the world. Still again I repeat: *The determinant
element in the longing for the Return was the desire to remain
Jewish.* As the Hasideans, in Maccabean days, fought only
for the minimum conditions that would permit them to continue the spiritual search, so the Jewishly orientated Zionists sought in Palestine only the instrument for the perpetuation of the same search. Political self-determination as an
end in itself, the standard national functions as ideals, have
always been immoral concepts. Today they are the obvious
prelude to the suicide of the human species. If the Jews have
survived only to join this chorus, they would have done better to disappear two thousand years ago.

## REACTIVATION

From this paralysis on a phase of development, Judaism
and Zionism must now be rescued by reactivation. Perhaps
the metaphor is wrong; perhaps we have to do not with
paralysis but with a program of de-Judaization. In that

case the corrective is a return, *T'shuvah*, which must be preceded or accompanied by clarification.

Those who have thought of Zionism and a Jewish state, or of the modernizing of Judaism, as a way of making life easier for the Jew have been right only if they have given the word "easier," in this connection, a limited and special meaning: "easier" as implying the removal of certain cramping restrictions and unfruitful dangers, "easier" as implying the creation of circumstances for a new spurt of creative effort; but not "easier" in the sense of more soothing and less strenuous. This is not a time for tired people, and least of all for tired Jews.

This Judaism that I speak of is a world-wide enterprise, conducted by a group with a special history, tradition, training, technique, and life-outlook, with a bearing on the supreme problem of mankind, which is: "How to live"; which problem, as I shall argue in the next and closing chapter, has now narrowed down to: "How to remain alive." Within the body that conducts the enterprise, meaning those who call themselves Jews, many deviations and contradictions appear. For me power-seeking Jews, Jews who have accepted the competitive principle of life and its ritual, Jews to whom wealth, political influence, social prominence are aims and ideals and signs of grace, are the embodiment of the contradictions. So are Jews unperplexed, unhaunted by the imperfections of a society that helps to perpetuate these standards. They are no more Jewish to me than their like among the gentiles are Christians; yet they are Jewish, and the others are Christians, to this important extent: that they are identified with Judaism, as the others are with Christianity, and are therefore the better able to work corruption from within.

I am being arbitrary? I am only so with words and beliefs, and would not be with anything else. And if these

314

words and beliefs fail—I do not mean *my* words and beliefs, for these are not discoveries of mine, only restatements—then another kind of arbitrariness will decide the issue, making such arbitrariness as mine seem very mild indeed.

But to continue: those who wish to associate themselves with the Jewish contribution to world survival—for that is the issue now—cannot do so simply by accepting its moral principles; for Judaism is a method and a destiny as well as a revelation. Still less is it "Judaism" to have sound and decent social principles, know nothing about Judaism, and call oneself a Jew. I have mentioned the well-intentioned progressives who have been attracted by the social program of Labor Zionism, and rendered sensitive to their Jewish identity by the events of the last ten or fifteen years. This is not Judaism; it is only a prelude to the acquisition of Judaism. Judaism calls for education in the history of the Jewish enterprise and self-identification with it not simply by approval on general grounds, but by participation in it, and by the absorption and transmission of its tradition. A friendly attitude toward Jewishness, friendly acts toward Israel—this we expect from Christians. Much more is needed for the maintenance of that Jewish unity in time, space, and destiny which I have so often referred to; namely, the intellectual and moral arduousness of being Jewish, so that Zionism and the Jewish state and the modernizing of Judaism make life not "easier" for the Jew, but more strenuous.

The practical help that comes from such persons is imperfect, like the help that comes from rich Jews who know nothing of the moral implications of Judaism; imperfect, though in another way. The help of the latter has to be "filtered" into the Jewish state. Rich, reactionary Jews, personifications of the competitive principle on the economic side of human relations, have been heavy contributors to the building of the Jewish state. But their contributions, passing through the machinery of the Zionist Organization, have hitherto, and on the whole, served the co-operative and not the competitive spirit in Israel. The collectives of Israel have been created to a large extent with the funds of non-Israeli Jewish capitalists. Some of them knew what was happening and closed their eyes to it; others half-knew it; still others had not the slightest notion of what they were doing. The imperfection consisted in the failure of Israel to react on the donors; they did not apply to their Jewish and non-Jewish relationships outside of Israel the principles they were implementing in Israel! It was a loss to them, to Judaism and to mankind.

In the case of the socially conscious who do apply outside of Israel the principles they encourage in Israel, the imperfection (not absent in the others, of course) consists dominantly in cultural disassociation, which will lead to personal disassociation in the next generation, if not before. They do not make of their practical self-identification with Israel the occasion for a remaking of their relationship, and that of their children, to the accumulations of the Jewish experience.

And so, from another point of view, the two imperfections are similar after all. Neither the one group nor the other learns anything; each remains what it was before, morally and culturally; in both, the re-creation of the Jewish state is balked of its purpose, which is the perpetuation and re-activation of Judaism. The good they do falls short of its potential objective, and the "We"-and-"They" development between Israel and the rest of world Jewry, pregnant with fatal possibilities, is further encouraged.

# CHAPTER XXVI

## *The Twilight of Competitive Man*

❧

I MUST now bring together, for the close, the three strands of my thesis: the pagan, the Jewish, the Israeli. I must speak again of the competitive or power principle, in the individual and the nation; of the prophetic principle of co-operation in the individual and nation; and of the Jewish acceptance of the prophetic principle as national policy —or rather, national meaning. All this against the background of the urgent present.

In Chapter Eight of Book One, "The Evasion," I reached the conclusion that when we scrutinize intently what we call the will to power, we cannot discover any purpose that it serves. It is not prudential—it is not an aid to survival. It is not hedonistic—it does not contribute to appetitional enjoyment. On the contrary, it decreases or blocks appetitional enjoyment by making things desirable for their demonstrative value, not for the satisfaction they give to our appetites as such; it stands between us and the functional pleasures of consumption; besides which it grudges us the time and energy for pleasures (physical or intellectual), and makes life laborious, just as it makes life dangerous: the power-seeker is a poor insurance risk.

And so the purpose of the will to power in the individual baffles us; it contradicts itself out of intelligibility. Men apparently want power in order that they may win approval or applause. But applause is only the acknowledgment or shadow of power. Therefore men want power in order that they may possess the shadow of power. Or they may even forgo the applause, and content themselves with the thought that they could extract the applause if they wanted to. They are content with the shadow of the shadow.

Thus, in the individual, the competitive principle, which is the activation of the will to power, seems to be nothing but an aberration, as obstructive as it is dangerous.

Was there a time when the competitive principle, or the will to power, served a purpose for the individual? Perhaps. Anthropologists state that in the far-off days when men were food-gatherers, not more than five million human beings could find nourishment on the surface of our planet. In a food-gathering economy there is no room for co-operation; individuals have to compete for the existing supply, and competition means appetitional satisfaction and survival. The will to power, with all its emotional overtones, may therefore have had meaning and purpose.

In a hunting economy—the next stage—the food supply still remains what man finds it. A hunting economy is really a food-gathering economy, but the food is now mobile, and sometimes combative. Now there is room and demand for occasional and limited co-operation. Co-operation is man's peculiar weapon (we will ignore instinctive co-operation in animals) against the foods that flee or fight back, and against the food that would—literally—turn the tables on him. But as man becomes a breeder of animals and an agriculturist, a food-creator rather than a food-gatherer, the co-operative principle becomes increasingly important.

Competition, however, still remains basic. *Groups* now compete—for grazing grounds and for fertile soil. What now becomes increasingly unintelligible is *the competition with each other of individuals within the co-operative groups.*

In organized groups there appears for the first time a phenomenon that obviously could not appear without a group life: the tyrannical concept of a social standard. But what is a social standard? It is a level of subsistence on which the psychological element displaces the physical and the appetitional. It is (see once more the chapter "The Evasion") the acceptance of the comparative as the basis of existence. It has nothing to do, in itself, with survival and health, with appetites and appetitions, with æsthetic enjoyment, with the exercise of the intellectual faculties. It is "place, degree, and form." And the most important feature of a social standard, its special characteristic, is that it shall *not* be accessible to all members of the group.

At first it looks like a metaphysical perversity. It seems to have no place in the common-sense conduct of affairs. It has apparently divorced survival and appetitional pleasure from realities. Not what you are and have, but what you are and have by comparison with your neighbor determines the livability of life!

But if we take a larger view, if we consider the individual not for his own sake and in his own right, but merely as a unit in the group, we seem to discover a rational or intelligible purpose in the social standard. As long as groups compete with one another for the means of subsistence, the law of the group is: We must be militarily strong. The social standard is then the method by which the members of a group are kept on their toes, trained in combative will and efficiency. By maintaining a ceaseless and implacable competition with one another, the members of the group ensure the combative quality of the group as a whole. They keep in training by fighting with one another in order that they may, when necessary, be able the better to co-operate in fighting another group. Thus the behavior of the individual is not intelligible except in the larger context; the illusion of his personal aims, his personal striving for power, is not the key to his character; individuality of character becomes an absurdity.

It becomes something worse: namely, a crime against the group or state. To reject the competitive principle within the group is to prepare the decline of the fighting quality of the group as a whole. A group or nation is essentially a combative organization. Such co-operation as it encourages internally is only *esprit de corps*. There must be just enough of it to hold the group together—although very often even this sensible proviso is neglected and the group is split. But beyond this sensible proviso co-operation is definitely a sign of military or combative effeteness. An individual who wants to co-operate beyond the accepted minimum is undermining his country. He must be corrected, and if incorrigible, he must be suppressed, *gleichgeschaltet*, co-ordinated—that is, destroyed. All ideas that, by diminishing the competitive ardors of the social-standard struggle, diminish the fighting potential of the group, must be combated, derided, and denounced as immoral. A desire to co-operate with members of other groups is exceptionally monstrous. In a world of competing nations, the ruling powers must, by special training, by spiritual perversion, by systematic lying, prevent the spread of the co-operative principle. In short, in a Plato-Machiavelli-Hitler world we can have only Plato-Machiavelli-Hitler states, with only illusory spiritual freedom for the individual.

I have made two debatable but not unreasonable assumptions so far: first, that the co-operative principle was inapplicable between individuals (or families) in the early days of man, in the days of a food-gathering economy; second, that it was inapplicable between groups (tribes or nations) in the first stages of the period that followed, the period of cattle-breeding, agriculture, and industry. Or, to put it more cautiously and generally: there was a time in the history of man when his limited powers over nature made inevitable a competitive struggle for roots and fruits, then for hunting and grazing ground, then for tillable soil and other natural resources; out of that time, stretching back we do not know how many hundreds of thousands of years, man has brought with him the struggle for power.

What follows now is not an assumption, but the most undebatable and overwhelming fact in human history: *we have reached that stage in the control of nature at which the continuation of the struggle between groups means the destruction of the species as a whole.*

What remains now of the "logical" connection between the will to power and the struggle for survival, between the competitive principle and the military security of the group?

There are, it is true, some people who refuse to be convinced that this totally new situation is upon us. Perhaps they will never be convinced, for either the world will not destroy itself and then they can still believe there was no danger (you will never convince a fool of the reality of a danger you have averted for him), or else the world will destroy itself and they will be beyond convictions. Very extraordinary indeed are the debates that go on about us, and the assurances given us that the H-bomb is not definitely a practical achievement; that the present atom bombs cannot destroy more than a hundred thousand lives at a time; that the possibilities of bacteriological warfare are rather obscure; that an artificial satellite controlling the surface of the earth is still a remote theory. As though we had not learned long ago that scientific progress is not in a straight line, but in a curve of acceleration; as though it were not blindingly clear that somewhere along the curve lies the point marked: "Total Destruction of Civilization," or "Uninhabitability of the Planet," or "Uncontrollable Chain Reaction." Whether we shall reach that point in five years or ten, or fifty, it is plainly in view. There the curve may break off abruptly. The will to power, the competitive principle, has now become as unintelligible for the group as it has long been for the individual.

We may now examine the complex from another point of view.

I have all along made a third assumption, an extremely dubious one: namely, that combat plays the determinant role in the survival of groups. Actually, adaptation and re-production are perhaps the real determinants; history abounds in instances of the conquered outbreeding the conqueror. But I have made the assumption in order to give the combative philosophy every benefit of the doubt. Let us then concede that combat has been the mainspring of all progress, that competition is the order of life, and that in man competition has taken the fantastic psychological form of the will to power—man's distinctive and hitherto unknown instrument of survival, his unique contribution to the life-process and the true source of his supremacy. If that is so, the will to power as a fixation has now become the instrument of man's destruction.

The will to power is, in other words, a fatal hangover; it is a faculty, or attitude, or method, which (we will grant) was once helpful; but, continuing into a stage of human evolution to which it no longer applies, it has become suicidal.

So, if we persist in the boundless folly of trying to deduce laws of human relations from natural law, we must say of the will to power that it is a petrifaction of form. But it is not like the form-petrifaction of the oyster, which has permitted that species to survive unchanged for millions of years. It is rather like the petrifaction-in-size of the great saurians, which at first was their survival device, and afterwards became the cause of their decline. Or it is like the petrifaction in growth-pattern which (according to George Gaylord Simpson) was characteristic of a group of European stags. These had the habit of developing antlers that made up a greater and greater proportion of the animal as its body became larger. At first the habit was useful or adaptive; but they could not drop it when it ceased to be useful. The species disappeared, destroyed by its antlers; it killed itself with its device for living.

We may look for other analogies. We might compare this outdated persistence and habit of the will to power with the feudal strategy of the European aristocracy, which gave it dominance a thousand years ago, but which became obsolete in the face of the mercantilistic-democratic strategy of the rising middle classes; or it is like the obstinate will of the southern American states to perpetuate the slavery and plantation system in a land and age to which they were no longer suited. All of this by way of rough analogy, without too much insistence on the scientific accuracy of each example. In short, the competitive principle has reached its dialectic term: to insist on its "practical" usefulness today is evidence of a fatal petrifaction; it indicates the rapid approach of a time when man will disappear from the earth, like other species, some of which held the stage far longer than he will have done.

Yet all this talk, let it be intellectually incontrovertible, and emotionally a thousand times more cogent, is beside the point. It might tell us what we ought to do, but it will not provide us with the drive to do it. For it is once again an attempt to find a rational foundation for the moral code, to deduce from naturalistic considerations an inspiration to right behavior, whereas that cannot even give us a guide to safety.

It is the mechanistic philosophy in which I once wandered hopelessly. It is also the best that paganism can give us: the Stoic philosophy which equates morality with health —indeed, with survival.

I have said: "You do not improve the moral insight of people by threatening them with public disaster. The approaching destruction of the world, visible to all as the consequence of our viciousness, could not make us better." The appeal to prudence is at best a stopgap. It may well be that the destruction of the world will be delayed a decade or two by fear alone—aided perhaps by initial incompetence. But to rely on fear for the continuation of the species is a horror that cannot endure. What we seldom think about is the remoter future: if the human species is to survive, it must survive under the eternal shadow of its own scientific omnipotence for evil. As long as we live, we shall have the capacity to destroy the earth at will, and we shall have it in increasing measure from decade to decade. The means will be accessible first to the mightier nations, then to the smaller ones, then perhaps to sub-national groups.

And with what shall we face this prospect? With the gentlemanly gesture? With the gallantry of the game, with the rules of cricket, the manly honesty of the prize-fight ring, and the honorable dueling-code of the Heidelberg students?

The answer was given a long time ago by a cycle of prophets evolving in the Jewish people. These, denying the principle of the will to power in the individual, saw that this denial is useless unless it is extended to the nation. Unless the nation is a moral thing, the individual cannot be moral. Therefore they laid the moral injunction on both individual and nation. Or we may say that the nation that produced prophetism strove to lay this injunction upon itself: strove and failed, and strove again and failed again, and went on striving, knowing that this was the only possible answer.

Where the moral, co-operative principle comes from is not to our purpose. We must only know that it does not come from natural law, and therefore cannot be deduced from it; we must know further that the attempt to deduce it from natural law is the way in which we deny it.

The Jewish people became, as a people, the imperfect embodiment of this liberation from the mechanical cycle of nature. For a number of centuries on its own soil, and for a larger number in dispersed exile, it has struggled with its destiny, realizing it fitfully, fragmentarily, but with an extraordinary general consistency. Out of its struggles there went forth to the world a message inviting the other nations to the same destiny; and if this world has meaning, it will be revealed only in the acceptance of the invitation.

Today the Jewish people is attempting to re-create, in the land of its original self-realization, a form of life that will again express its moral destiny; and perhaps this form will be more successful in cleansing it of its imperfections, and in clarifying its message. It is not inevitable that this should be so; it is not inevitable that the species called man shall achieve the liberation of life from bondage. But this much has been made clear: the path of liberation lies in the direction the prophets have indicated, and if the Jewish people can overcome the external dangers that surround, and the internal corruptions that have crept into, its re-creative effort, it will have fulfilled the purpose it set out with thousands of years ago.